Understanding Verbal Relations

Series Editors

The International Institute
on Verbal Relations

Linda J. Hayes
Steven C. Hayes
University of Nevada

Understanding Verbal Relations

The Second and Third International Institute on Verbal Relations

Edited by

Steven C. Hayes
Linda J. Hayes
University of Nevada

CONTEXT PRESS
Reno, Nevada

Understanding Verbal Relations: The Second and Third International Institutes on Verbal Relations / edited by Steven C. Hayes and Linda J. Hayes

Paperback. 224 pp. Includes bibliographies.

ISBN 1-878978-01-2

© 1992 CONTEXT PRESS
933 Gear Street, Reno, NV 89503-2729

All rights reserved

No part of this book my be reproduced, stored in a retrieval system, or transmitted in any form or by any means, electronic, mechanical, photocopying, microfilming, recording, or otherwise, without written permission from the Publisher

Printed in the United States of America

To our sibs:

*Gregory
Suzanne
(SCH)*

*Leslie
Richard
(LJH)*

Contributors

Gudfinna S. Bjarnadottir, *West Virginia University*
Philip N. Chase, *West Virginia University*
Maria Martha Hubner d'Oliveira, *Universidade de Sao Paulo*
W. V. Dube, *E. K. Shriver Center and Northeastern University*
Linda J. Hayes, *University of Nevada*
Steven C. Hayes, *University of Nevada*
James G. Holland, *University of Pittsburgh and University of South Florida*
J. B. Kledaras, *E. K. Shriver Center and Northeastern University*
Maria Amelia Matos, *Universidade de Sao Paulo*
W. J. McIlvane, *E. K. Shriver Center and Northeastern University*
Ullin T. Place, *University of Wales, Bangor*
Hayne W. Reese, *West Virginia University*
Emilio Ribes Inesta, *Universidad de Guadalajara*
Tania M. S. de Ros, *Universidade Federal De Sao Carlos*
Julio C. de Rose, *Universidade Federal De Sao Carlos*
Ana Lucia Rossito, *Universidade Federal De Sao Carlos*
Murray Sidman, *New England Center for Autism*
Kathryn J. Saunders, *University of Kansas Bureau of Child Research*
Richard R. Saunders, *University of Kansas Bureau of Child Research*
Deisy G. de Souza, *Universidade Federal De Sao Carlos*
Joseph E. Spradlin, *University of Kansas Bureau of Child Research*
L. T. Stoddard, *E. K. Shriver Center and Northeastern University*

Preface

The last decade has seen a series of rapid developments in contemporary behavioral approaches to language. Two areas of research have been particularly responsible for these changes: a) research on the impact of verbal rules and instructions, and b) research on derived stimulus relations, including stimulus equivalence, exclusion, and other forms of relational responding.

The explosion of research in these areas is recent. The time frame has been too short to assimilate these new data fully into behavioral perspectives on a variety of important topics. It is already clear, however, that these research developments will almost certainly lead to major theoretical modifications in many areas of behavioral psychology. Some analyses have emerged that make contact with contemporary cognitive analyses of particular topics, although with interesting differences. The nature of the continuity between human and non-human behavior is being reconsidered.

For many years Skinner's theoretical analysis of language has had wide support in the behavioral community, and has constituted the framework for behavioral analyses of many other forms of complex human action. The empirical and theoretical literature on rules and derived stimulus relations have posed a serious challenge to Skinner's authority on these issues. It now seems to be widely agreed that his analysis cannot accommodate the implications of this empirical work without extensive modification of some of its central concepts. The lack of confidence in Skinner's work in this area spreads readily to traditional behavior analytic conceptualizations of other forms of complex human behavior, such as thinking, problem solving, and imagining. This is a period of great flux within the behavior analytic group, and there seems to be every reason to believe that this will increase as many previously settled issues are reexamined.

Thus, this volume should be read as one small step in the ongoing development of a research and theoretical tradition. Guided by Skinner's analysis, behavior analysis once viewed verbal events as *essentially* similar to all other psychological events, and thus had little fundamental reason to do research in the area. Many behavior analysts still hold to that view, but the zeitgeist is changing. Today, many behavior analysts seem actively open to the possibility that verbal events involve unique processes and principles, and thus the view that research on verbal relations is possibly fundamental research, as "basic" as research on direct contingency control or classical conditioning.

The International Institute on Verbal Relations should be seen in the context of the excitement and controversy entailed by these two polarities. The purpose of the Institute, now approaching its Fourth rendition (to be held in Japan in the summer of 1992), is to examine empirical and theoretical developments in verbal relations in detail so that substantive developments can be distinguished from a chaotic embrace of all things new on the one hand or a rigid rejection of theoretical innovation on the other.

The conferences are deliberately structured to bring together basic and applied psychologists, those active in the study of verbal relations and those who are not, and North Americans and other researchers around the world. Almost all of the participants are behavior analysts, and those that are not are thoroughly knowledgeable about the approach. By bringing such a diverse group together, possible changes and new developments are placed into the broad context of the behavior analytic approach considered as a whole. This is a context that is most likely to ignore proposed changes that are merely fadish. Conversely, the experts in these volumes are well positioned to identify and to promulgate developments that are significant.

The Institutes have been supported by many people, both with time and with money. The Second International Institute on Verbal Relations was supported in part by the National Autonomous University of Mexico. The Local Organizer was Emilio Ribes, who located a fantastic conference site (the conquistador Cortez's summer home), organized the participation of Mexican behavior analysts, and in so many other ways made the conference possible.

The Third International Institute on Verbal Relations was supported in part by a grants to D. G. de Souza (FAPESP Grant no. 88/0430-1) and to Julio de Rose (CNPq Grant no. 403580/88-9). These generous grants provided travel and per diem funds for many of the participants. The Local Organizers were Deisy de Souza and Marie Amelia Matos, who worked tirelessly to locate a site (a beautiful facility in the Brazilian mountains), and generate funding, and to coordinate visits by the North American participants with many Universities around Brazil. These visits, to deliver workshops and courses, in turn also helped support the travel of participants, and thus we are indebted to the many Brazilian Universities that took part.

Finally, we appreciate the support of the University of Nevada, which has provided part of the means to organize these Institutes.

Steven C. Hayes
Linda J. Hayes
Reno, NV
January, 1992

About the Series

Three International Institutes on Verbal Relations have been held. The first was held in Bad Kreuznach, West Germany in June of 1986, the second in Tequesquitengo, Mexico in June 1988 and the third in Aguas de Lindoia, Brazil in January 1989. The fourth will be held at Mt. Fugi, Japan in July 1992. Additional Institutes are planned.

The structure of each of the Institutes has been roughly the same. About 10-12 psychologists from around the world have been asked to participate as primary speakers, including several from the host country. About 15-20 other psychologists and students serve as observers and discussants. The Institute extends over a period of about five days. Each day, two to three talks are given. Each talk is discussed by the entire group, lead by a discussion leader. General discussion then extends into the wee hours of the morning.

Proceedings of each of the Institutes are being published by CONTEXT PRESS. Linda J. Hayes and Steven C. Hayes are editors of the series. The proceedings of the First International Institute on Verbal Relations were published in 1991 under the title **Dialogues on Verbal Behavior**, edited by Linda J. Hayes & Philip N. Chase. It is available for $34.95 plus $3 shipping and handing from CONTEXT PRESS, 933 Gear St., Reno, NV 89503-2729. This volume presents the Second and Third International Institutes. The proceedings of the Fourth International Institute on Verbal Relations will be available in early 1993.

Table of Contents

Part 1
Derived Stimulus Relations: Empirical Findings

Chapter 1
Equivalence Relations: Some Basic Considerations 15
Murray Sidman, *New England Center for Autism*

Chapter 2
The Stability of Equivalence Classes 29
Joseph E. Spradlin, Kathryn J. Saunders, and Richard R. Saunders
University of Kansas Bureau of Child Research

Chapter 3
Stimulus-Reinforcer Relations and Conditional Discrimination 43
W. J. McIlvane, W. V. Dube, J. B. Kledaras, J. C. de Rose, and
L. T. Stoddard
E. K. Shriver Center and Northeastern University

Chapter 4
Stimulus Equivalence and Generalization in Reading After Matching to Sample by Exclusion 69
Julio C. de Rose, Deisy G. de Souza, Ana Lucia Rossito, and
Tania M. S. de Rose
Universidade Federal De Sao Carlos

Chapter 5
Equivalence Relations and Reading 83
Maria Amelia Matos and Maria Martha Hubner d'Oliveira
Universidade de Sao Paulo

Part 2
Derived Stimulus Relations: Theoretical Analyses

Chapter 6
Equivalence as Process 97
Linda J. Hayes, *University of Nevada*

Chapter 7
Verbal Relations, Time and Suicide 109
Steven C. Hayes, *University of Nevada*

Part 3
Rules and Verbal Formulae

Chapter 8
Rules as Nonverbal Entities 121
Hayne W. Reese, *West Virginia University*

Chapter 9
**Behavioral Contingency
Semantics and the Correspondence Theory of Truth** 135
Ullin T. Place, *University of Wales, Bangor*

Chapter 10
Problem Solving by Algorithms and Heuristics 153
Hayne W. Reese, *West Virginia University*

Chapter 11
**Instructing Variability:
Some Features of a Problem-Solving Repertoire** 181
Philip N. Chase, Gudfinna S. Bjarnadottir, *West Virginia University*

Part 4
Other Topics in the Analysis of Verbal Relations

Chapter 12

Language and the Continuity of Species 197
    James G. Holland
    University of Pittsburgh & University of South Florida

Chapter 13

An Analysis of Thinking 209
    Emilio Ribes Inesta, *Universidad de Guadalajara*

Part 1
Derived Stimulus Relations: Empirical Findings

Chapter 1

Equivalence Relations: Some Basic Considerations

Murray Sidman
New England Center for Autism

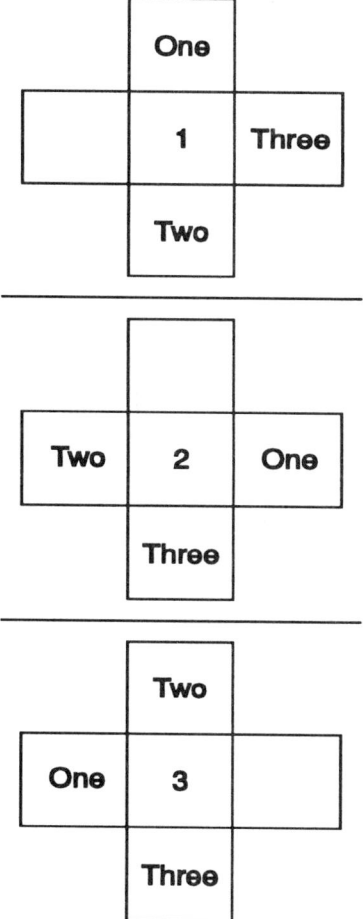

Figure 1. Diagram of the first set of conditional discriminations taught, with numerals as samples and English number names as comparisons.

The concept of stimulus equivalence is being called on more and more frequently to support behavioral accounts of cognition and language. Occasionally, in our eagerness to extend behavior analysis to these exciting areas, we ignore or even sweep under the rug some of our problems of experimental technique and data interpretation. It is important, therefore, to stop every now and then, and review what we think we know. In our haste to extend what we think we know, what unsolved problems have we left behind?

The Basic Findings

Let us start out with a quick review of a basic experiment. We use a standard conditional-discrimination procedure, often called arbitrary or symbolic matching to sample (e.g., Cumming & Berryman, 1965). As in Figure 1, we present the subject with a sample stimulus on the center key of a 5-key display, and with comparison stimuli on three of the four outer keys. Here, the sample can be any one of three numerals – 1, 2, or 3 -- and the comparisons are three English words – the number names, one, two, and three. The stimuli, of course, vary in sequence and position from trial to trial.

A child, adult, or monkey who has not yet learned to relate numerals and their printed names, is taught to do so by standard reinforcement procedures. By selecting a name that (for us) matches the numeral, the subject produces a reinforcer – a candy, coin, point, food pellet, or whatever we have found will keep that particular subject working and learning. The subject learns to select one of the comparison words conditionally upon the particular sample digit that is in the center.

After having learned to do this, can the subject be said to read numbers and number names? At this point, we do not know. Watching a monkey and a child doing this task, we cannot see any difference. And yet, we want to believe that something different is happening in the two cases. This is, after all, just a simplified version of standard tests for reading comprehension. The basic equivalence paradigm provides a way to find out whether comprehension is involved in either subject's performance.

To prepare for the critical test, we teach a second task, illustrated in Figure 2. Now, the sample is always an English word, one of the number names that were comparisons in the first task. The comparisons are three Portuguese number names. The subject learns to select Portuguese number-name comparisons conditionally upon English number-name samples.

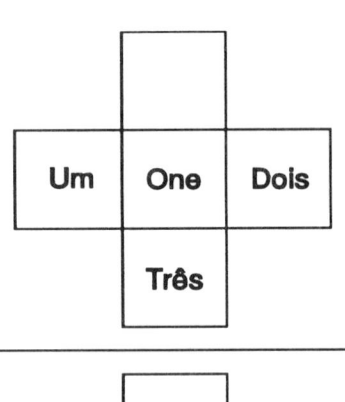

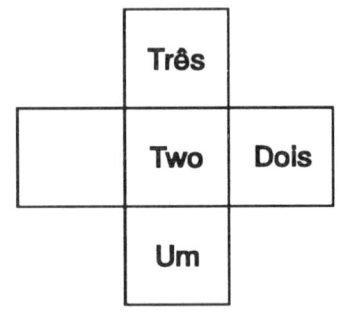

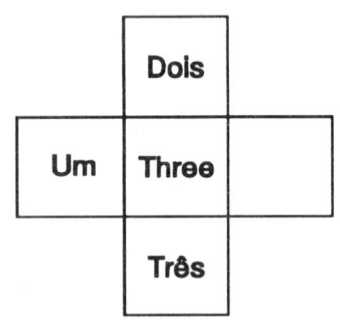

Figure 2. Diagram of the second set of conditional discriminations taught, with English number names (formerly comparisons) as samples, and Portuguese number names as comparisons.

Can we now say that the printed English and Portuguese number names mean the same thing to the subject? Do "Two" and "Dois" represent the same numeral? Can we say, as many would like, that the child can read number names in two languages, but the monkey is just doing conditional discriminations? We still do not know, but we are now ready to shed our preconceptions and answer these questions objectively.

We give our subjects a task they were not able to do before. Figure 3 shows some of the test trials. With Portuguese words as samples, we determine whether a subject will select the appropriate numeral. To avoid telling subjects what we expect, we do not reinforce the selections.

Many replications of this and similar teaching and testing procedures, with many kinds of stimuli, and with many kinds of human subjects (but not yet unequivocally with nonhumans), permit us to predict confidently that the subject will succeed in matching Portuguese words to the numerals. The test will show new performances emerging, performances that we did not explicitly teach. (See, for example, McDonagh, McIlvane, & Stoddard, 1984; Saunders, Wachter, & Spradlin, 1988; Sidman, 1971; Sidman, Kirk & Willson-Morris, 1985; Spradlin, Cotter, & Baxley, 1973).

We can then say that the two tasks we taught directly (Figures 1 and 2) did involve reading comprehension. We can say that the digit, "1," the English word, "One," and the Portuguese word, "Um," mean the same thing to our subject; and we can say the same for what we might call the "Twos" and the "Threes."

Equivalence Relations

To explain why this is a decisive test for comprehension requires a small theory. Given the results we have now seen so regularly, it seems reasonable to suggest that for many subjects, the conditional relations between sample and comparison stimuli are also equivalence relations. If this theoretical proposition is correct in any particular case -- if the conditional-

Equivalence: Some Basic Considerations

discrimination procedures have also generated equivalence relations — then the subject's new performances on the test are predictable: The new conditional discriminations **must** emerge. If the conditional relations are not equivalence relations, then the subject will not succeed on the test.

The statement that conditional relations may also be equivalence relations is a theory simply because the subject's behavior shows us only the conditional relations between sample and comparison stimuli. We cannot see equivalence relations; we have to infer them from the results of the test.

On what grounds do we claim that our test is a test for equivalence? To justify this claim requires a definition of equivalence relations. The mathematical definition requires that any equivalence relation possess three properties: reflexivity, symmetry, and transitivity. We extend our theory by suggesting a behavioral test for each one of those relational properties (Sidman, Rauzin, Lazar, Cunningham, Tailby, & Carrigan, 1982; Sidman & Tailby, 1982). In a behavioral context, one could, of course, define equivalence any way one wants. The definition we have started with, however, has proven so consistent and useful that to violate it would only destroy its utility in behavioral analysis.

Figure 4 illustrates how the conditional discriminations depicted in Figures 1, 2, and 3 enter into our definition of equivalence, and how we can tell whether the explicitly taught conditional relations are also equivalence relations. In Figure 4, stimuli presented singly, as samples, are shown in separate boxes; the same stimuli, when presented three at a time as comparisons, are all shown in the same box. Arrows always point from samples to comparisons.

Reflexivity

To be an equivalence relation, a conditional relation must be reflexive; stimuli that are conditionally related to each other must show the same relation to themselves. Figure 4 shows the three reflexivity tests (labelled REFL on the left side): Will the subject relate each stimulus to itself? For example, given "3" as a sample (the uppermost test), will the subject select that same numeral when given "1," "2," and "3" as comparisons? Given the English word, "Three," as the sample, will the subject select that same word from the English comparisons? We can ask the same question about the Portuguese words. A subject who behaves this way without explicit reinforcement is showing generalized identity matching with the stimuli we are using — the test for reflexivity.

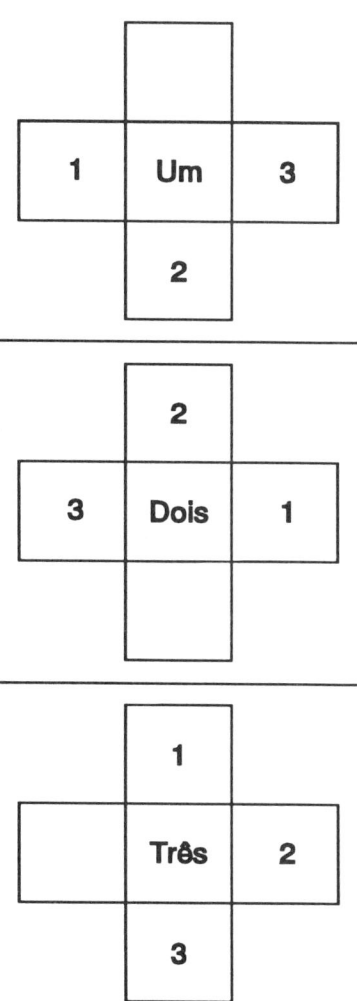

Figure 3. Diagram of the conditional discriminations tested after subject has learned the relations shown in Figures 1 and 2. Here, the Portuguese names are samples, and the numerals are comparisons.

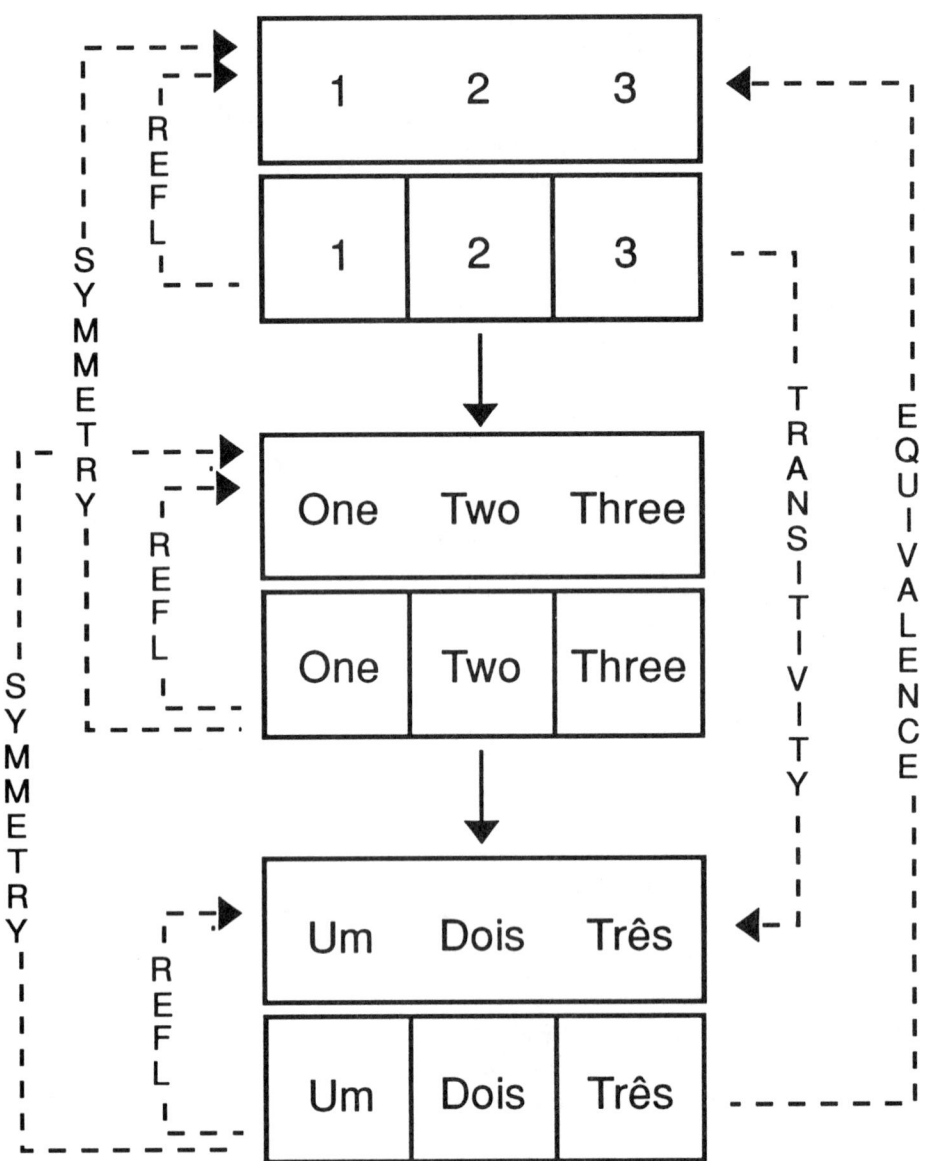

Figure 4. Each arrow points from samples to comparisons. The solid arrows in the center indicate the two sets of conditional discriminations that were explicitly taught: digit samples (presented one at a time) with English-name comparisons (presented three at a time), and English-name samples with Portuguese-name comparisons. The dotted arrows indicate emergent conditional discriminations, not explicitly taught. Illustrated here are the three tests for reflexivity (REFL), the two SYMMETRY tests, the TRANSITIVITY test, and the EQUIVALENCE test.

Symmetry

The second requirement for equivalence is that the relation be symmetric; sample and comparison must be interchangeable in function. In symmetric conditional relations, sample stimuli will function effectively as comparisons, with the former comparisons as samples.

Figure 4 shows the two symmetry tests. If the explicitly taught conditional relation between sample numerals and English-name comparisons is symmetric, the subject will then be able to relate the names as samples to the numerals as comparisons (the upper symmetry test). The relations between English and Portuguese names will also be symmetric (the lower symmetry test).

Transitivity

The third requirement for equivalence is that the conditional relations be transitive. A labelled arrow on the righthand side of Figure 4 denotes the transitivity test: Having learned to relate numeral samples to English-name comparisons, and English samples to Portuguese-name comparisons, the subject must then be able to relate numeral samples to Portuguese comparisons.

The reflexivity, symmetry and transitivity tests yield new conditional discriminations, never explicitly taught but derived from the conditional discriminations that were explicitly taught. It is important to note that either symmetry or transitivity could emerge without the other. The subject could fail to show transitivity while succeeding on one or both symmetry tests, or could succeed on the transitivity test even though unable to relate Portuguese samples to English comparisons, or English samples to numeral comparisons.

The Equivalence Test

In the final test (denoted by the other labelled arrow on the righthand side of Figure 4), the subject demonstrates conditional relations between Portuguese samples and numeral comparisons. Now we can see how the existence of equivalence relations makes these derived relations inevitable.

First, reflexivity establishes the identity of each stimulus -- from occasion to occasion, from place to place, from function to function, etc. Second, symmetry establishes two sets of untaught relations: between Portuguese samples and English comparisons, and between English samples and numeral comparisons. Third, the two sets of relations made possible by symmetry can themselves be tested for transitivity. If they are transitive, the subject will match Portuguese samples to numeral comparisons.

I have, however, labelled this not transitivity, but equivalence. This requires some explanation. We noted that simple transitivity (matching numeral samples to Portuguese comparisons) might emerge even in the absence of symmetry. Unlike simple transitivity, however, equivalence (matching Portuguese samples to numeral comparisons) could not emerge unless both of the explicitly taught relations were symmetric, and the symmetric relations transitive. In the equivalence test, transitivity and symmetry are no longer independent. The subject could not do the equivalence test unless both sets of directly-taught relations possessed all the properties of equivalence relations.

Utility of the Definition

Our definition of equivalence, and the behavioral tests, are useful because they require certain kinds of consistencies in the data. For example, if a relation could show each property of equivalence separately, but yield a negative equivalence test, the definition would lose its utility. It would also be useless if a negative equivalence test were not accompanied by a negative test for at least one of the individual properties of equivalence relations.

Also, a positive equivalence test cannot coexist with a failure in even one of the other tests. If just one of the individual reflexivity, symmetry, or transitivity tests yielded negative results, we would also have to expect a negative equivalence test. For example, in the face of a negative symmetry or transitivity test, we would have to attribute a positive equivalence test to something other than equivalence. If we could not identify an artifact or procedural deficiency (Sidman, 1987), we would have to conclude that our behavioral tests for equivalence relations do not define a real behavioral process.

So far, the necessary consistencies have held up, with seeming exceptions traceable to artifacts (Barnes, 1990), to incomplete descriptions of controlling stimuli (Carrigan, 1986; Iversen, Sidman, & Carrigan, 1986; Johnson & Sidman, 1991; Sidman, 1980) or experimental procedures (Stikeleather & Sidman, 1990), or to unwarranted theoretical attribution of equivalence to members of other kinds of stimulus classes (Sidman, Wynne, Maguire, & Barnes, 1989). These empirical consistencies now permit the following additional theoretical statements.

When people talk about the dictionary meaning of words, or about words and their referents, or about symbol and substance, or about rule-governed versus contingency-governed behavior, or about other similar kinds of relations between stimuli of various kinds, we will find that the items being related are equivalent to each other. According to this theory, it is when equivalence classes exist that people say such things as "numerals are symbols for quantities," "numbers are the referents of number names," or "dois means two." Equivalence relations make it possible for us to manipulate numerals on paper and thereby determine the number of boxes that will fit into a truck, to drive to an unfamiliar location by consulting a map, to purchase specific items in a store after looking at a shopping list, to operate a computer after reading a manual, or to teach a person anything just by giving instructions. With the procedures outlined above, these theoretical statements are now directly testable.

This final theoretical suggestion deals not with the sources of equivalence, but simply with the relation between equivalence and some of the things that people quite typically say (aloud, or on paper, or via signs, etc.). Skinner (1957) stated that the meaning of verbal behavior (or any behavior, for that matter) lies in the variables which determine that behavior. Equivalence relations can be viewed as such a variable, one that helps to account both for what people say and for their reactions to what other people say. In particular, the existence of equivalence relations can account for such utterances as "meaning," "symbol," "referent," and "rule-governed."

The simple-minded theoretical statements I have made so far do not provide a model that requires, predicts, or explains the emergence of equivalence relations from conditional discriminations, or from any other source. I have simply proposed what appears to be a useful set of tests for determining whether or not equivalence relations exist between stimuli, and have indicated how equivalence relations may help us understand why we talk about such things as meanings, verbal referents, or symbols.

Because equivalence is always an inference, never directly observed, it is vital to have an unequivocal test for determining whether or not that inference is correct in any instance. Without such a test, loose applications of the concept of equivalence will inevitably erode whatever utility it may possess for the understanding of complex behavioral processes. Although the conditional-discrimination procedures of the test can themselves produce equivalence relations, they need be neither the only nor even the most common procedures for doing so; the test itself is independent of any theory of where equivalence comes from.

It turns out that the very procedure of testing for equivalence causes a person to relate stimuli in new ways, i.e., to acquire new "knowledge" (Sidman, 1978) without having explicitly been reinforced for doing so. The test procedures do provide a practical technique for teaching such knowledge. The use of conditional discriminations (matching to sample) to generate equivalence relations is most evident in the classroom, when vocabularies are being taught. It also turns out that the equivalence relation can act as a transfer vehicle for adding new members to other kinds of classes (de Rose, McIlvane, Dube, Galpin, & Stoddard, 1988; Lazar, 1977; Lazar & Kotlarchyk, 1986; Sidman et al., 1989; Sigurdardottir, Green, & Saunders, 1990; Silverman, Anderson, Marshall, & Baer, 1986; Wulfert & Hayes, 1988). But the source of equivalence relations is still a matter of conjecture (Dugdale & Lowe, 1990; Hayes & Hayes, 1989; Sidman, 1990).

Equivalence Relations and Verbal Rules

It has been suggested that language may be necessary for the emergence of equivalence relations (e.g., Dugdale & Lowe, 1990). This is an easy assumption to make, since it is obvious that the statement of a verbal rule can establish equivalence relations. For example, one can instruct an experimental subject as follows: First, "Stimulus A1 goes with Stimulus B1, and B1 with C1;" second, "Any two or more stimuli that go with the same stimulus also go with each other." Such instructions can, of course, suffice to yield a positive equivalence test, not because of experimental contingencies but because of the subject's experiences before coming into the laboratory. Indeed, if the subject has a particular verbal history, the relation "goes with" may already be an equivalence relation, and the second instruction will not even be necessary; just telling the subject that particular stimuli "go with" each other may be sufficient to establish equivalence relations.

It is not clear, however, that verbal rules are necessary for the establishment of equivalence relations. That rules can give rise to equivalence relations does not mean that equivalence relations require rules. Also, to say that the derived relations indicative of equivalence must be products of verbal rules begs the question of where the verbal rules come from, and of how oral, written, or signed statements can generate behavior that is consistent with contingencies a listener or reader has never experienced. What does it mean to say that rules "specify" contingencies (Skinner, 1969)?

How is it that relations between noises that come out of our mouths can have the same effects on a listener as relations between other environmental events that the noises "specify?" The suggestion I made above was that equivalence relations between the noises and the events make such correspondences possible.

How is it that we react in many of the same ways both to a stove that is hot and to the words "hot stove," even though we may never have experienced a hot stove? Equivalence relations between the words and the actual hot stove would make this possible.

How is it that I can say, "A miniature kangaroo dances on the shore of the moon crater," when I have never before spoken, heard, or read that particular sequence of words? And how is it that others can understand that sentence even though they have never heard it or most of its component juxtapositions before? This first-time, grammatically correct sentence would be made possible by equivalence relations between members of grammatical classes (nouns, verbs, adjectives, etc.), and between members of sequence classes (first, second, etc.).

Thus, "kangaroo" is grammatically equivalent to other members of the class "noun," and "dances" to other members of the class, "verb." And, relative to verbs, members of the noun class (in English) are also in the class, "firsts;" relative to nouns, members of the verb class are also in the class, "seconds." Membership in the two equivalence classes "noun" and "first" places "kangaroo" in front of "dances." A similar analysis can be made of other parts of the sentence.

But, except for initial data from a few experiments (Lazar, 1977; Sigurdardottir et al., 1990), these are all conjectures. Until we have answered the question of whether rules give rise to equivalence, or equivalence makes rules possible, we are going to have to be careful about our experimental procedures in investigations of equivalence. If we tell our subject that stimuli "go with" each other (or that they "match each other," "belong together," "are the same," "go first" or "go second," etc.), the data may then tell more about the subject's verbal history than about the effects of current experimental operations. The instruction may even make the subject's subsequent behavior insensitive to our experimental manipulations.

A subject may, of course, derive a verbal rule even when we use only nonverbal contingencies. In such instances, however, we can be sure, at the least, that our experimental manipulations gave rise to the verbal rule. Given that equivalence relations make the correspondence between the contingencies and the words possible, we can be reassured that our experimental procedures have produced both the subject's verbalization and the equivalence relations we are studying.

Equivalence as a Fundamental Stimulus Function

The question of whether verbal rules are necessary for the establishment of equivalence relations may never be settled to everyone's satisfaction unless truly language-deficient subjects, like pigeons or chimpanzees, can be shown to form equivalence relations. Although it is clear that their ability to do so is, at best, limited, we are still far from certain that nonhumans are incapable of equivalence relations (see, e.g., D'Amato, Salmon, Loukas, & Tomie, 1985; Dugdale & Lowe, 1990; Lipkens, Kop, & Matthijs, 1988; McIntire, Cleary, & Thompson, 1987; Sidman et al., 1982; Vaughan, W., 1988).

If it does turn out that verbal rules are not necessary, and that verbal chaining (Dugdale & Lowe, 1990; Lowe, 1986; McIntire et al., 1987; Sidman, Cresson, & Willson-Morris, 1974) is not a sufficient explanation, then we will have to consider the possibility that equivalence is a fundamental stimulus function. I have pointed out elsewhere (Sidman, 1990) that we have good reasons even now for believing that equivalence, like reinforcement, discrimination, etc., represents a primitive stimulus function, not derivable from other behavioral processes.

If the emergence of equivalence relations between stimuli were a fundamental stimulus function, to be accepted as a given, how could it be that even humans do not always test positively for equivalence? Also, why do phenomena that equivalence is supposed to underlie not always happen? For example, the words "Route 128" on the map, and the road on which we are driving are equivalent when we are trying to find our way to an unfamiliar place, but we do not try to drive our car onto the words, or to illuminate the road with a reading light. We do not try to eat the word, "bread," or to swat the word, "fly."

To account for such seeming anomalies, we remind ourselves, and demonstrate experimentally, that equivalence relations come under contextual control (Bush, Sidman, & de Rose, 1989; Kennedy & Laitinen, 1988; Sidman, 1986; Wulfert & Hayes, 1988). Other circumstances determine whether, and when, stimuli are equivalent.

But to suggest that equivalence is a primitive stimulus function is to imply that the equivalence relations emerge first, before experience in different contexts modifies or breaks them down. We really would, for example, eat the word "bread," did we not learn through experience or through rules that words, even when equivalent to foods, are not eatable. This is just the opposite of the notion that rules are needed to create equivalence relations. The suggestion here is not that rules establish equivalence relations, but that rules break down or circumscribe equivalence relations.

Coming from an entirely different direction, Piaget (1963/1929) arrived at a similar conclusion. In discussing "Words and Things" (pp. 55-60), he stated, " ... the child cannot distinguish a real house, for example, from the ... name of the house" (p. 55). Piaget went on to say, "It will, therefore, be interesting to see at what age children can distinguish the word which designates it from the thing itself" (p. 56), and he came to the conclusion " ... that it is between 10 or 11 that the child becomes aware of thoughts or of words as distinct from the things of which

Equivalence: Some Basic Considerations

he thinks" (p. 60).

If equivalence relations come into existence before rules specify or limit them, we will have to consider the possibility that stimuli become equivalent for the same reason they become reinforcing, discriminative, eliciting, or emotional – simply because we are made that way. We do not yet have evidence that requires us to dismiss this possibility. There are experiments to be done here, before we move too far along the road to theory about either the source of equivalence relations, or about the relevance of verbal rules.

When Does Equivalence Emerge?

Another area of confusion arises from the suggestion that equivalence, or the individual properties that define equivalence, is established not when relations are explicitly taught, but during the tests (Sidman et al., 1985). With reference to Figure 4, for example, the notion is that although the learning of relations between numerals and their names, or between English and Portuguese names, establishes prerequisites, the equivalence relations form only when they are tested – in this instance, when the relations between Portuguese samples and numeral comparisons are tested. Going a step further, the suggestion was made that even symmetry does not exist until it is tested.

An objection to this notion is that we often see equivalence emerging even though we have tested neither symmetry nor transitivity. But equivalence requires symmetry and transitivity, so if those prerequisites do not exist until they are tested, how could we obtain a positive result in an equivalence test?

A similar problem exists with respect to the long-established principle that differential reinforcement is necessary for the establishment of simple discriminations. An objection to this notion is that we often see subjects discriminating stimuli before there has been any opportunity for differential reinforcement. After a few reinforcements for pecking a lighted key, a pigeon may never peck dark keys even though doing so has not been extinguished.

Such discriminations come about because other variables than differential reinforcement also affect stimulus control. Even with neither reinforcement in their presence nor extinction in their absence, some stimuli may be discriminated because of what has been called their salience, or because some stimulus control is, perhaps, "prewired," or because of a subject's particular discriminative history. These, however, are instances in which stimulus control comes about independently of our efforts as experimenters or teachers. It remains true that the only way we can guarantee stimulus control is to provide differential reinforcement.

A similar situation exists with respect to equivalence relations. A conditional relation may prove symmetric and transitive for reasons that have little to do with our experimental procedures, and will thereby yield a positive equivalence test. But it remains true that the only way we can guarantee equivalence is to do the test.

The necessity for doing the test in order to ensure equivalence arises from the fact that any stimulus can be, and usually is, a member of more than one class. In Figure 4, the numeral 1 belongs not only to the 3-member equivalence class for which our explicit teaching procedures established the prerequisites, but is also a member of other classes: "numbers" (vs. letters), "vertical" (shape), "single" (quantity), "small" (amount), "high" (quality), etc. On a test trial, the subject could choose a comparison on the basis of any of its class memberships.

For example, given a first equivalence test trial with Um as the sample, and faced with a choice between the numerals 1 and 2 (like Figure 4, but only 2 comparisons), the subject will not choose 1 because it is a number, since the other comparison is also a number. The subject might choose 1, however, because it is vertical, like the sides of the letters in the sample. With the test being run in extinction, no differential consequence informs the subject whether his choice was correct or not.

But then on the next trial, with Dois as the sample, and the numerals 2 and 3 as comparisons, verticality is not available as a possible basis for choice. The subject may now select 2 because dividing the number of letters in the sample by 2 gives 2 as the answer; or 3 might be selected because that is closer to the number of letters in the sample.

On the next trial, with Três as the sample, and 1 and 3 as comparisons, a subject who had selected the second option on the previous trial could do so again (3 is closer to the number of letters in the sample); a subject who had selected the first option (dividing by 2) would no longer have it available, so some other features of the stimuli or their relations would determine which comparison is selected.

Eventually, the subject would choose on the basis of equivalence-class membership of sample and comparison (although it might prove necessary to test first for symmetry or transitivity, as in Sidman et al., 1985; Sidman, Willson-Morris, & Kirk, 1986). This basis -- stimuli related by equivalence – would then remain an available option on every subsequent trial. From then on, the subject's choice on each test trial would be consistent with the formation of the expected equivalence classes.

An "armchair" analysis of the tests for equivalence, or for the individual properties of equivalence, tells us that some such selection process must take place. The participation of each stimulus in more than one class, and the possibility of several different kinds of relations between samples and comparisons, make some kind of a winnowing process necessary. When equivalence does emerge immediately, its rapidity must, like discriminations that occur without differential reinforcement, be attributed to uncontrolled variables. A critical factor is the construction of the test trials, particularly the "negative" stimuli in each trial. The speed with which the test shows itself positive will depend on the differentiating characteristics of the comparison stimuli. The fewer the possible controlling relations between samples and comparisons, the more rapidly will the relation being tested emerge. If many competing relations are possible, many trials may be required for the emergence of the one basis for choice that remains consistent from trial to trial.

This process would, of course, explain why equivalence, even when tested without reinforcement, sometimes emerges immediately and sometimes only after many trials (e.g., Devany, Hayes, & Nelson, 1986; Lazar, Davis-Lang, & Sanchez, 1984; Sidman et al., 1986; Sigurdardottir et al., 1990; Spradlin et al., 1973). But why, one must ask, should a subject come consistently to select only those comparisons that are related in a consistent way to the samples?

Here, a particular reinforcement history is required. In the experimental setting or in similar situations elsewhere, the subject must have learned, first, that each trial (or "problem") has a correct choice (or "answer"); and second, that each trial has only one correct choice. Without such a history, there is no reason why the subject's choices in a test without reinforcement should show any consistency at all, let alone the kind of consistency that the experimenter is looking for.

Such a selective process during the test can explain the delayed emergence of equivalence relations. It also permits another rather startling prediction: Even without explicitly teaching any prerequisite conditional relations, one should be able to produce the emergence of any kind of stimulus class or any relation one wants between samples and comparisons during the reinforced tests. That is to say, given a subject with the appropriate general history noted above, it should be possible to teach anything one wants to teach about relations between stimuli without giving the subject any differential reinforcement. All that would be required are appropriately designed test trials.

Harrison and Green (1990) have provided an impressive confirmation of this prediction. They presented subjects with a series of 2-choice conditional-discrimination trials, as illustrated in Table 1. Each trial had one of two possible samples, S1 or S2. Each trial also had one of two comparisons, C1 along with S1, and C2 along with S2. A second comparison, selected from a lengthy list, varied from trial to trial, but occasionally C1 and C2 were presented together. The subjects ended up always selecting C1 when S1 was the sample, and C2 when S2 was the sample. But the trials were run in extinction; no differential consequences were given for any of the subjects' choices. Consistency from trial to trial was the only possible basis for choice. (Harrison and Green then went on to show that the sample and the chosen comparison on each trial were related by equivalence.)

It remains, now, to determine how far this can be carried. In principle there is no limit. It should be possible to generate any relation one wants between sample and comparison, for example, color, form, size, oddity, order, identity or consistency of any arbitrary characteristic. All that should be required is to ensure that selections on the basis of any undesired relations are possible on only some of the trials, and that selection on the basis of the desired relations is possible on every trial.

This is what it means to assert that equivalence emerges during the test. Equivalence is only one of the possible relations that may exist between sample and comparison stimuli. Whether equivalence or some other relation emerges during a test will depend on the structure of the test trials. The prerequisites for equivalence relations must already have been established, but until the test, none of the subject's behavior need actually have been controlled by these potential equivalence relations. That this has happened is suggested when a subject says, after several inconsistent choices during the test, "Oh, now I see what this is all about," and then goes on to show equivalence (e.g., Bush et al., 1989). The only way to guarantee the emergence of equivalence relations is to test for them with test trials that permit no other consistent controlling relation between sample and comparison.

Table 1

List of the trial types (sample and comparison stimuli) presented to the subjects (in mixed orders) without reinforcement (after Harrison & Green, 1990).

SAMPLE
COMPARISONS

S1 ———> C1 X1
S1 ———> C1 X2
S1 ———> C1 X3
.   .
.   .
.   .
S1 ———> C1 Xn
S1 ———> C1 C2

———————————————

S2 ———> C2 Y1
S2 ———> C2 Y2
S2 ———> C2 Y3
.   .
.   .
.   .
S2 ———> C2 Yn

References

Barnes, T., & Sidman, M. (1990). *Equivalence without symmetry? A stimulus artifact.* Unpublished M.A. thesis, Northeastern University, Boston.

Bush, K. M., Sidman, M., & de Rose, T. (1989). Contextual control of emergent equivalence relations. *Journal of the Experimental Analysis of Behavior, 51,* 29-45.

Carrigan, P. F. (1986). *Conditional discrimination and transitive relations: A theoretical and experimental analysis.* Unpublished Ph.D. dissertation, Northeastern University, Boston.

Cumming, W. W., & Berryman, R. (1965). The complex discriminated operant: Studies of matching-to-sample and related problems. In D. I. Mostofsky (Ed.), *Stimulus generalization* (pp. 284-330). Stanford, CA: Stanford University Press.

D'Amato, M.R., Salmon, D., Loukas, E., & Tomie, A. (1985) Symmetry and transitivity of conditional relations in monkeys (*Cebus apella*) and pigeons (*Columba livia*). *Journal of the Experimental Analysis of Behavior, 44,* 35-47.

de Rose, J. C., McIlvane, W. J., Dube, W. V., Galpin, V. C., & Stoddard, L. T. (1988). Emergent simple discrimination established by indirect relation to differential consequences. *Journal of the Experimental Analysis of Behavior, 50,* 1-20.

Devany, J. M., Hayes, S. C., & Nelson, R. O. (1986). Equivalence class formation in language-able and language-disabled children. *Journal of the Experimental Analysis of Behavior, 46,* 243-257.

Dugdale, N. & Lowe, C. F. (1990). Naming and stimulus equivalence. In D. E. Blackman & H. Lejeune (Eds.), *Behaviour analysis in theory and practice: Contributions and controversies.* (pp. 115-138). Hillsdale, NJ: Erlbaum.

Harrison, R. & Green, G. (1990). Development of conditional and equivalence relations without differential consequences. *Journal of the Experimental Analysis of Behavior, 54,* 225-237.

Hayes, S. C. & Hayes, L. J. (1989). The verbal action of the listener as the basis for rule-governance. In S. C. Hayes (Ed.), *Rule-governed behavior: Cognition, contingencies, and instructional control* (pp. 153-190). New York: Plenum.

Iversen, I. H., Sidman, M., & Carrigan, P. (1986) Stimulus definition in conditional discriminations. *Journal of the Experimental Analysis of Behavior, 45,* 297-304.

Johnson, C., & Sidman, M. (1991). *Stimulus classes established by sample-and-S- conditional discrimination performance.* (Symposium presentation at the meeting of the Association for behavior Analysis, Atlanta, GA).

Kennedy, C. H., & Laitinen, R. (1988). Second-order conditional control of symmetric and transitive stimulus relations: The influence of order effects. *Psychological Record, 38,* 437-446.

Lazar, R. (1977) Extending sequence-class membership with matching to sample. *Journal of the Experimental Analysis of Behavior, 27,* 381-392.

Lazar, R. M., Davis-Lang, D., & Sanchez, L. (1984). The formation of visual stimulus equivalences in children. *Journal of the Experimental Analysis of Behavior, 41,* 251-266.

Lazar, R. M., & Kotlarchyk, B. J. (1986). Second-order control of sequence-class equivalences in children. *Behaviour Processes, 13,* 205-215.

Lipkens, R., Kop, P. F. M., & Matthijs, W. (1988). A test of symmetry and transitivity in the conditional discrimination performances of pigeons. *Journal of the Experimental Analysis of Behavior, 49,* 395-409.

Lowe, C. F. (1986, May). *The role of verbal behavior in the emergence of equivalence relations.* Paper presented at the meeting of the Association for Behavior Analysis, Milwaukee, WI.

McDonagh, E. C., McIlvane, W. J., & Stoddard, L. T. (1984). Teaching coin equivalences via matching to sample. *Applied Research in Mental Retardation, 5,* 177-197.

McIntire, K. D., Cleary, J., & Thompson, T. (1987). Conditional relations by monkeys: Reflexivity, symmetry, and transitivity. *Journal of the Experimental Analysis of Behavior, 47,* 279-285.

Piaget, J. (1963). *The child's conception of the world.* (J. & A. Tomlinson, Trans.). New Jersey: Littlefield, Adams. (Original English translation published 1929 by Routledge & Kegan Paul, Ltd., London).

Saunders, R. R., Wachter, J., & Spradlin, J. E. (1988) Establishing auditory stimulus control over an eight-member equivalence class via conditional discrimination procedures. *Journal of the Experimental Analysis of Behavior, 49,* 95-115.

Sidman, M. (1971). Reading and auditory-visual equivalences. *Journal of Speech and Hearing Research, 14,* 5-13.

Sidman, M. (1978). Remarks. *Behaviorism, 6,* 265-268.

Sidman, M. (1980). A note on the measurement of conditional discrimination. *Journal of the Experimental Analysis of Behavior, 33,* 285-289.

Sidman, M. (1986). Functional analysis of emergent verbal classes. In T. Thompson & M. D. Zeiler (Eds.), *Analysis and integration of behavioral units* (pp. 213-245). Hillsdale, NJ: Erlbaum.

Sidman, M. (1987). Two choices are not enough. *Behavior Analysis, 22*, 11-18.

Sidman, M. (1990). Equivalence relations: Where do they come from? In D. E. Blackman & H. Lejeune (Eds.), *Behaviour analysis in theory and practice: Contributions and controversies.* (pp. 93-114). Hillsdale, NJ: Erlbaum.

Sidman, M., Cresson, O., Jr., & Willson-Morris, M. (1974). Acquisition of matching to sample via mediated transfer. *Journal of the Experimental Analysis of Behavior, 22*, 261-273.

Sidman, M., Kirk, B., & Willson-Morris, M. (1985). Six-member stimulus classes generated by conditional-discrimination procedures. *Journal of the Experimental Analysis of Behavior, 43*, 21-42.

Sidman, M., Rauzin, R., Lazar, R., Cunningham, S., Tailby, W., & Carrigan, P. (1982). A search for symmetry in the conditional discriminations of rhesus monkeys, baboons, and children. *Journal of the Experimental Analysis of Behavior, 37*, 23-44.

Sidman, M., & Tailby, W. (1982). Conditional discrimination vs. matching to sample: An expansion of the testing paradigm. *Journal of the Experimental Analysis of Behavior, 37*, 5-22.

Sidman, M., Willson-Morris, M., & Kirk, B. (1986). Matching-to-sample procedures and the development of equivalence relations: The role of naming. *Analysis and Intervention in Developmental Disabilities, 6*, 1-19.

Sidman, M., Wynne, C. K., Maguire, R. W., & Barnes, T. (1989). Functional classes and equivalence relations. *Journal of the Experimental Analysis of Behavior, 52*, 261-274.

Sigurdardottir, Z. G., Green, G., & Saunders, R. R. (1990). Equivalence classes generated by sequence training. *Journal of the Experimental Analysis of Behavior, 53*, 47-63.

Silverman, K., Anderson, S. R., Marshall, A. M., & Baer, D. M. (1986) Establishing and generalizing audience control of new language repertoires. *Analysis and Intervention in Developmental Disabilities, 6*, 21-40.

Skinner, B. F. (1957) *Verbal behavior.* New York: Appleton-Century-Crofts.

Skinner, B. F. (1969). *Contingencies of reinforcement: A theoretical analysis.* New York: Appleton-Century-Crofts.

Spradlin, J. E., Cotter, V. W., & Baxley, N. (1973). Establishing a conditional discrimination without direct training: A study of transfer with retarded adolescents. *American Journal of Mental Deficiency, 77* 556-566.

Stikeleather, G., & Sidman, M. (1990). An instance of spurious equivalence relations. *The Analysis of Verbal Behavior, 8*, 1-11.

Vaughan, W., Jr. (1988). Formation of equivalence sets in pigeons. *Journal of Experimental Psychology: Animal Behavior Processes, 14*, 36-42.

Wulfert, E., & Hayes, S. C. (1988). Transfer of a conditioned ordering response through conditional equivalence classes. *Journal of the Experimental Analysis of Behavior, 50*, 125-144.

Chapter 2

The Stability of Equivalence Classes

Joseph E. Spradlin
Kathryn J. Saunders
Richard R. Saunders
University of Kansas

There have been numerous demonstrations of the development of stimulus classes with a variety of procedures and in a range of human subjects (de Rose, McIlvane, Dube, Galpin, & Stoddard, 1988; Dube, McIlvane, Maguire, Mackay, & Stoddard, 1989; Saunders, Saunders, Kirby, & Spradlin, 1988; Saunders, Wachter, & Spradlin, 1988; Sidman, 1971; Sidman & Cresson, 1973; Sidman, Cresson, & Willson-Morris, 1974; Sidman, Kirk, & Willson-Morris, 1985; Sidman, Willson-Morris, & Kirk, 1986; Spradlin, Cotter, & Baxley, 1973; Spradlin & Saunders, 1986; Stromer & Osborne, 1982; Wetherby, Karlan, & Spradlin, 1983). In the special case of equivalence classes (Sidman & Tailby, 1982), a few of the possible relations between the stimuli in a set are directly trained, allowing other relations between the stimuli in the set to emerge.

As in any area of experimental investigation, once a phenomenon has been demonstrated under a variety of conditions questions begin to arise that go beyond mere replication. In the case of stimulus classes, particularly equivalence classes, some of these questions are: "How stable are these classes over time? What happens when the trained relations that serve as prerequisites for emergent relations are changed through training? What kind of a model would account for data regarding stability across time and the effects of changed prerequisite relations?" These questions have led to the current chapter that will: (a) summarize research that demonstrates the stability of classes over time, (b) present a network model for explaining the stability of classes, and (c) evaluate the network model in terms of current data on the development of classes and on the effects of modifying the prerequisite relations for class development.

Research on Stability and Durability

There have been few attempts to determine whether stimulus classes remain intact after a period of weeks or months without intervening experience on either the trained conditional discriminations or the derived relations. One of the few was an unpublished report by Hollis (1987) of a study based on Sidman's (1971) study of reading equivalences. Like Sidman, Hollis began with subjects who correctly named pictures of a number of objects and who selected pictures of these objects in response to their spoken names. However, they did not read the names of these objects (name the printed words), select the printed words in response to their spoken names, or match pictures to the related printed words. In this study, the stimuli were divided into three sets; within each set, the subjects were taught one of the relations not previously demonstrated. For the first set, subjects were taught to name orally the printed words, with the second set of stimuli, subjects were taught to select the printed words in response to their spoken names; and with the third set, subjects were taught to select the printed words that matched the pictures. Thus, as shown in Figure 1, the relation trained in each set was a relation that would allow for the derivation of the two remaining untrained relations. After this training, all subjects exhibited nearly 100% correct responses on both the trained and untrained relations. Then, after intervals of 110 to 206 days without intervening laboratory experience, the subjects were retested. Tests were made in the absence of reinforcement. Performances on the untrained relations ranged from 72% to 87% correct. Although accuracy on the untrained relations had decreased, the percentages of correct responses were still far above chance. However, because the stimuli in the sets were common in the everyday environments of Hollis' subjects, the performances that were maintained could have been due to practice occurring outside of the experimental setting.

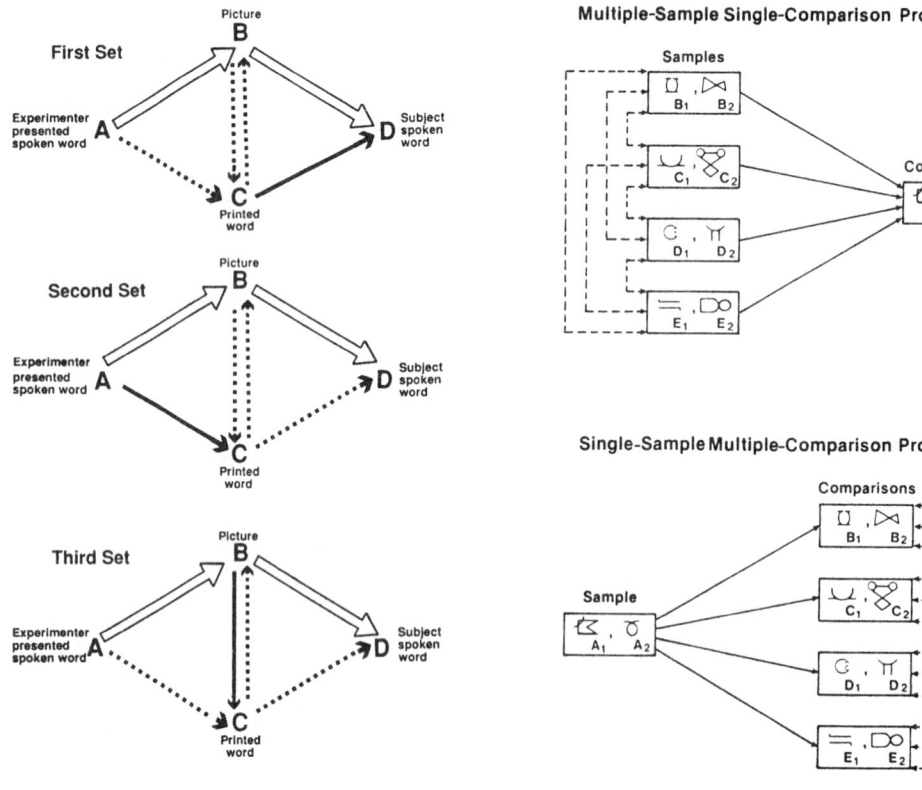

Figure 1. A schematic of the Hollis (1987) training and testing procedures. The wide arrows refer to the prerequisite relations that the subjects exhibited prior to entering the experiment. The subjects could select the pictures in response to the names and name the pictures. The solid narrow arrows indicate which additional relation was trained for each of the three sets and the dashed-line arrows indicate which relations emerged without direct training.

Figure 2. A schematic of the first phase of training and testing procedures reported by Saunders, Wachter, and Spradlin (1988). The solid arrows indicate trained relations between sample and comparison stimuli with the same numerical subscript. The dashed-arrow lines indicate the combined tests for symmetry and transitivity among samples and among comparisons with the same subscript. (Copyright 1988 by the Society for the Experimental Analysis of Behavior, Inc.)

In a study that bears on the issue of intervening practice, Saunders, Wachter, and Spradlin (1988) trained relations among letter-like nonsense visual stimuli, rather than among pictures, printed words, and spoken words. The tests for stable performance in this study were conducted between 2 to 5 months after the extensive and complex training and testing described below. First, the subjects acquired four conditional discriminations according to one of the two schematics shown in Figure 2. Two of the subjects were trained in the version in the upper panel of Figure 2 and two with the version in the lower panel. Once the subjects had demonstrated a high level of performance on these discriminations, they were tested for symmetry alone and then simultaneously for symmetry and transitivity, a test Bush, Sidman, and de Rose (1989) referred to as a test for equivalence. All four subjects eventually demonstrated 100% correct responding on both the symmetry tests and the tests for equivalence. These performances showed the emergence of one-node equivalence relations. (Nodes are stimuli that link two or more other stimuli (Fields, Verhave, & Fath, 1984).)

Second, the subjects were given training on three additional conditional discriminations combined with one of the conditional discriminations that had been learned in the previous phase, as shown in Figure 3. Once again subjects demonstrated perfect or near perfect performance on symmetry and one-node equivalence tests.

Third, the subjects were given training in which all seven conditional discriminations were intermixed. Once they had shown nearly perfect performance on these discriminations, they were presented two-node equivalence tests, appropriate to their preceding training, as shown in the two schematics in Figure 4.

During these tests, both the test trials and the baseline trials were presented without differential reinforcement. Once again the performances were nearly perfect. Fourth, the subjects were taught to select one of two comparison stimuli, E_1 and E_2, depending on whether the auditory sample "Cadoo" or "Sompta" was presented, as shown in Figure 5.

Next, the subjects were tested to determine if these auditory samples also controlled responses to the remaining seven stimuli in their respective stimulus classes. For three of the subjects, the performances were nearly perfect. The fourth subject performed at 50% correct. This subject was then given training involving the auditory samples and a second pair of visual

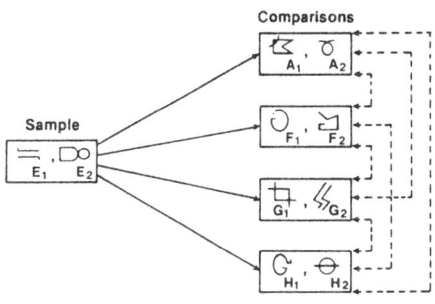

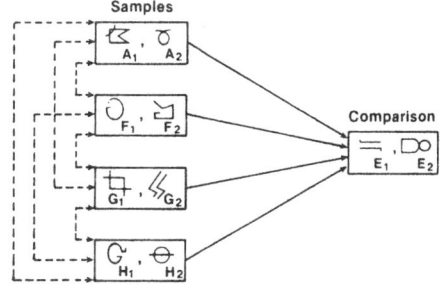

Figure 3. A schematic of the second phase of training and testing procedures reported by Saunders, Wachter, and Spradlin (1988). The solid arrows indicate trained relations between sample and comparison stimuli with the same numerical subscript. The dashed-arrow lines indicate the combined tests for symmetry and transitivity among samples and among comparisons with the same subscript. (Copyright 1988 by the Society for the Experimental Analysis of Behavior, Inc.)

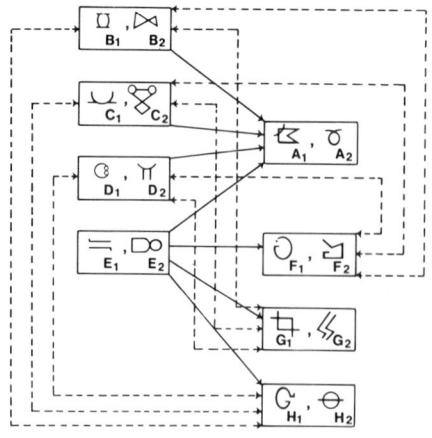

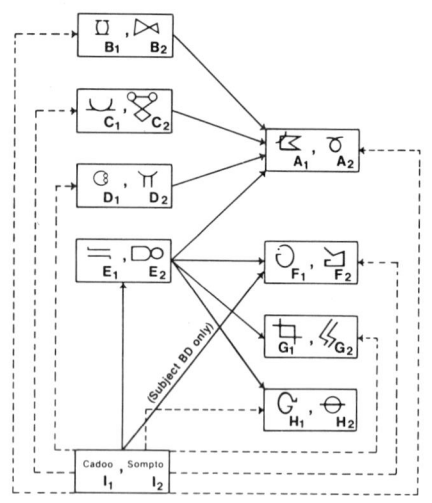

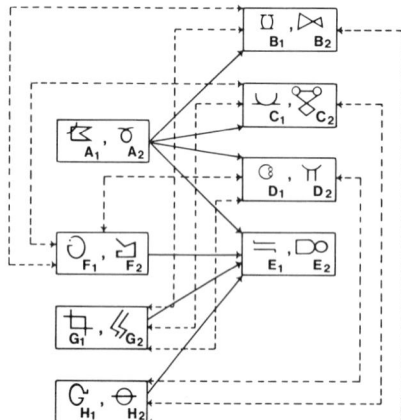

Figure 4. A schematic of the third phase of procedures reported by Saunders, Wachter, and Spradlin (1988). The solid arrows indicate trained relations completed during the first two phases. The dashed-arrow lines indicate the combined tests for symmetry and transitivity among samples and among comparisons with the same subscript that were linked by two nodes. (Copyright 1988 by the Society for the Experimental Analysis of Behavior, Inc.)

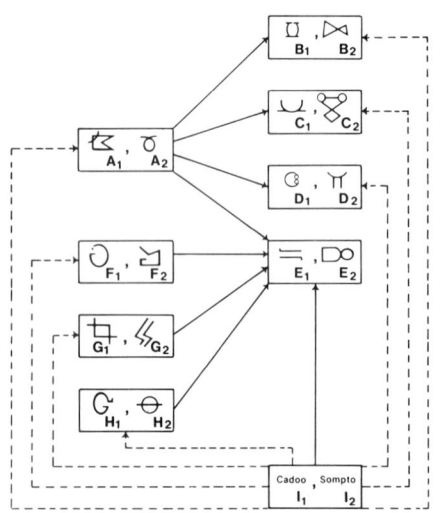

Figure 5. A schematic of the fourth phase of training and testing procedures reported by Saunders, Wachter, and Spradlin (1988). Solid arrows indicate trained relations completed during the first two phases and the training in the current phase. Dashed-arrow lines indicate the tests for the untrained relations. (Copyright 1988 by the Society for the Experimental Analysis of Behavior, Inc.)

stimuli as comparisons. After this was done, performance on class probes was 100% correct. The subjects then discontinued coming to the laboratory for periods of 2 to 5 months. Following this absence, the subjects were retested under nonreinforcement conditions for both the baseline and class relations. Three of the subjects' performances were initially at 90% or better on both baseline and class tests. The remaining subject performed at below 50% on both baseline and class tests during the first return session. However, when given two additional sessions, still without reinforcement, the subject gradually achieved 100% correct performance on both baseline and test trials.

The studies by Saunders, Wachter, and Spradlin (1988) and Hollis (1987) demonstrate that the derived relations of an equivalence class may be maintained across time and that intervening practice with the stimuli is not necessary for such maintenance. The study also demonstrates that having a large number of stimuli in a class is not a deterrent to class maintenance. Finally, the data suggest that, even though the initial retest performance may not be indicative of class maintenance, the baseline and class relations may gradually be recovered across repeated sessions with unreinforced trials.

A Network Model

What kind of model would describe the findings presented above? Saunders, Wachter, and Spradlin (1988) proposed a network model as being consistent with data that demonstrated that (1) equivalence performances with large classes of stimuli were maintained over several months without practice, and (2) when the baseline and derived relations were not maintained they were sometimes recovered during repeated unreinforced baseline and test trials. Their logic was as follows:

Start with a single conditional discrimination as shown in the top panel of Figure 6 in which the A-B relation is trained and the B-A relation emerges (showing the property of symmetry in the A-B relation). If anything disturbs or breaks down the A-B and B-A relations, there is no basis for their recovery other than retraining.

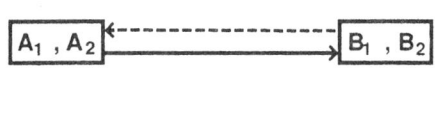

Suppose, however, that not only is an A-B relation trained but also an A-C relation as shown in the middle panel of Figure 6. Suppose further that symmetry and transitivity are demonstrated. If the A-B relations are disturbed and the relations involving A and C and B and C are maintained, A-B can be derived readily by the maintained relations in the same way that the B-C and C-B relations were originally derived.

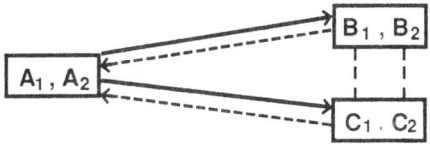

To take the example one step further, one can expand the set of conditional discrimina-

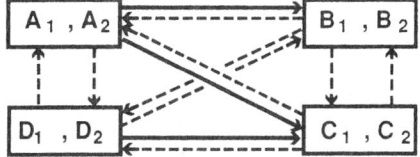

Figure 6. A schematic in three panels showing the increase in the number of derivation routes to the A-B and B-A relations as the number of stimuli in the class is increased. The solid arrows indicate trained relations and the dashed-line arrows indicate untrained relations.

tions to include four stimuli, as shown in the lower panel of Figure 6. If all of the derived relations are demonstrated, and if A-B relations are disturbed, the A-B relations are derivable as long as either the A-C and B-C relations are intact or the A-D and B-D relations are intact.

As the number of stimuli within each equivalence class increases, the number of possible ways of recovering the A-B relation is increased dramatically. As long as some key relations within the class have been tested and demonstrated and as long as the "to be recovered" relations are presented in sessions including these intact relations, it is easy to see how recovery might occur across repeated tests under extinction conditions.

Then the network model need not imply that relations are demonstrated with equal probability; it is not an all-or-none model. Indeed, an all-or-none model seems incongruent with demonstrations that sometimes during initial testing for derived relations performance starts out at near chance levels and gradually increases to 100% correct in the absence of reinforcement. An all-or-none model is also incongruent with the gradual recovery of both baseline and derived performances in the absence of reinforcement. Finally, an all-or-none network seems incongruent with higher order control of equivalence classes. So, it appears that if a network model is to be congruent with the data concerning stimulus classes, it must allow that some of the relations between stimuli in the network could emerge more readily or be more stable over time.

What might account for the gradual demonstration of some of the emergent relations in an equivalence class? Although direct reinforcement of the prerequisite relations may be said to extend to all of the other possible relations within the class (Sidman & Tailby, 1982), this does not rule out the possibility that other sources of control might also exist that would affect equivalence test trial performance. In fact, a number of sources of control might affect performance on test trials.

One source of control might be physical similarity. Although the baseline arbitrary matching training no doubt reduces the likelihood of control by physical similarity between the sample and comparison stimuli, it may not eliminate similarity as a source of control. Perhaps on some early test trials the subject simply selects on the basis of stimulus similarity. On another trial, the subject may respond on the basis of equivalence; that type of control may then also be probable on the next test trial. With repeated tests the subject "learns" that equivalence is a basis for responding to all probes while similarity only allows for selection on some trials. Hence, when equivalence is the only consistent basis for responding this becomes the consistent mode of response. Perhaps what happens with repeated tests is the weakening of competing sources of control. Although on any specific test trial the subject's response is controlled by a specific source of control, the sources may vary across trials. Repeated tests may strengthen the source of control that is possible across all test trials. This is simply a restatement of Devany, Hayes, and Nelson's (1986) explanation of why subjects sometimes show improvement on equivalence tests across unreinforced sessions.

The number of nodes separating any two stimuli during training can also affect the likelihood that a relation between the two stimuli will be demonstrated immediately. If a subject is given A-B, B-C, C-D, and D-E training, performance on the three node A-E relation is completely dependent on the one node A-C, B-D, C-E, relations (Sidman, Kirk, & Willson-Morris, 1985). Furthermore one would not expect the A-E relation to be demonstrated unless the two node A-D, B-E relations were demonstrated (except via some arbitrary matching pattern unrelated to the preceding training). So early in testing it would not be surprising to find that the relations between stimuli separated by one node are demonstrated on more opportunities than are those separated by two or more nodes. However, with repeated testing of one-node, two-node, and three-node relations, it would not be surprising if the three-node relations were gradually strengthened because of their relation to lower node relations. This premise was verified by Fields, Adams,

Verhave, and Newman (1990) in classes containing one- and two-node relations.

A network model must acknowledge the possibility that different sources of control act on emergent relations. This seems to be congruent with most of the facts involving gradual demonstration of stimulus class development or the gradual recovery of stimulus classes after periods of time without exposure. Although we believe the fit between the network model and existing data is compelling, it should be noted that the notion of a network of relations that influence re-emergence is highly speculative. There are no completed studies that compare the retention of relations involved in equivalence classes and relations involved in independent conditional discriminations. Perhaps unrelated conditional discriminations are equally stable over time. It might be that long term stable performance and/or re-emergence occurs because of overtraining. Prior to testing for equivalence, baseline relations are usually trained to a high level of accuracy, then presented under intermittent reinforcement conditions, and then presented under extinction conditions. Finally, an extensive testing series is presented. Perhaps this overtraining accounts for the long term stable performance on tests for equivalence relations.

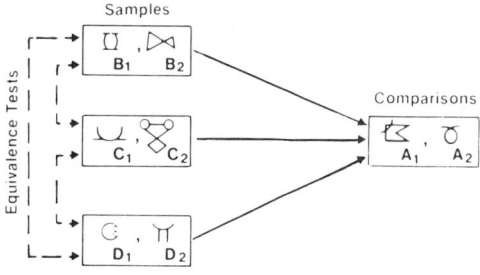

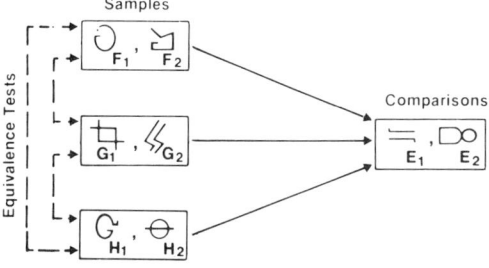

Figure 7. A schematic shown in two panels of the first two phases of training and testing procedures reported in Experiment 2 of Saunders, Saunders, Kirby, and Spradlin (1988). The solid arrows indicate trained relations between sample and comparison stimuli with the same numerical subscript. The dashed-arrow lines indicate the combined tests for symmetry and transitivity among samples with the same subscript. (Copyright 1988 by the Society for the Experimental Analysis of Behavior, Inc.)

Research on Altering Prerequisite Performances

The network model was originally proposed to account for the stability of large classes in which particular member relations may have weakened. Thus far, we have not discussed the results of efforts to change member relations through explicit training. When explicit contingencies for responding on some relations are altered, we might expect to see changes in performance on other relations among stimuli in the class. Such manipulations provide at least two opportunities to make observations relevant to the stability of relations involved in stimulus classes. First, how easily may selections on conditional discriminations be reversed when doing so alters class membership for the stimuli involved? Second, does reversal of a key prerequisite conditional discrimination result in changes in relations derived from it?

Saunders, Saunders, Kirby, and Spradlin (1988) conducted a series of experiments on the merging of existing classes via unreinforced selection that bears on both of these questions.

In Experiment 2 of their report, three mildly retarded subjects were given training to establish two equivalence classes as shown in the upper panel of Figure 7. That is, they were trained to select comparison A_1 in response to samples B_1, C_1, and D_1; and comparison A_2 in response to samples B_2, C_2, and D_2. All of these subjects' performances demonstrated the development of equivalence classes. Two more classes were then established, as shown in the lower panel of Figure 7. The subjects were taught to select comparison E_1 in response to samples F_1, G_1, and H_1 and to select E_2 in response to F_2, G_2, and H_2. Once again the performances of all three subjects demonstrated the development of equivalence classes.

Figure 8. A schematic of the unreinforced selection trials to which subjects in Experiment 2 of Saunders, Saunders, Kirby, and Spradlin (1988) were exposed following the first two phases of training and testing.

At this point the subjects were given a series of sessions in which F_1 and F_2 stimuli were presented as samples and A_1 and A_2 stimuli were presented as comparisons as shown in Figure 8. No differential programmed consequences followed any response during this phase. However, within three sessions all three subjects were selecting the A_1 stimulus when F_1 was presented as the sample and the A_2 stimulus when F_2 was presented as the sample. When these trials were interspersed among baseline trials, performance on all trials remained at 100%. Subjects were then presented sessions in which the one- and three-node equivalence probes shown in Figure 9 were introduced. The performance of all three subjects indicated that the four classes had merged into two according to their performances on the unreinforced conditional selection trials (A-F). That is, B_1, C_1, and D_1, had merged with F_1, G_1, and H_1, and B_2, C_2, and D_2, had merged with F_2, G_2, and H_2.

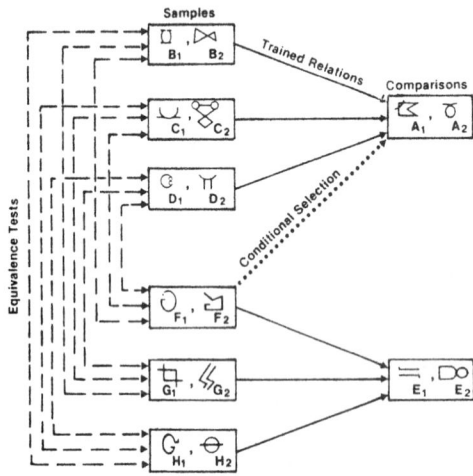

Figure 9. A schematic of the final phase of testing procedures reported in Experiment 2 of Saunders, Saunders, Kirby, and Spradlin (1988). The solid arrows indicate trained relations between sample and comparison stimuli conducted in earlier phases. The dotted-line arrow indicates the unreinforced selections permitted during the preceding phase. The dashed-arrow lines indicate the combined tests for symmetry and transitivity among samples linked by one and three nodes.
(Copyright 1988 by the Society for the Experimental Analysis of Behavior, Inc.)

After the demonstration of the merger of classes the subjects were given training with the F and A stimuli in which selections opposite to those made earlier were reinforced. That is, reinforcement was delivered each time subjects selected A_2 when F_1 was presented as a sample and A_1 when F_2 was presented as a sample. Once a subject reached criterion under this training condition, these F-A conditional discrimination trials were interspersed with the original baseline trials under nonreinforcement conditions.

Two of the three subjects immediately

reverted back to their initially unreinforced selections on F-A discrimination trials. The third subject's performance varied from 37% to 100% correct across four sessions on F-A trials. In addition, for this subject, errors occurred on the F-E discrimination of the original baseline. Twenty-three sessions were required to demonstrate maintenance of correct performances on the unreinforced baseline trials and the reversed F-A trials. For the two subjects who reverted back to their initial unreinforced F-A performance when the F-A trials were interspersed in the original baseline conditions, the establishment of this performance was not easy, requiring 14 and 38 sessions before correct performance was maintained on the unreinforced baseline trials and the reversed F-A trials.

These data suggest that it is difficult to reverse relations when doing so would alter the class membership of the stimuli involved–at least when the relations occur within the context of the existing classes. Once the F-A reversal was maintained in the context of the other relations in the existing classes, probes to determine how the reversal had affected class merger were introduced. For two subjects, responses on probe trials were virtually identical to those made during the first test for merger of the classes. For the third subject, performance on probes was the same as it had been prior to the reversal except for probes involving the F stimuli. On these probes, performance was in line with the F-A reversal training. In essence, F_1 had now been assigned to the 2 class and F_2 to the 1 class for this one subject. However, the initial merged classes remained quite stable. In summary, once small classes had merged into larger classes, the derived relations indicating larger classes were extremely resistant to alteration. That is, although reinforcement procedures could be used to alter performances on the specific conditional discriminations that were central to initial class merger, altering these performances had little or no effect on the performances that showed the merger.

Recent research conducted in our laboratory also bears on the resistance of emergent relations to rearrangement by changed performances on prerequisite conditional discriminations. Two normal subjects, one 12 and one 8 years of age, were given training as shown in Figure 10. Once the subjects had demonstrated nearly 100% correct responding on a mixture of the four conditional discriminations (A-B, B-C, C-D, and D-E), they were tested for all of the untrained relations involving the E stimuli (except E-D, symmetry). These included the three-node transitivity test (A-E), the two-node transitivity test (B-E), the one-node C-E test, and the combined tests for transitivity and symmetry E-A, E-B, and E-C. The 12-year-old subject made no errors in two sessions (12 probe trials per session) while the 8-year-old subject made one error in three probe sessions. Then the D-E discrimination was reversed from what it was during initial training; that is the subjects were taught to select E_2 in response to sample D_1 and E_1 in response to D_2.

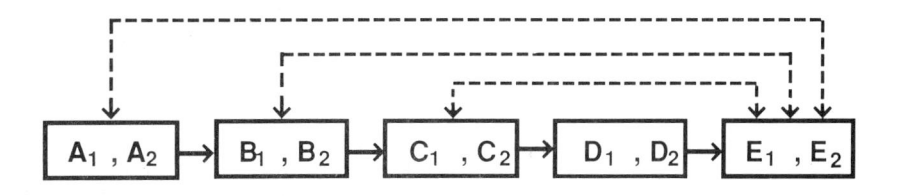

Figure 10. A schematic of the training and testing for two normal subjects. The solid arrows indicate the relations trained among stimuli with the same subscript. The dashed-line arrows indicated the untrained relations tested.

For the 8-year-old subject, it took only two sessions of training to establish 100% reversed responding. Then, performance on a mixture of reversed D-E relations and the original A-B, B-C, and C-D relations presented under extinction conditions remained at above 95% correct. For the 12-year-old subject, D-E reversal required only two training sessions. However, when D-E trials were introduced into the original A-B, B-C, and C-D baseline, the subject responded by reversing all discriminations. It then took 22 sessions of remedial training before the subject reached criterion with the D-E reversal and the original baseline. After each subject maintained the reversed D-E discrimination in the initial baseline, probe trials as described above were reintroduced. In general, both subjects responded to the probe trials as they had after initial training. Both subjects initially made a small number of responses to probes that would be in line with their reversed D-E training. That is, they occasionally selected A_1, B_1, or C_1 in response to E_2 or selected A_2, B_2, or C_2 in response to E_1. However, such performance never occurred on more than 25% of the probe trials and, after repeated probe sessions, both subjects resumed responding exactly as they had after their initial baseline training. This was true even though reversed responding on the D-E conditional discrimination was maintained.

The data from the last two studies suggest that changing a key prerequisite relation within the context of a large network does not necessarily result in changes in other relations in that network. In a sense, the changed relation exists independently of the others. Based on the network model, one might suppose that this finding would be more likely when single relations are changed within large classes. This is because all of the relations in the class are multiply determined. That is, although the now changed relation was initially crucial to the development of emergent relations, once a network has formed, it is not the sole determinant of any other relations. Based on this line of reasoning, one might make two predictions. First, when the majority of the relations involved in a stimulus class are altered, alterations in the remaining relations in the class would be expected. Second, when only one relation in a class is changed, one might expect less stability within smaller (e.g., three-member) classes relative to larger classes.

A study by Spradlin, Cotter, and Baxley (1973) addressed the first prediction. In this study, **all** of the prerequisite baseline relations were changed subsequent to the demonstration of emergent relations. Spradlin et al. (1973) initially trained A-C, B-C, and A-D relations, then tested for the B-D relations as shown in Figure 11. As one would expect, on probe trials the subjects selected comparison stimulus D_1 in the presence of sample stimulus B_1 and comparison stimulus D_2 in response to sample stimulus B_2. The subjects were then retrained to select comparison stimuli C_2 and D_2 in the presence of sample A_1 and comparison stimuli C_1 and D_1 in the presence of sample A_2. Likewise, the subjects were trained to select C_2 in the presence of B_1, and C_1 in the presence of B_2. After this training, when the B-D test was made the subjects selected D_1 in the presence of B_2 and D_2 in the presence of B_1. So, with extensive retraining, the classes of A_1, B_1, C_1, and D_1 and A_2, B_2, C_2, and D_2 had now been changed to A_1, B_1, C_2, D_2 and A_2, B_2, C_1, D_1.

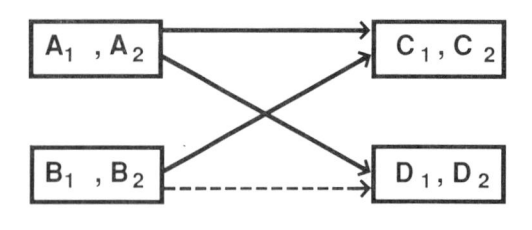

Figure 11. A schematic of the training and testing procedures described in Spradlin, Cotter, and Baxley (1973). The solid arrows indicate trained relations among stimuli with the same subscript. The dashed-line arrows indicated the untrained relations tested.

The second prediction is addressed in a study by Pilgrim and Galizio (1990). These authors taught college students A-B and A-C relations, then tested the A-A, B-B, C-C identity relations, the B-A and C-A symmetry relations and the B-C and C-B relations. As expected these subjects' responses demonstrated equivalence. Then, for two subjects, the contingencies for the A-C relations were reversed so that selection of C_1 in the presence of A_2 was reinforced and selection of C_2 in the presence of A_1 was reinforced. One subject's performance of the B-C and C-B relations changed for one session (the sixth), then returned to the prereversed state while the performance of the other subject on these relations became unstable. Both subjects showed extensive changes on symmetry test trials. These data suggest that small classes are less resistant to change, a finding that is in accordance with the network model. It should be noted, however, that conclusions drawn from comparisons across procedures and subject populations that are as different as those across the studies presented in this chapter must be tentative.

A study currently being conducted in our laboratory is designed to assess the interplay between class size and the effects of reversal manipulations. The study is a follow-up of the previously described study involving two normal children in which one prerequisite relation for a five-member class was reversed after tests for emergent relations had been made. Selections on test trials were largely unchanged for one subject and completely unchanged for the second. In the present study one child learned C-D-E relations and showed emergent C-E and E-C relations (3-member classes). Reversal of the D-E relations resulted in mixed performance on test trials: responses on C-E trials were largely the same as those prior to the D-E reversal while responses on E-C trials were consistent with the reversed relation. Although these responses might seem incompatible, it should be remembered that both were made possible by the training procedure (one before and one after the reversal). An alternative interpretation might hold that the subject was simply responding conditionally, with the **specific** sample-comparison relations demonstrated no longer determined by the training procedure. This conditional responding might occur because reinforcement for conditional responding was the most consistent feature of the subject's experimental history (Saunders, Saunders, Kirby, & Spradlin, 1988). Regardless of the specific sources of control involved, these results suggest greater disruption of smaller classes after the alteration of a single prerequisite relation—a finding congruent with the network model.

The network interpretation becomes less clear, however, when additional findings of Pilgrim and Galizio (1990) are considered. After the initial training and testing sequences described above, three other subjects were exposed to a procedure that generated inconsistent responding on the A-C trials, thus providing no basis for consistent responding on B-C and C-B trials (except that provided by the initial training and testing sequence). This manipulation did not change responding on B-C and C-B trials or on symmetry test trials. For two of these subjects, A-C selections were then reversed as they had been for the subjects mentioned previously who had not been previously exposed to contingencies generating inconsistent responding. B-C and C-B responses did not change for either subject and symmetry test responses changed for one subject only. The results for the latter two subjects again suggest stability of derived relations after modification of the baseline prerequisite relations. The latter findings seem to be incongruent with the network model, because stability was shown within a small class. Saunders, Saunders, Kirby, and Spradlin (1988) noted that the results of their reversal manipulation indicated that, once demonstrated, emergent relations may no longer be dependent on their prerequisites. Perhaps this observation provides the most parsimonious explanation.

Another set of findings might also seem incongruent with the network model. More recent research in our laboratory suggests that there are conditions under which emergent relations within relatively large classes are not resistant to change and, in fact, do change in the direction of new or reversed contingencies. The 12-year-old boy discussed above was brought back after 1 year to determine if the results of the prior study would be replicated if new classes were taught via the A-B, B-C, C-D, D-E procedure. Conditions were the same as for the previous study with the exception that **prior to** the initial tests for equivalence the D-E relation was reversed from that which was initially trained. When tests were made, derived relations were in line with the current baseline relations. That is, the formation of two classes was demonstrated: [A_1, B_1, C_1, D_1, and E_2] and [A_2, B_2, C_2, D_2, and E_1] as shown by E-A, E-B, E-C, and E-D tests for derived relations. Next the initial D_1-E_1 and D_2-E_2 relations were re-established. When tests for the derived relations involving the E_1 and E_2 stimuli were made, the class membership of the E stimuli was shown to have reversed in accordance with the training on the baseline relations. These findings have been replicated with another preadolescent normal child who had no previous experience in studies of equivalence classes.

Thus, studies in which a prerequisite conditional discrimination is reversed yield differing results that are not completely described by the simple network model discussed thus far. The critical variables for these varying results have not been fully specified. However, data from studies on the conditional control of classes may provide a clue. In these studies, the original and the reversed prerequisite relation(s) are associated with different second order discriminative stimuli that provide the contexts for the intended differential performances. These contextual stimuli then typically are shown to control performance on test trials. That is, class membership is shown to be flexible and under contextual control.

These findings suggest the following interpretation: procedures involving the reversal of key prerequisites provide the basis for more than one set of relations to be demonstrated on test trials. However, when no explicit contextual stimulus is provided, the source of control of the specific relations demonstrated is unpredictable. Sometimes contextual control may be established even though there is no experimenter designated contextual stimulus. The contextual stimuli may be the altered prerequisite relations themselves (i.e., whether the original or reversed selections have most recently been reinforced) and some procedures may be more likely to establish contextual control by the reversed relation than others. This possibility is strengthened by the observation that, in studies in which the reversal of prerequisite relations results in marked changes in derived relationships, an operation has been performed that made the stimuli for which the class membership was to be changed (those involved in the reversed relations) quite unique from the remaining stimuli within the classes prior to the first test for equivalence involving these stimuli. For example, the procedure described above involving reversing the D-E relations prior to making any tests for equivalence, the relations between A, B, C, and D stimuli were not reversed. The E stimuli and their relationship to the D stimuli were then unique with respect to their history in training; other pairs of stimuli had no such history.

Another form of contextual control that may determine whether or not the class membership of a particular stimulus is shown to be flexible (in combination with the altered prerequisite relations) may be identified. A subject's history on similar tasks may determine whether performance on test trials changes as a result of changes in the prerequisite relations. We are not aware of any studies explicitly attempting such a manipulation, but some of the results of the study by Pilgrim and Galizio (1990) may be suggestive. In that study, two college students were exposed to the A-C reversal condition after being exposed to an intermediate condition in which random contingencies produced inconsistent selections on A-C trials. Test trial selections were unchanged in this intermediate condition, probably because there was no basis for alternative consistent selections and subjects with a history of reinforcement for conditional responding tend to respond conditionally. When next exposed to conditions that did provide a consistent basis for change (complete reversal of A-C, as for the initial two subjects) selections on equivalence test trials remained as in the initial and intermediate training conditions, and A-C symmetry test selections reversed for only one subject. In essence, the intermediate condition may have served to instruct these subjects not to change despite changes in contingencies on prerequisite relations.

As mentioned earlier, two other subjects who were exposed to the A-C reversal condition and retesting of derived relations without the intermediate condition showed at least some disruption of performance on equivalence tests. One subject apparently responded inconsistently across test trials. That is, responses were consistent with both the initial training and the reversal training (either B_1 or B_2 could be matched with either C_1 or C_2). The second subject made a complete reversal during the sixth test session after reversal training, then shifted back. This once again indicates a lack of conditional control. Both subjects showed extensive change on tests for symmetry of the A-C relations.

Conclusion

In summary, certain key findings concerning equivalence class performance have been presented. These are:

1. High levels of correct performance on numerous trained and derived relations are maintained even after several months without intervening practice.

2. Sometimes, after a period of several months, when baseline trials and tests for derived relations are presented, accuracy on both baseline trials and derived relations is initially low. However, with repeated testing in the absence of differential reinforcement, performance on both baseline and test trials improves to 100% correct.

3. It may be very difficult to change the relationships between stimuli of the original baseline after tests for the derived relations of an equivalence class have been made.

4. Sometimes, even after reversals such as those mentioned under item 3 are established, performance on tests for equivalence does not change.

5. If tests for emergent relations are not made until after key prerequisite relations are reversed, emergent relations may be shown to vary with reversals in the prerequisite relations. That is, derived relations are more likely to change according to changes in the baseline conditions.

6. Equivalence classes can be brought under conditional control. That is, in the presence of X_1, $[A_1, B_1, C_1, D_1]$ and $[A_2, B_2, C_2,$ and $D_2]$ may constitute the equivalence classes. In the presence of X_2, stimuli $[A_1, B_1, C_2, D_2]$, and $[A_2, B_2, C_1,$ and $D_1]$ may constitute the equivalence classes.

These facts concerning equivalence classes seem congruent with a network model only if the classes have two characteristics. First, sources of control other than those of the experimenter-designated prerequisite relations may influence performance on test trials. Second, the specific relations among stimuli within classes must be under contextual control. Without these characteristics, it is difficult to imagine how equivalence classes could play a role in complex human functioning. Further research on the generality of these characteristics will be necessary for further evaluation of the network model for explaining the stability and durability of stimulus classes.

Some of the research cited in this chapter was supported in part by Federal NICHD grants 5-P30HD02528 and 1-P01HD18955 to the Bureau of Child Research, University of Kansas.

References

Bush, K. M., Sidman, M., & de Rose, T. (1989). Contextual control of emergent equivalence relations. *Journal of the Experimental Analysis of Behavior, 51,* 29-45.

de Rose, J. C., McIlvane, W. J., Dube, W. V., Galpin, V. C., & Stoddard, L. T. (1988). Emergent simple discrimination established by indirect relation to differential consequences. *Journal of the Experimental Analysis of Behavior, 50,* 1-20.

Devany, J. M., Hayes, S. C., & Nelson, R. O. (1986). Equivalence class formation in language-able and language-disabled children. *Journal of the Experimental Analysis of Behavior, 46*, 243-257.

Dube, W. V., McIlvane, W. J., Maguire, R. W., Mackay, H. A., & Stoddard, L. T. (1989). Stimulus class formation and stimulus-reinforcer relations. *Journal of the Experimental Analysis of Behavior, 51*, 65-76.

Fields, L., Adams, B. J., Verhave, T., & Newman, S. (1990). The effects of nodality on the formation of equivalence classes. *Journal of the Experimental Analysis of Behavior, 53*, 345-358.

Fields, L., Verhave, T., & Fath, S. (1984). Stimulus equivalence and transitive associations: A methodological analysis. *Journal of the Experimental Analysis of Behavior, 42*, 143-157.

Hollis, J. H. (1987). *Reading vocabulary acquisition and retention in developmentally disabled children.* Working Paper in Child Development, Child Language Program, Lawrence: University of Kansas.

Pilgrim, C., & Galizio, M. (1990). Relations between baseline contingencies and equivalence probe performances. *Journal of the Experimental Analysis of Behavior, 54*, 213-224.

Saunders, R. R., Saunders, K. J., Kirby, K. C., & Spradlin, J. E. (1988). The merger and development of equivalence classes by unreinforced conditional selection of comparison stimuli. *Journal of the Experimental Analysis of Behavior, 50*, 145-162.

Saunders, R. R., Wachter, J., & Spradlin, J. E. (1988). Establishing auditory stimulus control over an eight-member equivalence class via conditional discrimination procedures. *Journal of the Experimental Analysis of Behavior, 49*, 95-115.

Sidman, M. (1971). Reading and auditory-visual equivalences. *Journal of Speech and Hearing Research, 14*, 5-13.

Sidman, M., & Cresson, O., Jr. (1973). Reading and crossmodal transfer of stimulus equivalences in severe retardation. *American Journal of Mental Deficiency, 77*, 515-523.

Sidman, M., Cresson, O., Jr., & Willson-Morris, M. (1974). Acquisition of matching to sample via mediated transfer. *Journal of the Experimental Analysis of Behavior, 22*, 261-273.

Sidman, M., Kirk, B., & Willson-Morris, M. (1985). Six-member stimulus classes generated by conditional-discrimination procedures. *Journal of the Experimental Analysis of Behavior, 43*, 21-42.

Sidman, M., & Tailby, W. (1982). Conditional discrimination vs. matching to sample: An expansion of the testing paradigm. *Journal of the Experimental Analysis of Behavior, 37*, 5-22.

Sidman, M., Willson-Morris, M., & Kirk, B. (1986). Matching-to-sample procedures and the development of equivalence relations: The role of naming. *Analysis and Intervention in Developmental Disabilities, 6*, 1-19.

Spradlin, J. E., Cotter, V. W., & Baxley, N. (1973). Establishing a conditional discrimination without direct training: A study of transfer with retarded adolescents. *American Journal of Mental Deficiency, 77*, 556-566.

Spradlin, J. E., & Saunders, R. R. (1986). The development of stimulus classes using match-to-sample procedures: Sample classification versus comparison classification. *Analysis and Intervention in Developmental Disabilities, 6*, 41-58.

Stromer, R., & Osborne, J. G. (1982). Control of adolescents' arbitrary matching-to-sample by positive and negative stimulus relations. *Journal of the Experimental Analysis of Behavior, 37*, 329-348.

Wetherby, B., Karlan, G. R., & Spradlin, J. E. (1983). The development of derived stimulus relations through training in arbitrary-matching sequences. *Journal of the Experimental Analysis of Behavior, 40*, 69-78.

Chapter 3

Stimulus-Reinforcer Relations and Conditional Discrimination

W. J. McIlvane
W. V. Dube
J. B. Kledaras
J. C. de Rose
L. T. Stoddard

E. K. Shriver Center and Northeastern University

Recently, the topics of stimulus equivalence and related phenomena have set the occasion for extensive activity involving many behavior analysts. Clearly, we see before us the potential for orderly study of what others term "the mind". In particular, we now see the opportunity to examine behavioral processes that may be important in the acquisition of behavioral repertoires that Skinner (1957) termed verbal. Many of us now are conducting experiments to analyze these processes, and so see our efforts as directly or indirectly pursuing a formal experimental analysis of verbal behavior.

In this chapter, we will discuss how certain reinforcement procedures influence the nature of conditional relations engendered by matching-to-sample procedures. We will describe some studies that have already been reported by other laboratories and some new ones that were conducted by us. Together, these studies will illustrate some experimental operations that permit one to look at processes that are not often examined by behavior analysts. One set of operations, for example, allows one to demonstrate that reinforcing stimuli can be members of stimulus equivalence classes. Finally, we will discuss how behavior generated by such operations may or may not be related conceptually to verbal operants termed "mands" by Skinner in *Verbal Behavior*. He defined the mand as "a verbal operant in which the response is reinforced by a characteristic consequence and is therefore under the functional control of relevant conditions of deprivation or aversive stimulation" (pp. 35-36).

To make the discussion familiar and concrete, let's consider the example of a young child who comes home from school to find his mother working in the kitchen. As this boy is accustomed to do at this time, he asks his mother for his afternoon snack by saying "May I please have some cookies and milk?" When this boy has made this request in the past, it has been followed by characteristic consequences – delivery of cookies and milk. Further, the request reflects the fact that the boy has not recently had cookies or milk; in this sense, then, he is both cookie- and milk-deprived. For these reasons, it seems reasonable to classify the boy's request as a mand for cookies and milk. To pursue the matter further, let's imagine that the boy's mother is at the same time enjoying some leftover Christmas fruitcake and eggnog which she offers to him instead. These foods do not suffice to end the verbal transaction, however. Rather, the boy says again (somewhat stridently this time) "I want cookies and milk". Now mother goes to the pantry and the refrigerator and gives the boy what he asked for. Only at this point does the verbal transaction end with the boy sitting down to consume his cookies and milk.

Consider what has happened here. The boy has emitted some verbal behavior, and produced some consequences. The initial consequences – the fruitcake and eggnog – would likely have functioned as reinforcers in other contexts. These consequences, however, are not those specified by the boy's mand, and they do not seem to be reinforcers in this context. Rather, the boy's behavior was not appreciably different from that which would be expected if the boy's mother had given him nothing at all. His more forceful repetition of the mand, in fact, recalls the more intense responding that is characteristic of early phases of an extinction condition.

One might be tempted to argue that the fruitcake and eggnog do not end the verbal transaction because the reinforcers specified by the boy's verbal behavior continue to be available and are more highly preferred. We can remove this possible confound by making a slight alteration in this hypothetical situation. Suppose instead that the boy had entered the kitchen in the identical state of deprivation, but that he had asked at first merely for some milk, intending to ask for the cookies afterwards. If mother responded by giving him some cookies, the boy might be puzzled and say something like "Thanks Mom, but where's the milk?" Thus, delivery of cookies – perhaps even a preferred reinforcer – does not complete the verbal transaction. Rather, the mand is repeated – albeit in a somewhat altered form – because the mand was for milk and not for cookies.

Outcome-Specific Reinforcement Procedures with Laboratory Animals

Does the behavior described in the hypothetical example represent an unusual case – one perhaps restricted to the unique characteristics of human verbal repertoires? Are mands the only case in which operant behavior depends critically upon not merely any set of reinforcing consequences but upon a specific set of consequences? Or might similar behavior be demonstrable under other circumstances and with other organisms? To begin, let's consider the pigeon working in the laboratory on a standard conditional-discrimination procedure. The experimental situation is illustrated in Figure 1, which shows two trials of a delayed arbitrary matching-to-sample task.

Here we see the familiar three-key experimental arrangement. A visual sample stimulus, either the color red or green, appears on the center key. A peck to the sample darkens all keys for a brief delay period – in this example, 3 seconds. After the delay, comparison stimuli, horizontal and vertical lines, appear on the side keys. If red was the sample most recently, a peck to the horizontal lines is followed by one reinforcer, water. If green was the most recent sample, however, a peck to the vertical lines is followed by a different reinforcer, grain. Pecks to vertical following red samples and to horizontal following green samples are never fol-

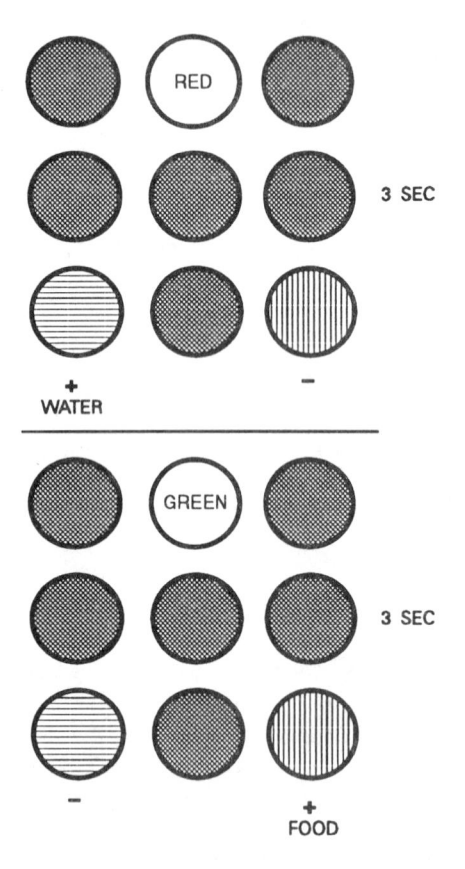

Figure 1. Delayed arbitrary matching-to-sample task displays (Peterson, Wheeler, & Armstrong, 1978).

Stimulus-Reinforcer Relations 45

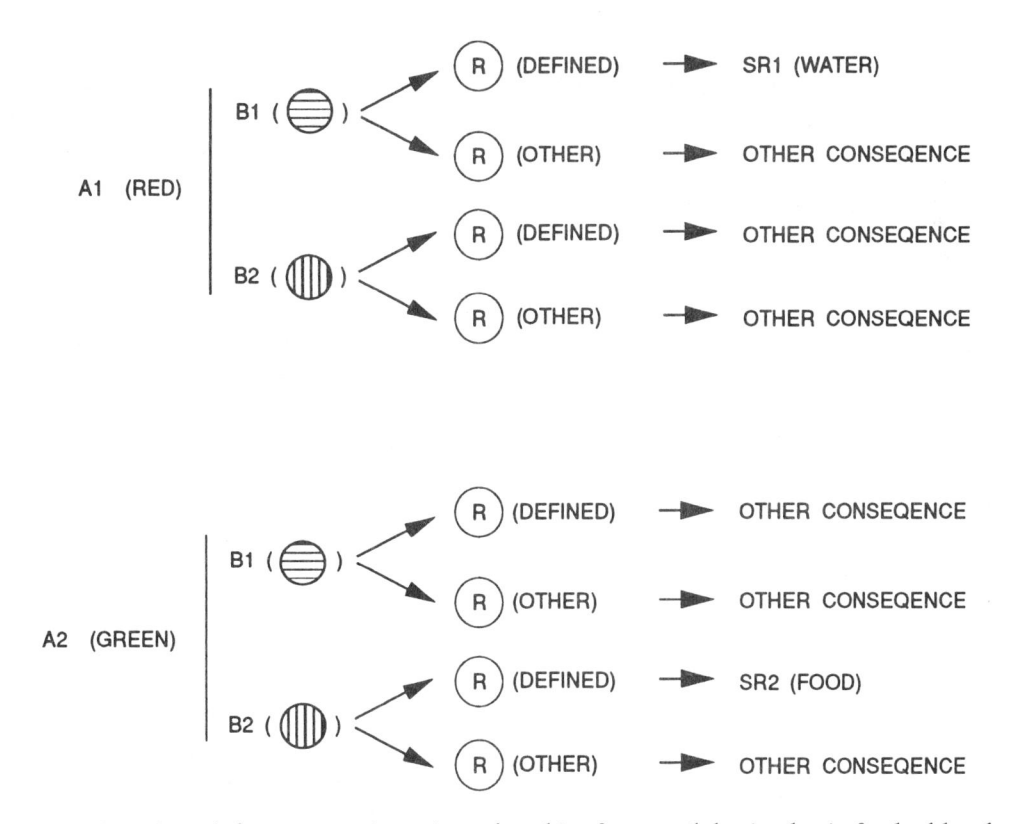

Figure 2. Reinforcement contingencies and resulting four-term behavioral units for the delayed matching-to-sample task shown in Figure 1. Sample stimuli are shown to the left of the vertical lines, and simultaneously displayed comparison stimuli are shown to the right. Selection of a comparison is shown by an encircled "R" (for "response"). The stimulus that follows selection is shown to the right of the encircled "R".

lowed by food or water. Thus, in this situation, one bit of behavior produces one reinforcer and another bit produces another reinforcer — a situation perhaps analogous to our earlier example of the boy, the cookies, and the milk.

Figure 2 diagrams the reinforcement contingencies just described. The upper portion shows that one consequence, SR1, is made available when the defined response, a peck, is made to the key displaying horizontal lines, following a red sample. Other responses, or the defined response to the key displaying the other stimulus, have consequences other than SR1. In the lower portion, a different reinforcer, SR2, is made available when the defined response is made to a key displaying vertical lines following a green sample; any other behavior has consequences other than SR2.

The reinforcement contingencies diagrammed in Figure 2 also illustrate the fundamental four-term unit of analysis (Sidman, 1986). The definition of the unit specifies the relations of the sample (first term) and comparison (second term) stimuli with the defined response (third term) and a reinforcing stimulus (fourth term). One might argue that the critical elements in such units are the stimulus-stimulus relations among the samples and comparisons. In this view, the reinforcing stimulus would serve a purely motivational function, controlling only the frequency of the responses that demonstrate the relations, but could be otherwise functionally nondifferential.

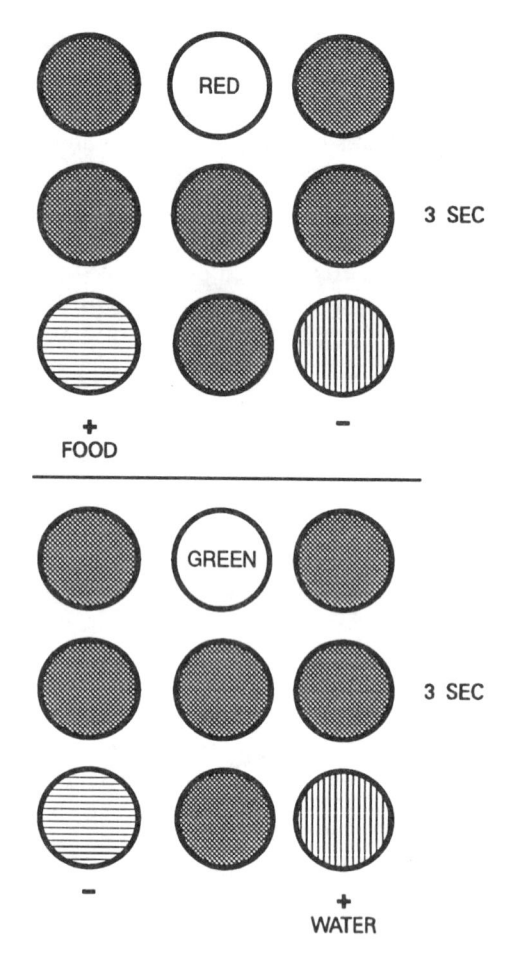

Figure 3. Outcome reversal for the delayed matching-to-sample task shown in Figure 1.

That view might naturally derive from the traditional practice of using a single reinforcing stimulus common to all units. However, this definition may not irreducibly specify all the elements of the behavior, as the term "unit" implies. In the diagram, we see that a complete specification of each unit includes a specific and unique reinforcing stimulus.

Effects of outcome reversal tests. A relatively simple test of whether the specific reinforcers do more than serve a motivational function is to examine what would happen if the reinforcing stimuli change places – if the original reinforcing contingencies diagrammed in Figure 1 were changed to those in Figure 3. Now, selections of horizontal conditionally upon red are followed by food – not water. Further, selections of vertical conditionally upon green are followed by water – not food. A rationale for this *outcome reversal* test is as follows: If the specific stimulus-reinforcer relations are in fact a critical element of these behaviors (i.e., part of the fundamental units) then changing them should disrupt the behavior. If, however, the sample-comparison stimulus-stimulus relations are the critical ones and the stimulus-reinforcer relations are not, then the behavior should be undisturbed. Such outcome reversal tests have been reported occasionally in the literature (Honig, Matheson, & Dodd, 1984; Peterson & Trapold, 1980, 1982; Peterson, Wheeler, & Armstrong, 1978). Figure 4 presents data from the study by Peterson and colleagues (1978).

The data show four pigeons' performances on the 3-second delayed arbitrary matching procedure illustrated in Figures 1 and 3. Each point represents the mean accuracy score for three successive sessions. The initial curve in each panel shows post-acquisition accuracy scores on the original task; the curves average about 90%. At the point labelled "outcome reversal", the consequence for selections of horizontal in the presence of red was changed to food; for selections of vertical in the presence of green, it was changed to water. For all subjects, accuracy scores following outcome reversal were substantially lower and declining, reaching about 50%. Thus, merely reversing the reinforcers led first to disruption and finally to abolition of a previously well-established conditional discrimination. These data lead to the conclusion that the reinforcers did more than merely modulate the frequency of the sample-comparison relations. Rather, the specific stimulus-reinforcer relations appeared critical to the maintenance of those relations.

Effects on delayed matching performance. Outcome-specific reinforcement procedures also appear to exert substantial influence on delayed matching-to-sample performance. A study by Edwards and colleagues provides a good example (Edwards, Jagielo, Zentall, & Hogan, 1982). The study used a group design and an identity matching-to-sample procedure with geometric-

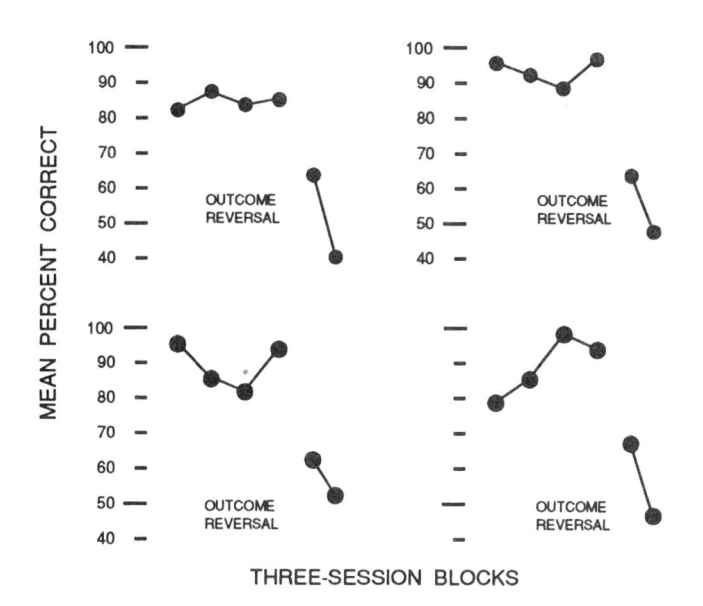

Figure 4. Pigeons' delayed matching-to-sample accuracy prior to and immediately following outcome reversal (Peterson, Wheeler, & Armstrong, 1978, Experiment 2).

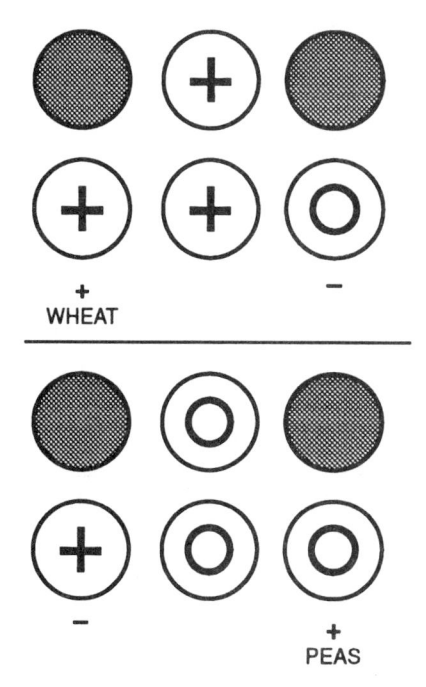

Figure 5. Identity matching-to-sample task displays (Edwards, Jagielo, Zentall, & Hogan, 1982).

form stimuli, as illustrated in Figure 5. For one group, selections of the plus comparison in the presence of the plus sample was followed by wheat, and selections of the circle comparison in the presence of the circle sample was followed by peas. For another group, identity-matching selections of both types were followed equally often by peas or wheat. Thereafter, the birds were given delayed matching-to-sample tests. Figure 6 shows accuracy scores with delays of 0, 1, and 2 seconds; solid and open points show the performance of birds trained with the outcome-specific and outcome-varied procedure, respectively. Note that the scores of the outcome-specific group are substantially higher at all delay values. Similar results have been reported in a number of other studies, all with pigeons as subjects (Brodigan & Peterson, 1976; DeLong & Wasserman, 1981; Honig et al., 1984; Peterson, 1984; Peterson et al., 1978; Peterson & Trapold, 1980; Peterson, Wheeler, & Trapold, 1980; Santi, 1989; Santi & Roberts, 1985). Enhanced delayed matching with outcome-specific procedures seems to be a highly reliable finding with these subjects.

Effects on acquisition of conditional discrimination. The outcome-specific procedure also appears to enhance acquisition of conditional-discrimination performances in both rats and pigeons (Carlson & Wielkiewicz, 1972, 1976; Fedorchak & Bolles, 1986; Peterson, 1984; Peterson & Trapold, 1982; Peterson et al., 1980; Trapold, 1970). For example, using wild and domestic pigeon subjects, Brodigan and Peterson (1976) compared acquisition of 0-delay arbitrary matching using outcome-specific and outcome-varied reinforcement procedures. Figure 7 shows some of their data. It shows percent correct accuracy scores for each of seven successive 300-trial blocks. Filled circles represent the performance of the birds exposed to the outcome-specific procedures and open circles that of the birds exposed to the outcome-varied procedure. Again, the outcome-

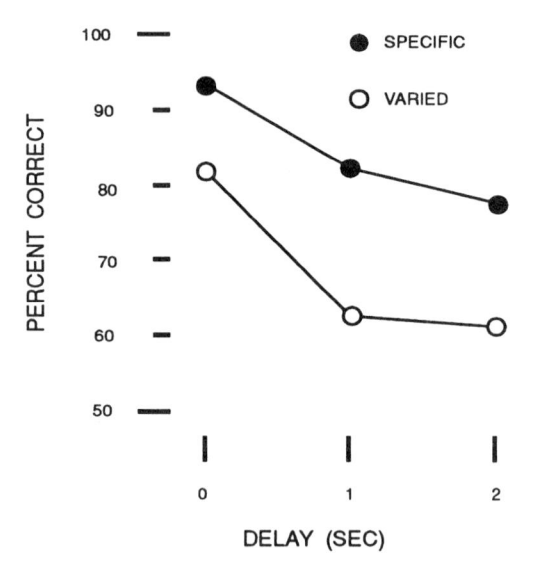

Figure 6. Pigeons' delayed matching-to-sample accuracy with outcome-specific (filled points) and outcome-varied (open points) procedures (Edwards, Jagielo, Zentall, & Hogan, 1982).

specific procedures seem to produce superior performance. Note, for example, the substantial separation of the functions for the domestic birds and the third-block performance differences for subjects of both types.

Stimulus-reinforcer relations and subsequent learning. A number of studies have examined the effects of specific stimulus-reinforcer relations on subsequent learning of conditional discriminations involving the same stimuli and reinforcers. Several studies have investigated the effects of response-independent stimulus-reinforcer pairings on subsequent discrimination learning (Carlson & Wielkiewicz, 1976; Kruse, Overmier, Konz, & Rokke, 1983; Peterson & Trapold, 1980; Trapold, 1970). For example, the study by Kruse and colleagues (1983) is represented in Figure 8. In the first stage of training, rats were given a series of discrete trials on which one of two response levers, L1 or L2, was presented in an irregular sequence. Pressing L1 was followed by presentation of a food pellet, SR1, and pressing L2 was followed by sucrose and water solution, SR2, as shown in the first row of Figure 8. In the second stage of training, all subjects were exposed to conditional-discrimination contingencies: Both response levers were simultaneously presented; in the presence of auditory stimuli A1 and A2, pressing L1 and L2, respectively, was followed by SR1 and SR2, respectively. The reinforcement contingencies are shown in the second row of Figure 8. The third stage of training consisted of response-independent pairings of a third auditory stimulus, A3, and a reinforcer (with the levers removed). For some subjects, A3 was

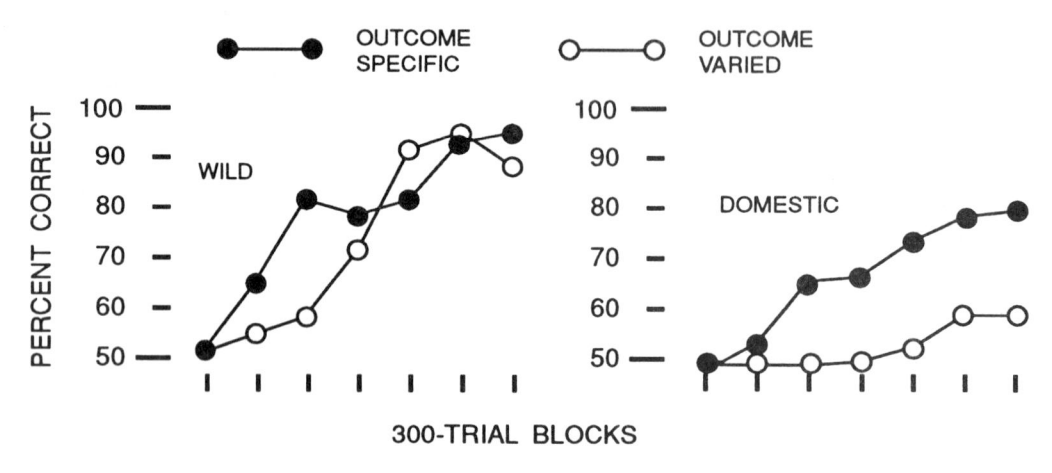

Figure 7. Acquisition of 0-delay arbitrary matching to sample for wild (left) and domestic (right) pigeons with outcome-specific (filled points) and outcome-varied (open points) procedures (Brodigan & Peterson, 1976).

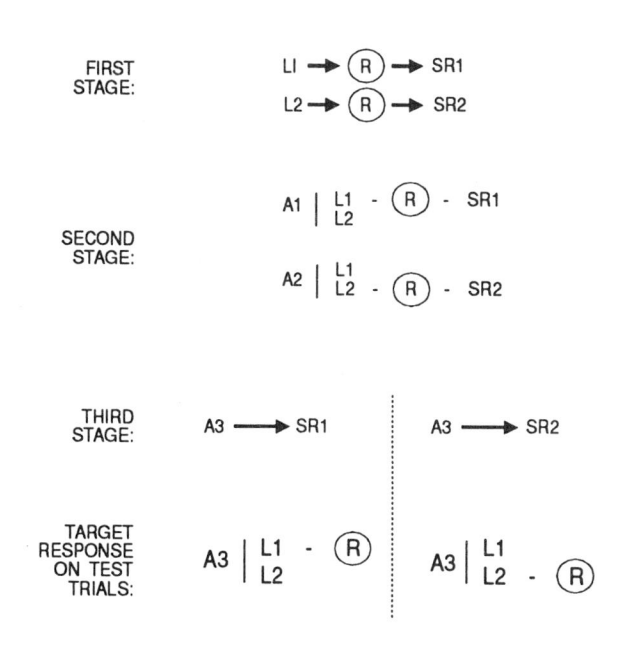

```
FIRST          L1 → (R) → SR1
STAGE:         L2 → (R) → SR2


                   A1 | L1  - (R) -  SR1
                        L2
SECOND
STAGE:
                   A2 | L1  - (R) -  SR2
                        L2


THIRD
STAGE:         A3 ——→ SR1        │        A3 ——→ SR2


TARGET
RESPONSE       A3 | L1 - (R)     │     A3 | L1
ON TEST             L2           │          L2  - (R)
TRIALS:
```

Figure 8. Reinforcement contingencies and test trials for Kruse, Overmier, Konze, and Rokke (1983). See Figure 2 caption for explanation of symbols.

followed immediately by presentation of SR1; for others, A3 was followed by SR2, as shown in the third row of Figure 8. Finally, a test of conditional control by A3 was given: Each subject received test trials on which A3 was presented along with L1 and L2. All responses on test trials were unreinforced, and test trials were intermixed with unreinforced baseline trials to verify maintenance of the conditional discrimination under extinction conditions.

Test results were given as the percent of "target" responses. For subjects who had received pairings of A3 and SR1, the target response was pressing L1; for subjects who had received pairings of A3 and SR2, it was pressing L2. The overall mean percent of target responses was 70% (median 74%); this score is significantly higher than chance, but also much lower than baseline accuracy in extinction, which averaged 94%. The results suggest that the training had established specific stimulus-reinforcer relations and that those relations may have led to conditional control by A3 on some test trials. In the first and second stages, relations were established between L1 and SR1, and between L2 and SR2; in the third stage, they were established between A3 and either SR1 or SR2. A target response may be described as one on which A3 effectively substituted for A1 or A2 as a conditional stimulus according to stimulus-reinforcer relations established earlier in training. On test trials, subjects showed a tendency to behave as though they had been exposed to the four-term contingencies that would have established the A3 conditional discrimination.

Other studies have employed concurrently or consecutively trained discriminations to examine the effects of stimulus-reinforcer relations on subsequent learning (Edwards et al., 1982; Honig et al., 1984; Peterson & Trapold, 1982). An experiment by Edwards and colleagues (1982, Experiment 1) is a good example; it is diagrammed in Figure 9. Three groups of pigeons were trained to perform two visual identity-matching tasks (the stimuli are represented as A1, A2, B1, and B2 in Figure 9). Pigeons in two of the groups, called here the consistent and inconsistent groups, were trained with identical reinforcer-specific contingencies, as shown in the upper portion of Figure 9. The reinforcers were wheat and corn. Subjects in the third group, a control group, were trained with varied reinforcement; they received wheat or corn with equal frequency for correct selections of all stimuli (not shown in Figure 9). After stable and accurate performance was achieved, all subjects were trained to perform arbitrary-matching tasks using combinations of the same stimuli displayed on the identity-matching tasks, as shown in the lower portion of Figure 9. For subjects in the consistent group, stimulus-reinforcer relations were consistent with any that might have been established previously. That is, correct selections of both sample and

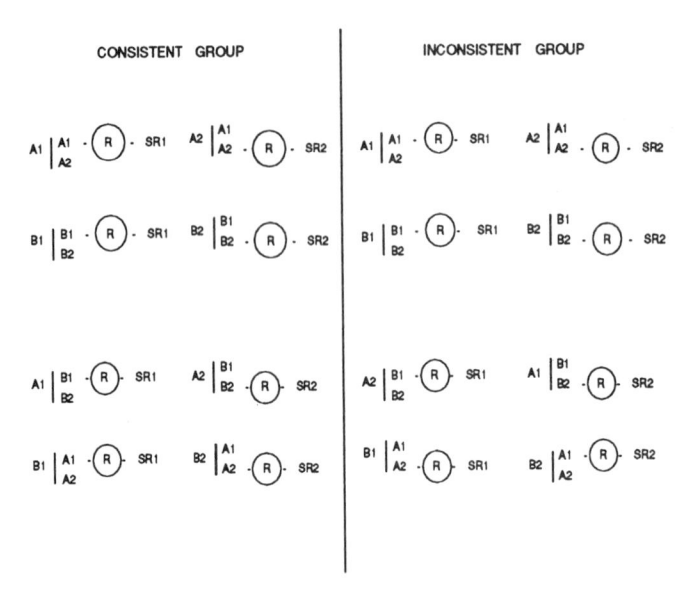

Figure 9. Reinforcement contingencies for Edwards, Jagielo, Zentall, & Hogan (1982; Experiment 1). See Figure 2 caption for explanation of symbols.

comparison stimuli had been followed by the same reinforcer on the identity-matching tasks. For subjects in the inconsistent group, selections of samples and correct comparisons had previously been followed by different reinforcers.

When the arbitrary-matching tasks were introduced, initial performances reflected the effects of earlier training. Data from the first arbitrary-matching session showed that (a) subjects in the varied control group performed at chance accuracy levels (mean approximately 51%), (b) subjects in the consistent group were significantly above chance (mean approximately 64%), and (c) subjects in the inconsistent group were below chance, but not significantly so (mean approximately 46%). Thus, from the earliest arbitrary-matching training trials, pigeons in both the consistent and inconsistent groups demonstrated some tendency to select a comparison stimulus that had been related previously to the same reinforcer as the sample stimulus. Although the effect was small, these subjects behaved as though they had already been exposed to the contingencies that would establish the discrimination shown in the lower left portion of Figure 9.

Summary of results with laboratory animals. The results presented above – disruption of conditional discrimination, enhanced delayed matching-to-sample performance, enhanced acquisition of conditional discrimination, and influences on subsequent learning – are not unusual. Rather, they represent a substantial number of experiments that have been conducted with different nonhuman species and with a variety of procedures. Surprisingly, however, it seems that many behavior analysts – a group with a well-documented interest in reinforcement variables – are not familiar with this work, perhaps because none of it has appeared in the *Journal of the Experimental Analysis of Behavior* (others have also noted this discrepancy, e.g., Williams [1984]).

Also of interest, there are certain formal similarities between some of the procedures used to study subsequent learning and those of stimulus-equivalence research with humans (e.g., Sidman & Tailby, 1982): Both types of studies examine performance on new discriminations as a function of prior training with the stimuli. Both ask, "If A is related to B, and B is related to C, what, then, is the status of the relation of A to C?". Of course there are also great differences, the primary one being whether "B" is a reinforcing stimulus or a discriminative stimulus. Nevertheless, those concerned with the issue of stimulus equivalence, particularly in nonhuman species, will find these data worth reviewing.

Outcome-Specific Reinforcement Procedures with Humans

The obvious and substantial influence of outcome-specific procedures with lower species leads obviously to the question of whether similar effects will be seen in human subjects. Our

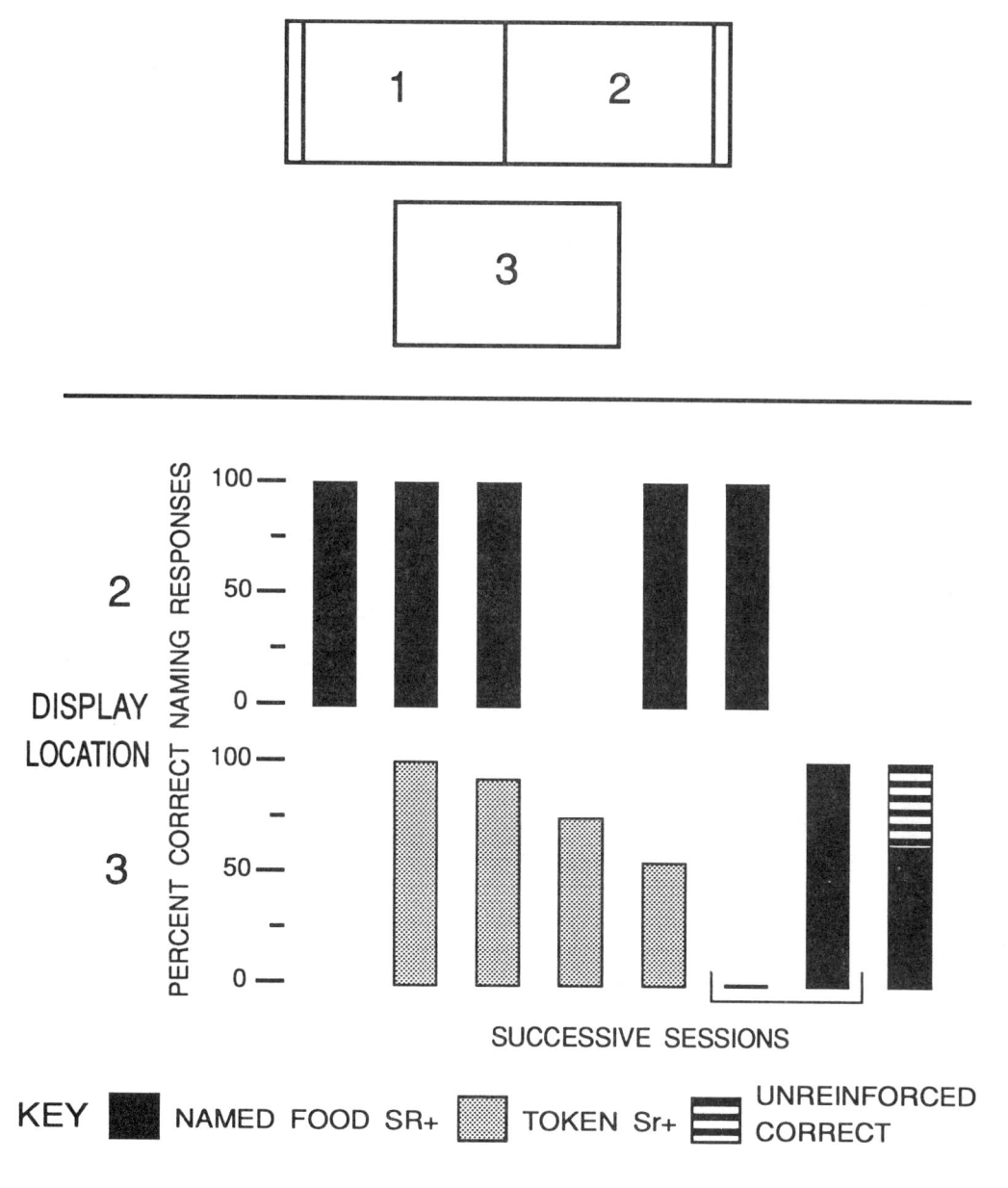

Figure 10. Upper portion: Three-compartment display. Compartments 1 and 2 have sliding Plexiglas doors; the Plexiglas front of compartment 3 does not open. Lower portion: Naming accuracy scores for a mentally retarded boy when foods to be named were displayed in compartment 2 (top row) and in compartment 3 (bottom row). Bars show accuracy when correct naming was reinforced with the food named (dark bars), was reinforced with tokens (gray bars), and was unreinforced (striped bars).

laboratory has been interested in this research area for some time. In this section, we will summarize the results of our studies as they relate to three relevant areas. First, are performances learned with outcome-specific reinforcement procedures disrupted if the reinforcement procedures are changed? Second, do outcome-specific reinforcement procedures enhance delayed matching? And third, will such procedures enhance acquisition of conditional discrimination?

Effects of switching reinforcement procedures. To date we have conducted outcome-reversal tests with only a few subjects. The work so far has not replicated the effects shown by Peterson and his colleagues. Conditional discriminations acquired under outcome-specific contingencies have not been disrupted by reversing or otherwise substituting reinforcers. However, we did obtain some possibly relevant data in a case where we weren't looking for it (McIlvane, Bass, O'Brien, Gerovac, & Stoddard, 1984). Those data were collected as part of an effort to develop automated programming procedures for teaching individuals with profound mental retardation (Stoddard, 1982; McIlvane, Kledaras, Dube, & Stoddard, 1989). The subject of this teaching study was an adolescent boy who could speak, but virtually all of his verbalizations were echoics. As a step in his remedial training, we wanted to teach him to name food items that were displayed before him in compartments in an automated teaching laboratory. The compartment display is illustrated in the upper portion of Figure 10. The top compartments (1 and 2) had clear, moveable Plexiglas doors, and we displayed foods in them for matching-to-sample training. For example, a piece of cookie might be displayed in one compartment and a cup of milk in the other, and the boy's task was to select one or the other item conditionally upon a name dictated by the experimenter. That is, if "Cookie" was spoken, he was to select the piece of cookie, and if "Milk" was spoken he was to select the cup instead. On a correct selection, he opened the door and consumed the comparison stimulus; the incorrect door was always locked.

As another part of his training, we sought to teach him to name the food items when they were displayed individually. That is, if the cup was displayed and the teacher said "What is that?", the boy was to say "Milk". At the time, we thought that we were teaching him to tact the foods. However, subsequent developments led us to conclude otherwise.

In teaching the naming task, the baseline was developed initially in compartment 2 (Figure 10, top). When a food item was displayed by itself, the boy was to speak its name aloud. When he did so correctly, he could open the door of the compartment and take and eat the food item that he had just named, as he did on match-to-sample trials. The food-reinforcement procedure, however, was a bit cumbersome, involving not only the time the boy took to eat the food but also some more or less elaborate activities on the part of the experimenter to screen the compartment and to load the food. For these and other reasons, we sought to change the task by (a) displaying the food to be named in the lower compartment (Figure 10, compartment 3) and (b) reinforcing the boy's naming responses with tokens. The tokens had previously been established as reinforcers in this and other settings, and were used routinely with him to teach and maintain behavior.

We expected that the change in the baseline would be quickly accomplished, and our initial results, shown in the lower portion of Figure 10, supported that expectation. The upper bars show accuracy scores for naming trials conducted in the original compartment (compartment 2) where correct responses continued to produce the food he named. The lower bars show the results of trials in the third compartment, which initially produced token reinforcement. At first, naming accuracy was 100% in both locations. However, in subsequent sessions naming of foods displayed in compartment 3 became progressively less accurate, dropping to about 50% correct in the fourth session. Thus, token reinforcement was apparently not maintaining the baseline. Note that naming responses to foods displayed in the original location continued to be perfectly accurate. Although his naming errors took several forms, a telling observation was that he most often gave the name "token" to foods displayed in compartment 3.

We sought to recover accurate naming in compartment 3 by changing the reinforcement procedure. Now correct naming responses were followed by the named food, delivered in compartment 2. Naming accuracy recovered immediately and was maintained even after an intermittent reinforcement schedule was introduced. These results suggest that our teaching procedure did not in fact establish tacting. Rather, it appears that the naming performances depended in a critical way on the reinforcers that supported them. Apparently, we had developed mands for the various food items, and the performance deteriorated when the food items were no longer forthcoming. Others have described similar experiences with nonhuman subjects. Savage-Rumbaugh (1984), for example, has reported findings like ours from her chimpanzee-language studies, and Pepperberg (1988) very recently described what appear to be similar findings with an African Grey parrot.

Effects on delayed matching performance. Again, we have studied only a few subjects, but so far our data are unlike those obtained with other species. Our initial study (Dube, Rocco, & McIlvane, 1989) was a systematic replication of the procedures reported by Edwards and colleagues (1982). Recall that the task was delayed identity matching. Figure 11 illustrates the procedure used with one of our subjects, a 43-year old moderately mentally retarded man. The stimuli were nonrepresentational forms and the outcomes for selections of each type were a sip of juice and a penny.

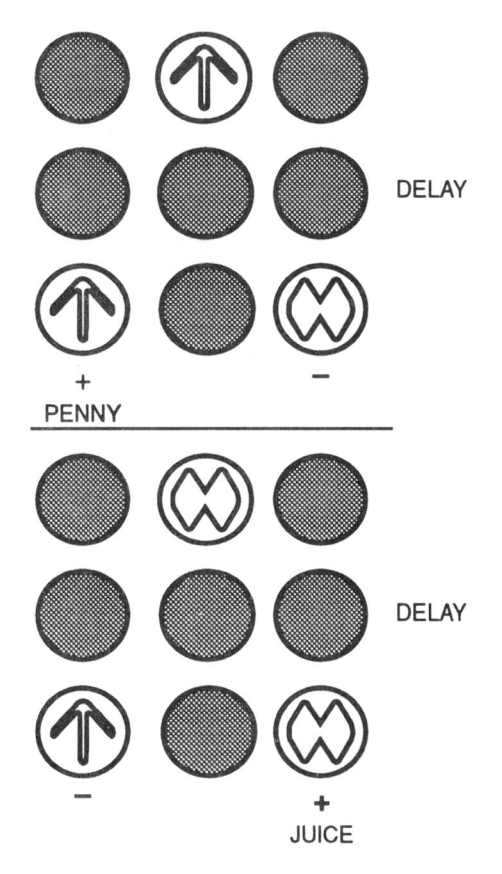

Figure 11. Delayed identity matching-to-sample task displays (Dube, Rocco, & McIlvane, 1989).

Figure 12 shows a portion of the subject's data. Plotted points are accuracy scores for successive sessions at 1- and 3-second delays under the outcome-specific and outcome-varied procedures. There is substantial variability at both delay values, and there is no evidence of enhanced performance under the specific conditions. The horizontal lines through each function give the mean accuracy scores under each condition, and they are virtually identical. These data are representative of results with three other mentally retarded subjects. At these and longer delays and with procedure changes such as increasing the number of comparison stimuli displayed on a trial, we found no evidence of enhanced delayed matching.

Effects on acquisition of conditional discrimination. This topic has been, relatively speaking, well studied in human subjects. Several studies have been reported and we have conducted others. Some have looked at the results of the published studies and concluded that outcome-specific reinforcement contingencies do enhance acquisition (e.g., Williams, 1984). This may be the case, but our opinion is that such conclusions are not as yet warranted by the data. The most widely cited study was reported by Litt and Schreibman (1981). The procedure was two-comparison arbitrary auditory-visual matching-to-sample. Six autistic children were to select objects (barrette, hinge, etc.) conditionally upon their dictated names. The children were exposed to a series of problems, each of which had a different reinforcement procedure. The two

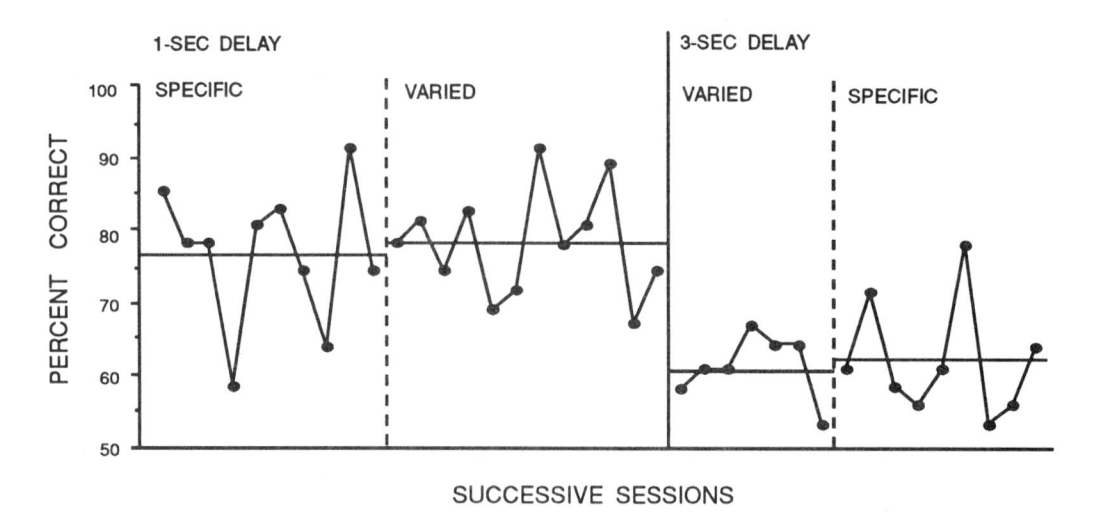

Figure 12. A mentally retarded man's delayed identity-matching accuracy with outcome-specific and outcome-varied procedures (Dube, Rocco, & McIlvane, 1989).

procedures considered here were outcome-specific procedures (like those illustrated in Figures 3 and 11) and outcome-varied procedures, where each of two reinforcing consequences was equally likely following correct responses to all stimuli.

Group data, analyzed via a number of statistical tests, showed that outcome-specific reinforcement produced faster learning than did the varied procedures. Like many group findings, however, these are a bit misleading. The left portion of Figure 13 shows the individual data for five children; the sixth didn't learn any discriminations at all despite protracted training, apparently with outcome-specific contingencies. The graphs plot the number of trials that each child required to meet the experimenter's accuracy criterion. Only Child 3's data suggest a meaningful difference between the outcome-specific and the outcome-varied procedure. Child 2 and Child 4 show some differences in favor of the outcome-specific procedure, but the criterion was such that these differences may have been due to as few as three errors. For the other two subjects (Children 1 and 5), there is no difference. Thus, in our judgment, the individual data only weakly support the conclusion drawn from the group data.

We recently followed up Litt and Schreibman's study, systematically replicating the procedures with five mentally retarded subjects. Three of them failed to learn any discriminations via the procedures, and the two who did learn showed no superiority of the outcome-specific procedure. Those data are plotted in the right portion of Figure 13. Note that both of our subjects merely learned each successive discrimination as or more rapidly than the preceding one – an apparent matching-to-sample learning set. This progressive improvement, also suggested in Litt and Schreibman's data for Child 4, tells us that the task may not have been optimally sensitive to specific reinforcer effects; other variables apparently influenced performance. Nonetheless, the data for only one or at most two of seven subjects suggest marked enhancement of acquisition by outcome-specific reinforcement procedures. Moreover, the effects shown in other published studies were either very weak (Saunders & Sailor, 1979) or perhaps dependent upon presenting selected aspects of group data (Shepp, 1962). Overmier (1988) has reported some enhancement of conditional discrimination acquisition in normally capable children, but his contribution is difficult to evaluate because details of the work have not yet been reported.

Effects on emergent behavior. To cast some new light on this problem, we have recently begun studies that ask whether outcome-specific reinforcement procedures enhance the formation or expansion of stimulus equivalence classes. One question, for example, is whether one is less likely to see the "gradual emergence" phenomenon with outcome-specific training procedures. Another question is whether outcome-specific procedures will facilitate the formation of unusually large classes — those involving five, six, or more members. However, pending the outcome of these studies, we think the proper interpretation of the findings so far would be that outcome-specific procedures do not substantially enhance acquisition in human subjects. In the next section, we will discuss one possible reason for why this may be true.

Summary: Relation of Nonhuman and Human Studies

The data so far suggest the following conclusions: Outcome-specific reinforcement procedures have pronounced effects upon rats' and pigeons' conditional-discrimination performances in a variety of situations. In contrast, those effects have not so far been routinely demonstrable in humans. Although none of our own studies may yet be considered definitive or complete, taken together, our results lead us to consider the possibility that outcome-specific procedures may have different effects with the two populations. Let us also suggest a reason why this relationship might hold.

Recall the studies of Jenkins and Moore (1973) and others who showed that the form of the pigeon's auto-shaped keypeck responses resembled those which occurred during consumption of the reinforcer. Birds emitted sharp, open-beaked pecks when the autoshaping stimulus preceded food delivery and slower, more sustained key contacts to stimuli that preceded water delivery. When pigeons are exposed to outcome-specific reinforcement procedures, similar response topographies have also been seen. Pigeons respond to samples that precede food differently from those that precede water (Brodigan & Peterson, 1976). These topography differences may be very important in accounting for enhanced acquisition and delayed matching-to-sample performance.

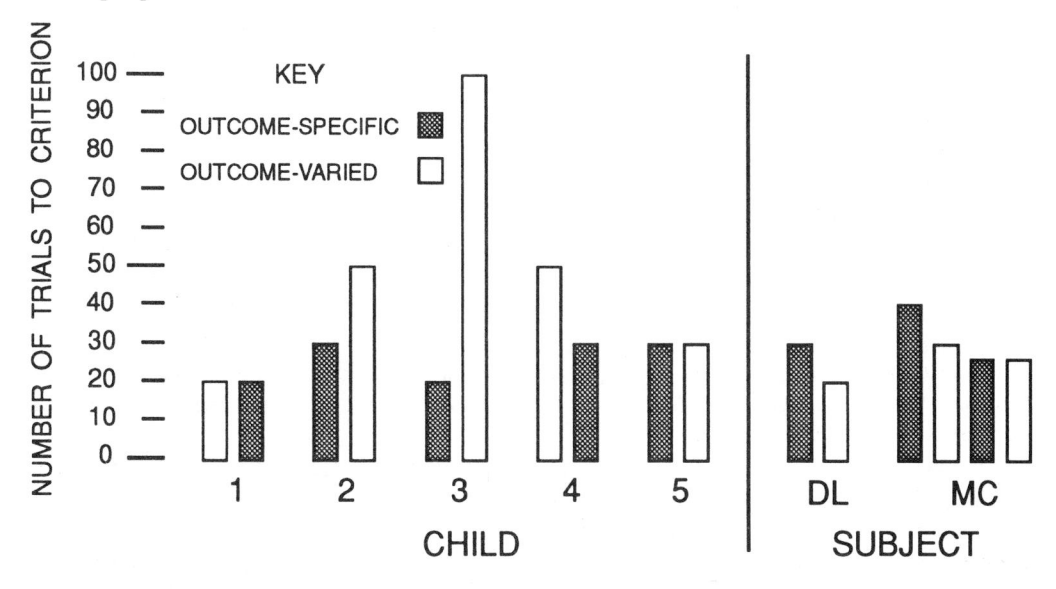

Figure 13. Acquisition of auditory-visual matching-to-sample performances with outcome-specific (dark bars) and outcome-varied (light bars) procedures. Left portion: Data for five autistic children (Litt & Schreibman, 1981). Right portion: Data for two mentally retarded adults.

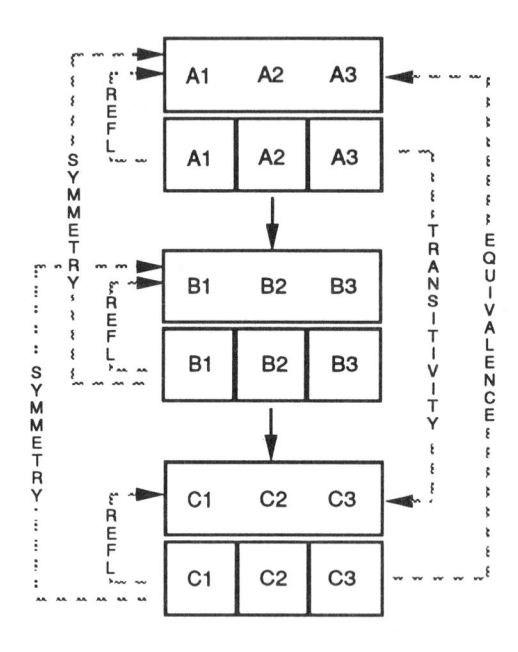

Figure 14. Stimulus equivalence training and testing paradigm. Stimuli that are simultaneously displayed as comparisons are shown in the larger rectangular boxes. Stimuli that alternate across trials as samples are shown in adjacent square boxes. Arrows representing arbitrary matching-to-sample performances point from samples to comparisons. Solid arrows illustrate performances that are directly trained; dashed arrows illustrate performances that emerge without direct training. The emergent performances demonstrate stimulus-stimulus relations exhibiting the properties of reflexivity (REFL), symmetry, transitivity, and equivalence.

Differential behavior to samples may, by itself, hasten pigeons' acquisition of conditional discrimination (e.g., Urcuioli, 1985); such behavior may also enhance performance on delayed matching-to-sample problems (Cohen, Brady, & Lowry, 1981). Perhaps outcome-specific procedures have their effects with pigeons because they tend to generate differential sample behaviors, which then may acquire discriminative control of behavior. If so, does performance enhancement with outcome-specific procedures occur if and only if those procedures generate some form of behavior that resembles sample-naming?

Whenever the question of naming occurs, of course, Pandora's box seems to open. Where do the names come from? A logical possibility is that they are a product of the stimulus-reinforcer relations rather than a cause. The pigeons clearly seem to learn something about the reinforcers that have followed particular samples; otherwise, the differential sample topographies are hard to explain. For human subjects, it seems likely that any analogous behavior would be verbal in nature – unless, of course, it can be shown that the topography of the human observing responses changes in relation to the reinforcer.

Stimulus-Reinforcer Learning in Humans

Although outcome-specific reinforcement procedures may not enhance some aspects of human conditional discrimination, they do have other effects of interest. For example, some of our recent research has asked whether the specific reinforcers can become members of stimulus equivalence classes (Dube, McIlvane, Mackay, & Stoddard, 1987; Dube, McIlvane, Maguire, Mackay, & Stoddard, 1989). To provide necessary context, we will briefly review some familiar stimulus equivalence procedures.

Figure 14 illustrates a now-standard stimulus equivalence training and testing paradigm (cf. Sidman, 1971; Sidman, Cresson, & Willson-Morris, 1974; Sidman & Tailby, 1982). When subjects select comparisons from Set B conditionally upon samples from Set A (AB matching) and also select comparisons from Set C conditionally upon samples from Set B (BC matching), equivalence relations are shown when subjects prove immediately capable of all of the other performances – CA, AC, CB, and BA.

The various four-term contingencies and resulting behavioral units are illustrated in the upper portion of Figure 15 using AB training as examples. Note that the units have three stimulus terms and a single response term. The emergent behavior shows that the first and second terms are members of stimulus equivalence classes. However, the fourth term – the reinforcer – is also a stimulus. Why does it not also become a member of the stimulus equivalence class? Probably because conditional discrimination could not be maintained if it did. If all of the stimuli related to the common reinforcer were then related to each other on that basis, the effect would likely interfere with discrimination among them.

The potential for that problem, however, is eliminated by using outcome-specific reinforcement procedures, illustrated in the lower portion of Figure 15. The elements of the behavioral units are the same as those shown above except for the reinforcers. With outcome-specific contingencies, all correct selections of A1, B1, and C1 are followed by reinforcer SR1 and those of A2, B2, and C2 are followed by SR2. As the stimulus designations in the diagrams imply, SR1 can now be related to stimuli marked 1 and SR2 can be related to those marked 2 without creating a situation in which all of the stimuli are potentially related to each other.

We have recently reported the outcome of training like this (Dube et al., 1987). Not only did the subjects match the stimuli from Sets A, B, and C with each other, they also matched those stimuli with the reinforcers themselves. That is, given B1 as a sample, subjects selected SR1 as a comparison; given B2 as a sample, they selected SR2. The study also provided another interesting finding. When new stimuli, D1 and D2, appeared on identity-matching trials, reinforced with SR1 and SR2, respectively, then the Set D stimuli entered the existing classes. D1 was matched with A1, B1, and C1, and D2 was matched with A2, B2, and C2.

In a followup study (Dube et al., 1989), these procedures were systematically replicated with new subjects and a less extensive baseline training procedure. Specifically, all trials that displayed reinforcers as samples and comparisons were omitted. Even without that potentially helpful context, however, the results were the same. Taken together, these studies provide good evidence that reinforcing stimuli can become members of stimulus equivalence classes.

In our current work, we are seeking to define the minimal experimental history for relating

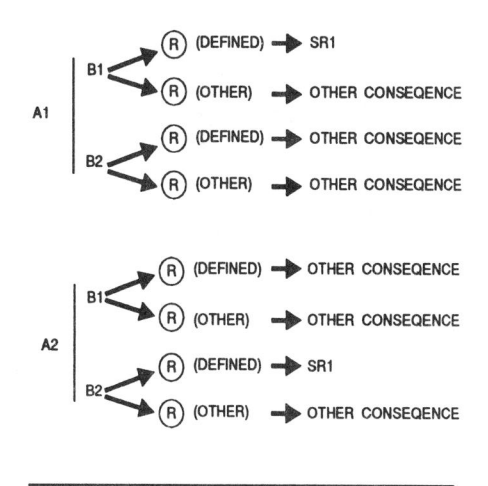

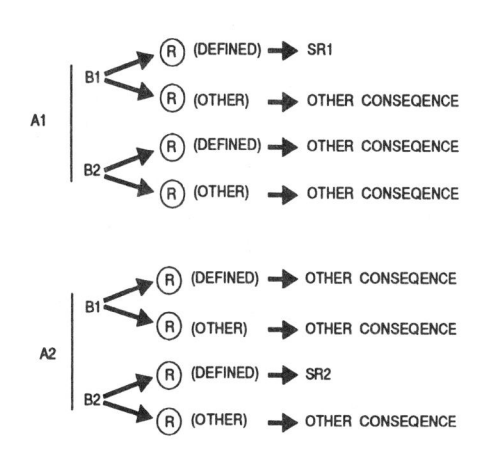

Figure 15. Upper portion: Nonspecific reinforcement contingencies and resulting four-term behavioral units for the AB matching-to-sample task shown in Figure 14. Lower portion: Outcome-specific reinforcement contingencies for the AB task.

IDENTITY-MATCHING BASELINE

A1 | A1 -(R)- SR1
   | A2

A2 | A1
   | A2 -(R)- SR2

B1 | B1 -(R)- SR1
   | B2

B2 | B1
   | B2 -(R)- SR2

PROBE TRIALS

A1 | B1 -(R)
   | B2

A2 | B1
   | B2 -(R)

B1 | A1 -(R)
   | A2

B2 | A1
   | A2 -(R)

REVERSAL BASELINE

A1 | A1 -(R)- SR2
   | A2

A2 | A1
   | A2 -(R)- SR1

B1 | B1 -(R)- SR1
   | B2

B2 | B1
   | B2 -(R)- SR2

PROBE TRIALS

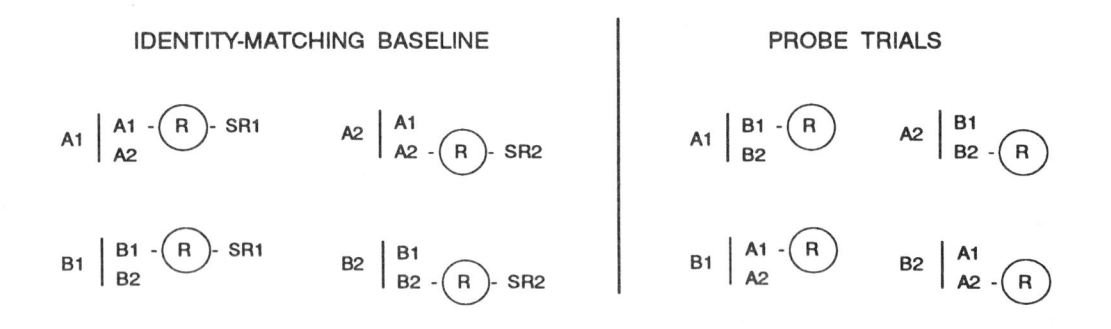

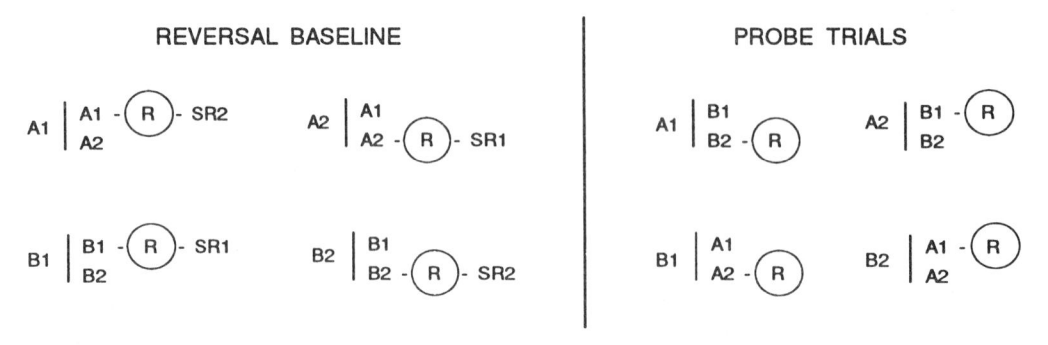

A1 | B1
   | B2 -(R)

A2 | B1 -(R)
   | B2

B1 | A1
   | A2 -(R)

B2 | A1 -(R)
   | A2

Figure 16. Identity-matching baseline and arbitrary-matching probe trials for an investigation of the minimal experimental history necessary for emergent matching based on stimulus-reinforcer relations. See Figure 2 caption for explanation of symbols.

stimuli on the basis of common relations to reinforcers. The upper portion of Figure 16 diagrams the procedures. Four different nonrepresentational forms (designated as A1, A2, B1, and B2 in Figure 16) served as samples and comparisons on identity-matching trials. Correct selections of A1 and B1 were followed by SR1, and those of A2 and B2 were followed by SR2 (upper left portion of Figure 16). Unreinforced probe trials then asked whether this history was sufficient to establish AB and BA arbitrary-matching performances shown in the upper right portion of Figure 16. That is, would subjects select B1 in the presence of A1, and B2 in the presence of A2, as well as the symmetrical counterparts of these performances?

Figure 17 shows the results for three subjects, all young men who were students at the New England Center for Autism. The histograms on the left give the percent of probe responses that were consistent with classes based on the relations with the specific reinforcing stimuli. Performances for two subjects, PN and RDP, were immediately consistent with the formation of those classes; those of subject JDB were not immediately consistent, but they became so with continued testing.

To control for the possibility that these results were the product of unsuspected primary stimulus generalization (or some other irrelevant form of control), we reversed the reinforcers for two of the baseline trial types. The lower portion of Figure 16 shows the procedures. In the reversal phase, selections of A1 were followed by SR2, and those of A2 were followed by SR1. Would the class membership of A1 and A2 change as a function of the changed reinforcement procedure? The data in the right portion of Figure 17 show the percent of probe responses consistent with reversed class membership (matching A1 with B2, and A2 with B1, as shown in

Figure 17. Results of probe trials illustrated in Figure 16, for Subjects PN, JDB, and RDP. Bars show the percent of probe responses consistent with stimulus class formation. Below each bar, letters show the performance tested and numbers in parentheses show the number of probe trials. Bars divided in two show the results of the first half (left) and second half (right) of the probe trials. Left portion: Original training contingencies (see Figure 16, upper portion). Right portion: Reversal training contingencies (Figure 16, lower portion).

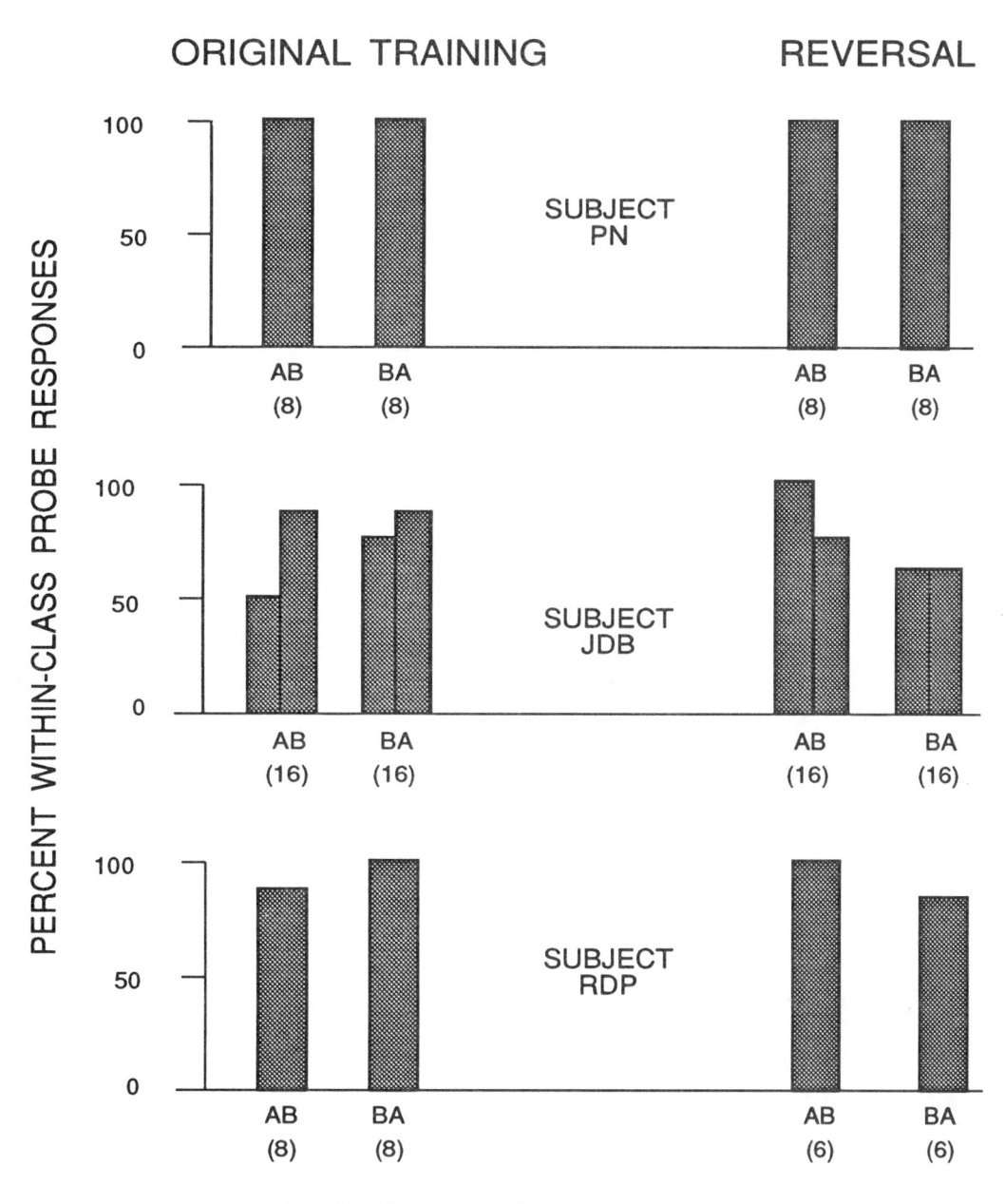

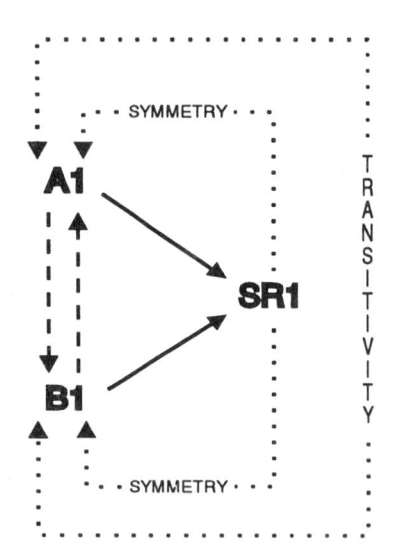

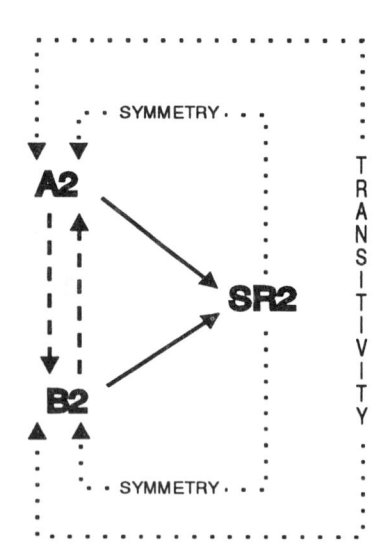

Figure 18. Analysis of the results shown in Figure 17 in terms of the "combined test for symmetry and transitivity" (Sidman & Tailby, 1982). Solid arrows illustrate stimulus-reinforcer relations established during identity-matching training. Dashed arrows illustrate emergent arbitrary-matching performances. Dotted arrows indicate symmetric and transitive relations among discriminative and reinforcing stimuli.

the lower right portion of Figure 16). For two subjects, performance was immediately consistent with the reversed reinforcer relations. For the third (JDB), the reversal procedure appeared only to disrupt the existing classes, but this outcome was sufficient to show that the original performance was probably not a product of similar physical characteristics.

One question raised by these findings is whether the emergent matching performances indicate that equivalence classes have formed. After all, the procedures are very different from the usual ones used to study stimulus equivalence. We offer the suggestion that equivalence classes do form. The rationale is similar to one originally proposed by Sidman and Tailby (1982), the so-called "combined" test for symmetry and transitivity, illustrated in Figure 18.

First, what relations are established during baseline training? Clearly, we have relations between the Set A stimuli and the reinforcers and also between the Set B stimuli and those same reinforcers. The emergence of AB and BA matching performances strongly implies that the relations between discriminative and reinforcing stimuli were relations of equivalence. If those relations were strictly unidirectional, there would be no basis for relation of A to B. Therefore, we conclude that these relations must be symmetrical and transitive, at least in some sense. The equivalence relation also implies that under some circumstances the subjects should relate the matching-to-sample forms with the reinforcers. Our first experiment (Dube et al., 1987) presented data confirming such relations, and we obtained similar results with one subject from our current study who was given similar tests.

As we noted above, there are some obvious formal similarities between the procedures we have just described and those used to study subsequent learning with other species, especially in the study by Edwards and colleagues (1982). However, while the human subjects generally demonstrated full-blown emergent matching performances, the effects with laboratory animals

Stimulus-Reinforcer Relations

were shown as savings in directly trained performances or weak tendencies toward conditional control. Are the differences between species simply a matter of degree, or do they represent different underlying behavioral processes? At present, we do not know; systematic replication of our procedures with laboratory animals will help answer this question.

Class membership based on positive and negative stimulus functions. The research just described shows that stimulus class membership can be based upon a common relationship with the same reinforcing outcome. Class membership based on common relations to consequences, however, does not necessarily require two (or more) different reinforcing consequences. Two diametrically opposed consequences – reinforcement and extinction – may serve as well, as Figure 19 (upper portion) might suggest. For example, suppose that we have two simple simultaneous discrimination problems involving nonrepresentative forms. The forms designated A1 and B1, respectively, are S+, and those designated A2 and B2 are S-. By the logic of the experiments described earlier, both A1 and B1 are potentially members of one class on the basis of their common S+ discriminative functions. Similarly, A2 and B2 are potentially members of another class based on their common S- discriminative functions.

How might we test for such class formation? One might take a straightforward approach, as follows. First, train the two simple-discrimination performances described above. Next, establish an arbitrary matching-to-sample baseline with different stimuli to provide some possibly helpful context. Finally, conduct matching-to-sample tests to ask the following question. When A1 is the sample, will the subject select B1, and vice versa? Conversely, when A2 is the sample, will the subject select B2, and vice versa? When we conducted such tests, we found that subjects usually selected the stimuli that functioned as S+ – those that were discriminative for

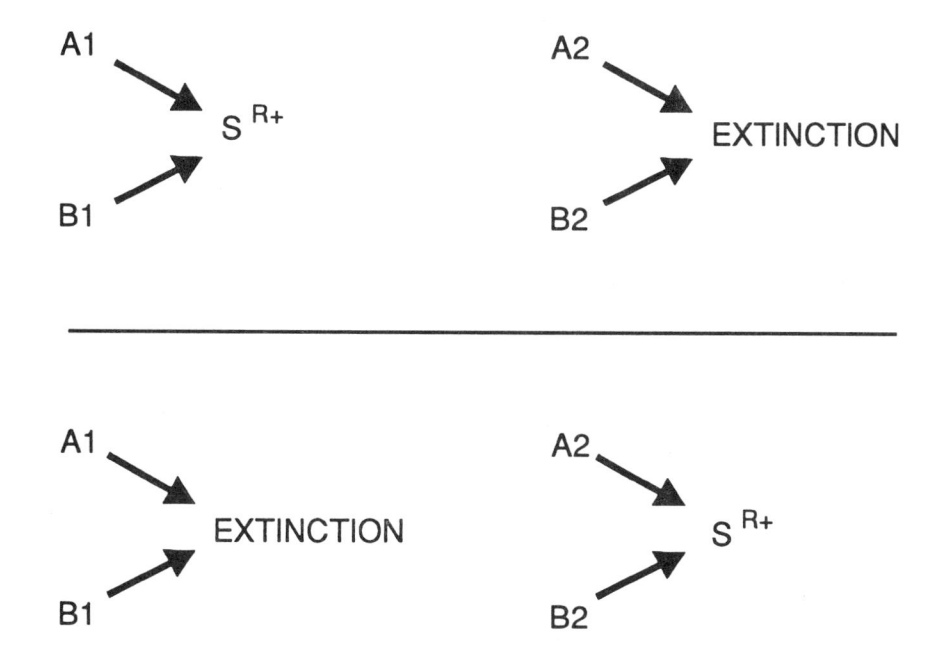

Figure 19. Upper portion: Relations of stimuli to consequences for two simple simultaneous discriminations. Lower portion: Yoked reversal of the A- and B-discriminations shown above.

reinforcement – regardless of what the sample was. (As usual, the subject did something sensible, but not what we were looking for.) Our attempts to find a way around this problem led to our recent studies that demonstrated transfer of simple discriminative functions via match-to-sample procedures (de Rose, McIlvane, Dube, Galpin, & Stoddard, 1988; de Rose, McIlvane, Dube, & Stoddard, 1988).

There is another approach, however, that shows how stimulus class formation on the basis of common discriminative function can be achieved. This approach is through repeated yoked reversals of simple discrimination, as illustrated schematically in Figure 19. In the first phase of training, the stimuli designated A1 and B1 are the positive stimuli and those designated A2 and B2 are the negative stimuli (upper portion). After that discrimination is acquired, the stimulus-consequence relations are reversed: A2 and B2 become the positive stimuli and A1 and B1 become the negative stimuli. After the reversed discrimination is mastered, the contingencies are re-reversed again and again such that reversal of either discrimination leads to an immediate untrained reversal of the other.

The first study of this type to be published was Vaughan (1988), whose subjects were pigeons. Two other studies with human subjects have extended the basic finding (McIlvane, Dube, Kledaras, Iennaco, & Stoddard, 1990; Sidman, Wynne, Maguire, & Barnes, 1989). These studies addressed not only the production of functional classes but also whether those classes were equivalence classes. Sidman and colleagues showed that functional classes need not always be equivalence classes.

To summarize all of this work, then, we may say without a doubt that stimuli that bear common relations to particular consequences will be related with each other under many circumstances. Questions about the range of these circumstances and the limits of such class formation remain to be answered, but the work is continuing.

Experimental Analysis of Stimulus-Reinforcer Relations and the Mand

We will conclude this chapter with a discussion of the possible relevance of the work on stimulus-reinforcer relations to the functional analysis of verbal behavior and the mand in particular. We frankly don't know whether our work is relevant to this topic. In this section, we will merely sketch out some thoughts on each side of the matter and make a few comments that might prove useful.

Points suggesting relevance. The class formation findings with outcome-specific procedures show that specific reinforcers can do more than merely provide motivational support for conditional-discrimination performances. Clearly, we could not fully describe the behavior engendered by those procedures without reference to those consequences and their specific relations with particular conditional and discriminative stimuli. In this regard, the specific reinforcers seem linked to specific conditional discriminations much in the same way as mands are linked to the consequences that they produce. These parallel linkages, of course, serve as the principal basis for suggesting that one type of performance may be related to another in some scientifically meaningful way.

Mere parallels, however, will not suffice by themselves. Rather, we will need experiments showing that variables that influence behaviors established with outcome-specific conditional-discrimination procedures also influence behaviors that are unquestionably mands. The procedure of switching reinforcers might be a good area for initial focus. We are not satisfied with the studies we have done so far; the fact that our subjects' performances did not deteriorate after outcome reversals may mean little. Intrinsic in our test situations were other possible reinforcers. For example, perhaps the experimenter's delivery of a reinforcer after every correct sample-matching selection (i.e., a "teacher's" approval) functioned as a reinforcer; that aspect of the situation did not change along with the specific-reinforcer contingencies.

Points suggesting irrelevance. The principal concern here comes from the definition of the mand itself as verbal behavior that "in contrast with other types of verbal operants ... has no specified relation to a prior stimulus" (Skinner, 1957, p. 36). Rather, the mand is under the functional control of an appropriate establishing operation or establishing stimulus (Michael, 1982). In our situation, of course, there are prior stimuli – the samples and the comparisons. Moreover, although matching-to-sample performances may function as verbal behavior (Michael, 1985), the situation does not much resemble that in which one would emit a mand. It is arranged by the experimenter and specific reinforcers are not continuously available. Instead, those that are available change from trial to trial conditionally upon the sample.

Nevertheless, the definitional and procedural differences may not be all that important. With respect to there being no prior stimulus, Skinner clearly intended to shift the emphasis onto the relevant motivational variables and away from discriminative stimuli. However, mands are often made under external stimulus control as well. As Skinner points out, the probability that a child will emit the mand "Candy!" increases when a listener holding candy is present (1957, pp. 52-53). As to the procedural differences, that same issue could be raised with respect to all of the equivalence work in relation to verbal behavior (e.g., Sidman, 1986; Stoddard & McIlvane, 1986; Wulfert & Hayes, 1988). Therefore, we seem to be back to the issue of relating our matching-to-sample procedures to the appropriate verbal categories.

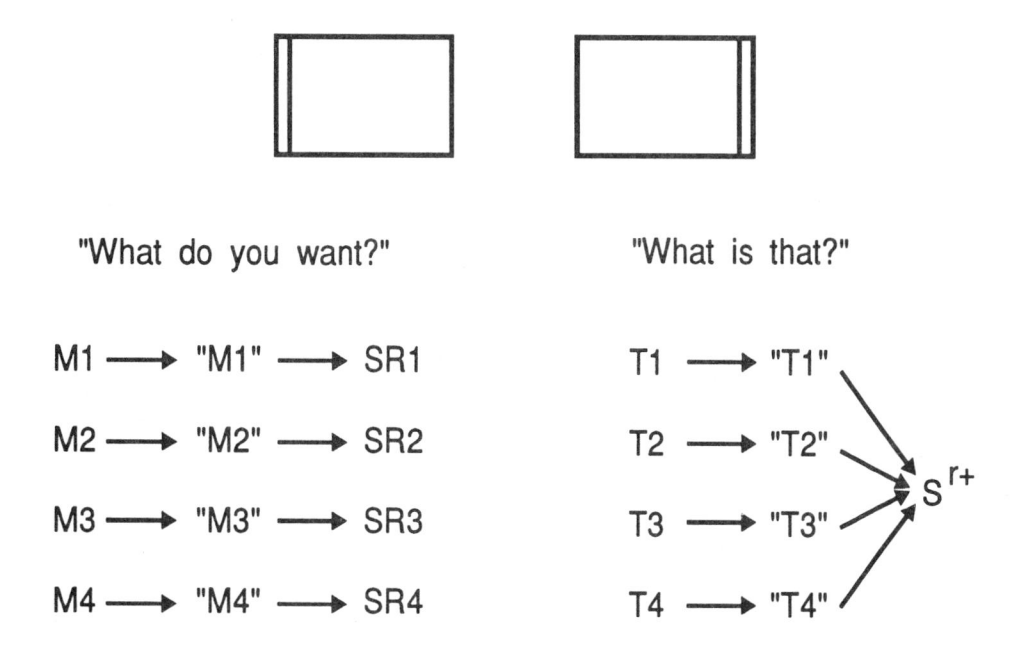

"What do you want?"   "What is that?"

M1 ⟶ "M1" ⟶ SR1   T1 ⟶ "T1"
M2 ⟶ "M2" ⟶ SR2   T2 ⟶ "T2"
M3 ⟶ "M3" ⟶ SR3   T3 ⟶ "T3"   ⟶ S^{r+}
M4 ⟶ "M4" ⟶ SR4   T4 ⟶ "T4"

Figure 20. Illustration of an experiment investigating the independence of tacts and mands. Rectangles above represent display compartments with Plexiglas doors. Objects M1-M4 are displayed only in the left compartment; correct naming ("M1", etc.) is followed by outcome-specific consequences (SR1, etc.). Objects T1-T4 are displayed only in the right compartment; for all objects, correct naming ("T1", etc.) is followed by the same conditioned reinforcer (S^{r+}).

One way, perhaps, might be to pursue what has been termed the functional independence of mands and tacts (Hall & Sundberg, 1987; Lamarre & Holland, 1985; Ribeiro, 1989; Sigafoos, Doss, & Reichle, 1989). Can we do so by means of matching-to-sample analogues? We will consider some possible ways. First, what do we mean by functional independence? Figure 20 provides an example in a context different from matching to sample; the figure shows two adjacent display compartments. In the left compartment, objects M1, M2, M3, and M4 are displayed successively, and the subject is to name them. Correct responses are followed by specific reinforcers. Recall that in our work with the severely retarded, the objects were actual foods, and the subject produced those same foods by naming them. In the right compartment, other objects, T1, T2, T3, and T4, are displayed and the subject is again to name them; with these items, however, correct naming responses produce a common, generalized reinforcer – a token – or some other kind of consequence that is not specific to each naming performance.

Let us say for the purposes of this argument that the performances on the left are indeed mands and those on the right are tacts. Functional independence would be indicated if the subject proves incapable of producing the name of the T-stimuli when they are displayed in the left compartment and the M-stimuli when displayed on the right. Results like those reported by Lamarre and Holland (1985) and Savage-Rumbaugh (1984) lead to the prediction that we may in fact see curious behavior like this sometimes in very young children, retarded subjects, and chimpanzees that have had language training.

Could we see something like the independence phenomenon in matching to sample with outcome-specific and outcome-varied procedures? Perhaps, but such an experiment will be difficult to design. One of the biggest problems to solve is that of multiple control; "pure" tacts or mands may be difficult or impossible to arrange given the demand characteristics of the matching-to-sample procedure.

Summary

To conclude, we will merely summarize a few main points. Outcome-specific reinforcement procedures seem to produce reliable and unusual effects in nonhumans' – primarily pigeons' – discrimination performances. With very few exceptions, those effects have not yet been shown in human subjects. Work with the human population, however, cannot be considered definitive. Not enough subjects have been studied, and the procedures used so far may not have been the correct ones. Outcome-specific procedures do lead to other interesting behavior in humans – primarily the formation of stimulus classes in which the reinforcer is a member. Studies of such classes may allow us to analyze behavioral processes relevant to distinctions between mands and tacts, but the methodology for doing so is not immediately obvious.

This research was supported by NICHD Grants HD 22218, HD 17445, HD 10210, and HD 04147 and in part by the Department of Mental Retardation of the Commonwealth of Massachusetts (Contract: 3403-8403-306). We thank Mr. Vincent Strully and the staff of the New England Center for Autism, and Mr. J. R. Robinson and the staff of the Day Development and Transition Center, Vinfen Corp. for their cooperation. Reprints are available from W. J. McIlvane or W. V. Dube, Behavior Analysis Department, Shriver Center, 200 Trapelo Rd., Waltham, MA 02254.

References

Brodigan, D. A., & Peterson, G. B. (1976). Two-choice conditional discrimination performance of pigeons as a function of reward expectancy, pre-choice delay, and domesticity. *Animal*

Learning and Behavior, 4, 121-124.

Carlson, J. G., & Wielkiewicz, R. M. (1972). Delay of reinforcement in instrumental discrimination learning of rats. *Journal of Comparative and Physiological Psychology, 81,* 365-370.

Carlson, J. G., & Wielkiewicz, R. M. (1976). Mediators of the effects of magnitude of reinforcement. *Learning and Motivation, 7,* 184-196.

Cohen, L. R., Brady, J., & Lowry, M. (1981). The role of differential responding in matching-to-sample and delayed matching performance. In M. L. Commons and J. A. Nevin (Eds.), *Quantitative analyses of behavior, Vol. 1, Discriminative properties of reinforcement* (pp. 345-364). Cambridge, MA: Ballinger.

de Long, R. E., & Wasserman, E. A. (1981). Effects of differential reinforcement expectancies on successive matching-to-sample performance in pigeons. *Journal of Experimental Psychology: Animal Behavior Processes, 7,* 394-412.

de Rose, J. C., McIlvane, W. J., Dube, W. V., Galpin, V. C., & Stoddard, L. T. (1988). Emergent simple discrimination established by indirect relation to differential consequences. *Journal of the Experimental Analysis of Behavior, 50,* 1-20.

de Rose, J. C., McIlvane, W. J., Dube, W. V., & Stoddard, L. T. (1988). Stimulus equivalence and functional equivalence in moderately retarded individuals' conditional discrimination. *Behavioural Processes, 17,* 167-175.

Dube, W. V., McIlvane, W. J., Mackay, H. A., & Stoddard, L. T. (1987). Stimulus class membership established via stimulus-reinforcer relations. *Journal of the Experimental Analysis of Behavior, 47,* 159-175.

Dube, W. V., McIlvane, W. J., Maguire, R. W., Mackay, H. A., & Stoddard, L. T. (1989). Stimulus class formation and stimulus-reinforcer relations. *Journal of the Experimental Analysis of Behavior, 51,* 65-76.

Dube, W. V., Rocco, F, J., & McIlvane, W. J. (1989). Delayed matching to sample with outcome-specific contingencies in mentally retarded humans. *The Psychological Record, 39,* 483-492.

Edwards, C. A., Jagielo, J. A., Zentall, T. R., & Hogan, D. E. (1982). Acquired equivalence and distinctiveness in matching to sample by pigeons: Mediation by reinforcer-specific expectancies. *Journal of Experimental Psychology: Animal Behavior Processes, 8,* 244-259.

Fedorchak, P. M., & Bolles, R. C. (1986). Differential outcome effect using a biologically neutral outcome difference. *Journal of Experimental Psychology: Animal Behavior Processes, 12,* 125-130.

Hall, G. & Sundberg, M. L. (1987). Teaching mands by manipulating conditioned establishing operations. *The Analysis of Verbal Behavior, 5,* 41-53.

Honig, W. K., Matheson, W. R., & Dodd, P. W. D. (1984). Outcome expectancies as mediators for discriminative responding. *Canadian Journal of Psychology, 38,* 196-217.

Jenkins, H. M., & Moore, B. R. (1973). The form of the auto-shaped response with food or water reinforcers. *Journal of the Experimental Analysis of Behavior, 20,* 163-181.

Kruse, J. M., Overmier, B., Konz, W. A., & Rokke, E. (1983). Pavlovian conditioned stimulus effects upon instrumental choice behavior are reinforcer specific. *Learning and Motivation, 14,* 165-181.

Lamarre, J., & Holland, J. G. (1985). The functional independence of mands and tacts. *Journal of the Experimental Analysis of Behavior, 43,* 5-19.

Litt, M. D., & Schreibman, L. (1981). Stimulus-specific reinforcement in the acquisition of receptive labels by autistic children. *Analysis and Intervention in Developmental Disabilities, 1,* 171-186.

McIlvane, W. J., Bass, R. W., O'Brien, J. M., Gerovac, B. J., & Stoddard, L. T. (1984). Spoken and signed naming of foods after receptive exclusion training in severe retardation. *Applied*

Research in Mental Retardation, 5, 1-27.

McIlvane, W. J., Dube, W. V., Kledaras, J. B., Iennaco, F. M., & Stoddard, L. T. (1990). Teaching relational discrimination to mentally retarded individuals: Some problems and possible solutions. *American Journal on Mental Retardation, 95,* 283-296.

McIlvane, W. J., Kledaras, J. B., Dube, W. V., & Stoddard, L. T. (1989). Automated instruction of severely and profoundly retarded individuals. In J. Mulick, & R. Antonak (Eds.), *Transitions in mental retardation,* Vol. 4 (pp. 15-76). Norwood, NJ: Ablex.

Michael, J. (1982). Distinguishing between discriminative and motivational functions of stimuli. *Journal of the Experimental Analysis of Behavior, 37,* 149-155.

Michael, J. (1985). Two kinds of verbal behavior plus a possible third. The *Analysis of Verbal Behavior, 3,* 2-4.

Overmier, J. B. (1988, May). *Expectations: From animal laboratory to the clinic.* Paper presented at the Meeting of the Midwest Psychological Association.

Pepperberg, I. M. (1988). Comprehension of "absence" by an African Grey parrot: Learning with respect to questions of same/different. *Journal of the Experimental Analysis of Behavior, 50,* 553-564.

Peterson, G. B. (1984). How expectancies guide behavior. In H. L. Roitblat, T. G. Bever, & H. S. Terrace (Eds.), *Animal cognition.* Hillsdale, NJ: Erlbaum.

Peterson, G. B., & Trapold, M. A. (1980). Effects of altering outcome expectancies on pigeons' delayed conditional discrimination performance. *Learning and Motivation, 11,* 267-288.

Peterson, G. B., & Trapold, M. A. (1982). Expectancy mediation of concurrent conditional discriminations. *American Journal of Psychology, 95,* 571-580.

Peterson, G. B., Wheeler, R. L., & Armstrong, G. D. (1978). Expectancies as mediators in the differential-reward conditional discrimination performance of pigeons. *Animal Learning and Behavior, 6,* 279-285.

Peterson, G. B., Wheeler, R. L., & Trapold, M. A. (1980). Enhancement of pigeons' conditional discrimination performance by expectancies of reinforcement and nonreinforcement. *Animal Learning and Behavior, 8,* 22-30.

Ribeiro, A. F. (1989). Correspondence in children's self-report: Tacting and manding aspects. *Journal of the Experimental Analysis of Behavior, 51,* 361-367.

Santi, A. (1989). Differential outcome expectancies and directed forgetting effects in pigeons. *Animal Learning and Behavior, 17,* 249-354.

Santi, A. & Roberts, W. A. (1985). Reinforcement expectancy and trial spacing effects in delayed matching-to-sample by pigeons. *Animal Learning and Behavior, 13,* 274-284.

Saunders, R. R., & Sailor, W. (1979). A comparison of three strategies of reinforcement on two-choice learning problems with severely retarded children. AAESPH Review, 4, 323-333.

Savage-Rumbaugh, E. S. (1984). Verbal behavior at a procedural level in the chimpanzee. *Journal of the Experimental Analysis of Behavior, 41,* 223-250.

Shepp, B. E. (1962). Some cue properties of anticipated rewards in discrimination learning of retardates. *Journal of Comparative and Physiological Psychology, 55,* 856-859.

Sidman, M. (1971). Reading and auditory-visual equivalences. *Journal of Speech and Hearing Research, 14,* 5-13.

Sidman, M. (1986). Functional analysis of emergent verbal classes. In T. Thompson & M. D. Zeiler (Eds.), *Analysis and integration of behavioral units* (pp. 213-245). Hillsdale, NJ: Erlbaum.

Sidman, M., Cresson, O., & Willson-Morris, M. (1974). Acquisition of matching to sample via mediated transfer. *Journal of the Experimental Analysis of Behavior, 22,* 261-273.

Sidman, M., & Tailby, W. (1982). Conditional discrimination vs. matching-to-sample: An expansion of the testing paradigm. *Journal of the Experimental Analysis of Behavior, 37,* 5-22.

Sidman, M., Wynne, C. K., Maguire, R. W., & Barnes, T. (1989). Functional classes and equivalence relations. *Journal of the Experimental Analysis of Behavior, 52,* 261-274.

Sigafoos, J., Doss, S., & Reichle, J. (1989). Developing mand and tact repertoires in persons with severe developmental disabilities using graphic symbols. *Research in Developmental Disabilities, 10,* 183-200.

Skinner, B. F. (1957). *Verbal behavior.* New York: Appleton-Century-Crofts.

Stoddard, L. T. (1982). An investigation of automated methods for teaching severely retarded individuals. In N. R. Ellis (Ed.), *International review of research in mental retardation* (pp. 163-207). New York: Academic Press.

Stoddard, L. T., & McIlvane, W. J. (1986). Stimulus control research and developmentally disabled individuals. *Analysis and Intervention in Developmental Disabilities, 6,* 155-178.

Trapold, M. (1970). Are expectancies based upon different positive reinforcing events discriminably different? *Learning and Motivation, 1,* 129-140.

Urcuioli, P. J. (1985). On the role of differential sample behaviors in matching-to-sample. *Journal of Experimental Psychology: Animal Behavior Processes, 11,* 502-519.

Williams, B. A. (1984). Stimulus control and associative learning. *Journal of the Experimental Analysis of Behavior, 42,* 469-483.

Wulfert, E., & Hayes, S. C. (1988). Transfer of a conditional ordering response through conditional equivalence classes. *Journal of the Experimental Analysis of Behavior, 50,* 125-144.

Chapter 4

Stimulus Equivalence and Generalization in Reading After Matching to Sample by Exclusion

Julio C. de Rose
Deisy G. de Souza*
Ana Lucia Rossito
Tania M. S. de Rose
Universidade Federal De Sao Carlos

We have been working for several years on a project to teach reading to lower socio-economic status children who are failing at regular school. The original purpose of our work was to design a program that could be massively applied to establish reading and writing in this population to help reduce the very high rate of failure that afflicts our school system, particularly in its first grade.

We are still pursuing this aim, but we will present here another aspect of our work. During the development and application of our reading program we have conducted a series of experiments investigating the acquisition of textual behavior from auditory-visual matching to sample. We also studied the formation of stimulus equivalence relations showing reading comprehension, and the acquisition of a repertoire of minimal units that enabled subjects to read untrained words.

The basic procedure consisted of matching to sample: the subject had to select one comparison stimulus from an array, based on a sample stimulus. Sample stimuli were either spoken words, printed words or pictures. Comparison stimuli were either printed words or pictures.

This experimental arrangement has been extensively investigated in the work of Sidman and his collaborators (e.g.: Mackay & Sidman, 1984; Sidman & Cresson, 1973; Sidman & Tailby, 1982). The methods and concepts introduced in these studies have done much to clarify the processes involved in textual behavior and reading comprehension.

Figure 1 presents a diagram illustrating Sidman's model; it also outlines part of our procedures. Our subjects were already able to match pictures to dictated words: when a particular word was spoken (the sample), they could select the corresponding picture (the comparison stimulus). This is represented by the thin arrow pointing from A to B in the diagram. They were also able to name pictures: this is represented by the thin B-D arrow in the diagram. The thick arrows represent what we explicitly taught to our subjects. The AC arrow indicates that subjects learned to match printed words (as comparison stimuli) to dictated words (as samples). We also taught the subjects to form the word from letters arranged in a random sequence (CE arrow). This was similar to the anagram composition used by Mackay and Sidman (1984) and Mackay (1985), but our subjects could see the printed word while they formed an identical word with the scattered letters. We taught this to increase the likelihood that subjects would pay attention to all the letters

---

*Now at Departamento de Processos Psicologicos Basicos, Universidade de Brasilia.

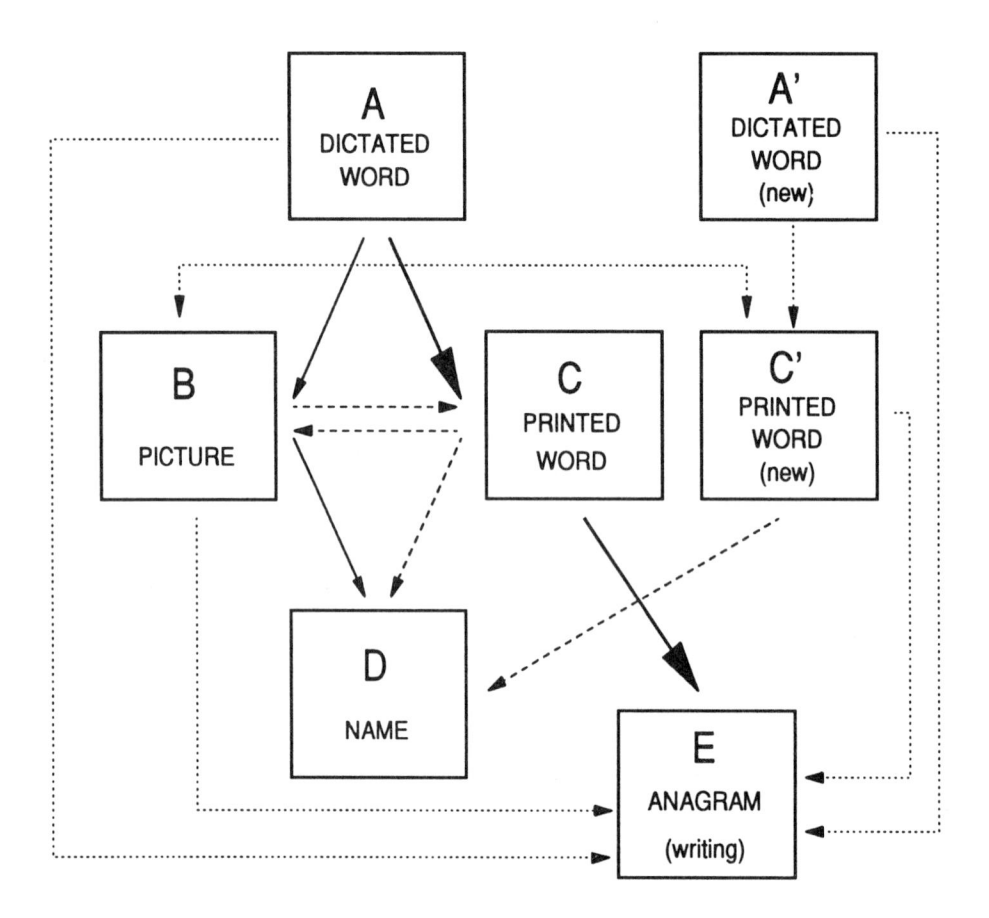

Figure 1. Schematic diagram of the network of matching-to-sample performances involved in reading and writing. Our subjects were already able to match spoken words to pictures —represented by the thin arrow pointing from A to B in the diagram. They were also able to name pictures — represented by the thin BD arrow in the diagram. The thick arrows represent what we explicitly taught to our subjects. Dashed arrows represent derived performances we tested—dotted arrows show other derived performances that might occur.

of the words they were learning to match. This performance has features in common with copying, but does not require the elaborate motor coordination involved in drawing the letters.

Heavily dashed arrows represent emergent performances: the C-D arrow is what Skinner calls textual behavior: naming the printed words. The B-C and C-B arrows represent matching printed words to pictures, and *vice-versa*. Given a picture, the subject selects the corresponding printed word, or given the printed word, the subject selects the corresponding picture. When these performances emerge from the training outlined in the diagram, we know that subjects have formed classes of equivalent stimuli involving printed and spoken words, and the corresponding pictures (Sidman & Cresson, 1973). These equivalences indicate that subjects do more than merely name the words: they read them with comprehension (Sidman & Cresson, 1973; Mackay & Sidman, 1984).

The fine dotted arrows in the diagram represent other derived performances that might emerge on the basis of stimulus equivalence. A to E would be writing on dictation, and B to E would be writing the name of pictures. In the present study we did not assess these performances.

Skinner points out that when people learn large textual units, they may gradually develop a minimal unit repertoire, so that syllables or letters would acquire control over the corresponding speech sounds. This repertoire enables people to read a variety of words without the necessity of learning them directly. This is necessary to achieve fluent reading.

The notion of minimal units is important in Skinner's analysis, not only of verbal behavior, but of several kinds of nonverbal behavior. This is one of the ways Skinner explains generation of new behavior. A new response may be produced through a combination of minimal operants: the particular combination may be new, but the minimal operants were already in the subject's repertoire. Matos and D'Oliveira (in this volume) have shown how this can occur in reading. It may also occur in writing, in echoic behavior, drawing, and so on.

Behavior analysts have long had an interest in emergent behavior, and how it can be explained by the individual's history. When confronted with behavior that seems novel behavioral theorists appeal to such concepts as class formation, verbal rules or instructions, or a repertoire of minimal units. Yet little experimental attention has been given to the notion of minimal units.

How are the minimal units acquired? They can be sometimes directly taught. That is the case with typing. We do not learn to type by typing several whole words, and eventually learning to type each individual key. Rather, we learn the keys, and this enables us to produce any word.

According to Skinner, the inverse process could also happen: the subject could learn larger units first, and then gradually acquire control by the smaller units. This might be one of the ways by which textual behavior could be generalized, enabling the individual to produce the name of virtually any new printed word.

In our studies, we investigated the emergence of textual units of this sort: this performance is represented by the arrow from C' to D. C' consisted of novel words, not directly taught to the subjects, but including minimal units contained in the words that they already learned. Other performances that we did not test would be represented by the arrows connecting C' to B and vice-versa, which would document stimulus equivalence regarding these new words, and A'to E, which represents writing these new words on dictation. This diagram probably represents most of what a literate person does, and it also permits the visualization of the many different ways in which these performances could be established.

In our Experiment 1 we used an exclusion procedure (Dixon, 1977; McIlvane & Stoddard, 1981) to increase the subject's repertoire of matching performances, represented by A-C in Figure 1. In this procedure a comparison stimulus from the baseline (that is, one that the subject has already learned to match to a particular sample) serves as a prompt for the subject to acquire a new matching relation. When a new sample is presented, the subject is likely to "exclude" the baseline comparison stimulus, and select a new one, eventually learning the relation between this new comparison stimulus and the new sample.

Our Experiment 1 was conducted to:

a) Verify whether oral naming of the trained words would emerge as a consequence of training the subjects to match printed comparisons to dictated samples (which in this case was accomplished via an exclusion procedure); that is, given A-C in the diagram, would we obtain the emergent performance C-D?

b) Investigate the emergence of reading comprehension, defined as equivalence between dictated words, printed words, and corresponding pictures. Equivalence would be documented by the B-C and C-B relations in our diagram.

c) Investigate whether subjects would be able to read words that were not explicitly taught (C'-D arrow in the diagram). The words in C' contained the same syllables of the words taught to the subject, but these syllables were recombined to generate new words.

The subjects in this experiment were six children who attended first or second grade (in the State of Sao Paulo, promotion from first to second grade is automatic, regardless of academic achievement). The teachers of these children judged that they made very little or no progress in learning to read; an independent evaluation conducted by the experimenters confirmed this.

Sessions were conducted in a quiet room at the subjects' school. Conditional discrimination trials were arranged on sheets of letter paper, and each sheet was enclosed in a transparent plastic envelope, mounted in a binder. Successive trials were presented by turning the sheets. Following every correct response, in training or testing trials, the subject was praised and told that his or her response was correct.

We began each session with a pre-test to see whether subjects could already name the words that we planned to teach in the session (henceforth called *training words*). We also verified whether subjects could or could not at first read two other words, which were composed of syllables in the training and previously learned (what we will call *baseline*) words. We will call these *generalization words*.

After this pre-test, exclusion training began. In an exclusion trial, two printed words were presented as comparison stimuli. One of them was a baseline word. The other was a training word. After the presentation of the comparison stimuli, the training word was dictated as a sample. In this situation we know that subjects are very likely to exclude the baseline comparison, and to select the new one (Dixon, 1977; McIlvane & Stoddard, 1981). In each session, we conducted four or five exclusion trials with each training word. In two of these trials, subjects were also required to compose the printed words with separate letters given in a random order. For each exclusion trial, there was a "novelty control" trial. In these, the comparison stimuli were a baseline word and a training word (printed), and the sample was the baseline word (dictated). This assured that selections based solely on novelty would not be consistently reinforced, thus requiring subjects to attend to the dictated sample.

After this matching to sample training, we could inquire: had the subjects learned to produce the name of the training words? And more: had the subjects learned to name the generalization words? A post-test was conducted to verify this.

Our program was arranged in a sequence of steps. To get the subjects to do exclusion, we needed a baseline. So, our first step was training the subjects to match three printed words to their dictated names. We did this with a matching to sample procedure, with three dictated words as samples and the corresponding printed words as comparison stimuli; an oral prompt was given in the initial trials.

Our second step was an equivalence test with the three baseline words: When the sample was a picture, the subject was asked to point to the picture and name it. Then two printed words were presented and the subject made a selection. When a printed word was the sample, the subject was also asked to point to it and name it, then the pictures were shown and the subject had to make a selection.

We then began exclusion training. The first two exclusion steps taught two words each. Then, in the following step, an equivalence test was conducted. This test included all the words taught so far. If the subject passed the test, the recently taught words were included in the baseline, serving as a basis for further exclusion. New words were taught in subsequent exclusion steps: from now on, four words were taught in each step. After each two exclusion steps, an equivalence test was conducted, and so on. At two points, in the middle and the end of the program, we conducted an extended generalization test. In this test we inserted probes to verify naming of 18 generalization words.

To summarize the results, it is first important to mention that subjects had a very high accuracy in matching responses. They virtually always excluded correctly.

Did correct exclusion result in the acquisition of naming the training words? Figure 2A shows the results for subject DB. Plus signs show naming scores in the pre-tests: they are very low, although occasionally we see the child giving correct answers in the pre-test. This becomes more common toward the end of the program. Diamonds represent naming in the post-tests. They are much higher than the pre-test scores. This indicates how many words the subject learned to name after the training in that particular session.

When post-test scores were not close to 100%, we repeated the step, as in the 4th and 12th step, and eventually scores got close to 100%. In equivalence steps, when the sample was a printed word, the subject had to name it as an observing response (this was required of subjects DB, EM and PR only after step 13). Reading the baseline words was also assessed in the extended generalization tests (Steps 9 and 19). The x's represent the accuracy of this response, indicating how well reading of baseline words was maintained. The results support the conclusion that this child learned to produce the names of the training words after exclusion training.

By the end of this training, the subject had acquired a repertoire of naming about 40 words. Did she at any point become able to read different words, not explicitly taught?

Figure 2B shows how this came about. Here, as before, the plus signs show pre-test scores,

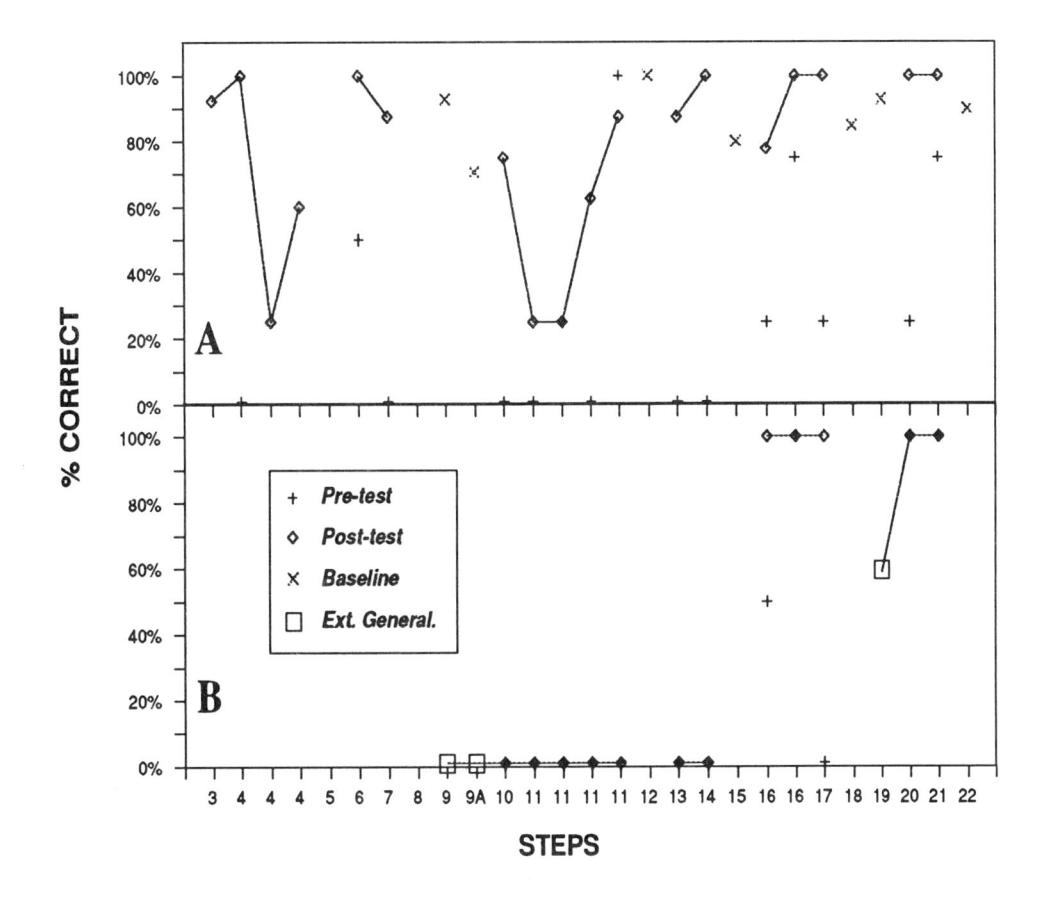

Figure 2. Accuracy of responses by Subject DB in reading probes with training words (Panel A), and with generalization words (Panel B).

and the diamonds show post-test scores. (The filled diamonds indicate identical pre-test and post-test scores). Notice that for this subject generalization probes began only after the 9th session. The boxes show results in the two extended generalization tests.

This subject shows no generalization until the 16th step. Then, it suddenly comes up, and continues. In the second extended generalization test the percent correct is higher than 50%. This means that the subject was able to name correctly ten generalization words. A naming response was considered correct when the whole word was named correctly; if the subject named correctly only part of a word, then the whole response was considered wrong.

Figure 3A shows results for subject NC. In this figure we see very rapid acquisition of oral naming of the training words. Generalization data, shown in Figure 3B are similar to our first subject in showing virtually no generalization in the initial part of the teaching program. For this subject, however, generalization occurs earlier and develops more gradually in the second half of the program until we see the subject naming generalization words with high accuracy in the final extended test.

Subject NA yielded very similar data, and EM showed even quicker generalization. NJ did

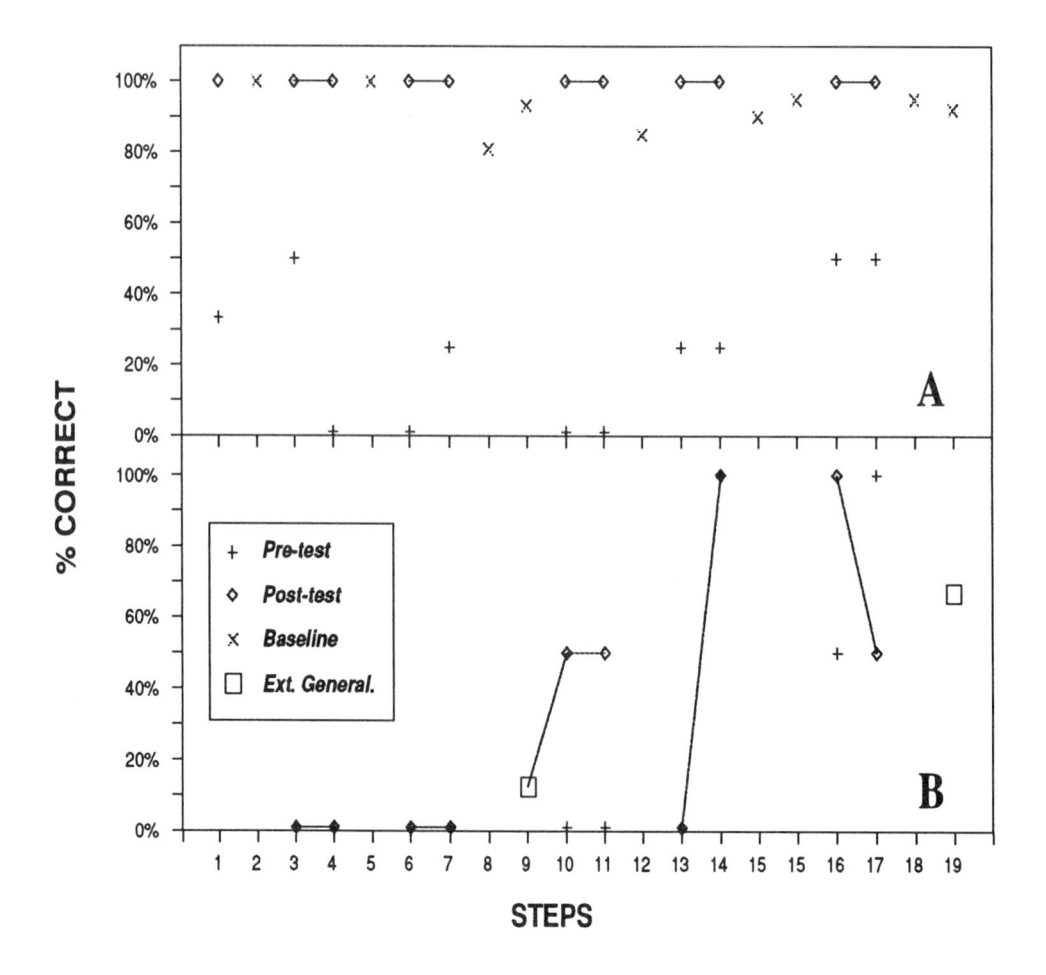

Figure 3. Accuracy of responses by Subject NC in reading probes with training words (Panel A), and with generalization words (Panel B).

not maintain reading of the baseline words, and abandoned school before completing the program. Another subject (PR) failed to learn the training words; more precisely, he was usually able to name the trained words in a step, but did not always maintain the baseline (which included all words trained in preceding steps). This may have happened partially because this subject missed many classes, and thus we were not able to conduct sessions with him two or three times per week, as we did with the others.

Subsequent experimentation showed many points of our program that needed revision. The choice of words for particular steps needed to be changed. We needed greater opportunity for maintaining and eventually retraining the baseline while advancing through the program.

In Experiment 1B we made several procedural changes, to control for a variety of features in our training and testing situation. First, we removed feedback from all testing trials. Subjects in Experiment 1B were never reinforced for oral naming of any words. We also tried to increase the amount of reinforcement in the training trials: we gave tokens that subjects could exchange for small toys. In the equivalence tests we eliminated the observing naming responses, and increased the number of comparison stimuli from two to three.

The subjects in this study were three children with school histories similar to the earlier subjects. Two to them showed the same pattern of results. The third subject also learned to name the baseline words, although he did that more slowly and with more repetitions of steps. This subject, however, reached the final steps without naming any generalization words.

We decided then to conduct generalization probes that did not require naming, and thus added to the equivalence tests some probes in which the samples were generalization words (this performance is represented as C'B in Figure 1). The subject's performance was initially near chance level, but the scores increased rapidly in successive steps. The extended generalization test (requiring the subject to name the words in unreinforced probes) was then conducted, and the naming scores increased gradually over successive repetitions of the test, reaching more than 60% on the fifth repetition[1].

We conducted an Experiment 2[2], in which we further analyzed the acquisition of minimal units. The subjects in this study were the four children who had completed the program in Experiment 1. They were now able to read most of the words of our language composed of two or three simple syllables. They could not yet read words containing what our first grade teachers call "difficulties". These are phonetical irregularities, or complex grapheme/phoneme combinations.

Table 1 presents a sample of our teaching program. In every step we taught four different words which contained a common "difficulty". For instance, in step 5 the four training words all contained the "difficulty" nh. Four different words, also containing nh were used only for generalization testing. All the other units (syllables and grapheme-phoneme units) were already familiar to the subject; the target difficulty constitutes the only feature of the word that the subject was supposedly unable to read. In this study, we used only social reinforcement, and responses in probe trials were never reinforced.

Every step started with a pre-test, in which we verified whether subjects could name the four training words and the four generalization words for that step. In this pre-test we also verified whether subjects could read the training words of the last step.

After the pre-test, exclusion training began. Each word appeared in four exclusion trials. The training word and a baseline word were displayed as comparison stimuli, and the training word was dictated as a sample. Each training word appeared also in four novelty control trials. We used these latter trials also as naming probes: the training word and a baseline word were displayed,

[2] *This experiment was conducted by D. G. de Souza, J. C. de Rose, O. M. Kubo and M. A. C. Liborio.*

Table 1
Sample of Training Sequence in Experiment 2

STEP	TRAINING WORDS		GENERALIZATION WORDS	
Target Unit: "nh"				
5	banha	minhoca	sonho	manha
	canhoto	lenha	vinho	pamonha
6	gafanhoto	unha	gatinho	inhame
	munheca	vinho	ninho	linha
7	sozinho	inhame	tamanho	picanha
	pinho	nenhuma	minha	punhado
8	façanha	ranheta	ninhada	medonho
	banhado	cozinha	galinha	caminho
Target Unit: "g"				
13	girafa	geada	vigia	ligeiro
	magico	tigela	mugido	geléia
14	gelatina	gemeo	regime	gilete
	pagina	relógio	genio	agito
15	megera	geladeira	gelado	fugitivo
	genio	colégio	agilidade	gíria
16	girino	regina	geranio	giovana
	magia	getúlio	geleira	lógico
Target Unit: "r" when not followed by a vowel				
25	gordo	martelo	argola	forte
	vergonha	carga	perna	farda
26	tartaruga	vermelho	verde	barba
	covarde	fornalha	largada	cortina
27	verdura	dorminhoco	mar	bordado
	armario	açucar	apertado	forca
28	mergulho	amargo	marmita	verdade
	torneira	calor	jornaleiro	diretor

and the baseline word was dictated as a sample. The subject pointed to the baseline printed word and this response was reinforced. The experimenter then asked the subject to name the other word (the training word). No feedback was given for this naming response. The exclusion and novelty control trials with the four training words were presented in a randomized order. After this training was completed, a post-test was conducted, verifying naming of the training words and generalization words.

Training with words containing the same "difficulty" continued along four successive steps

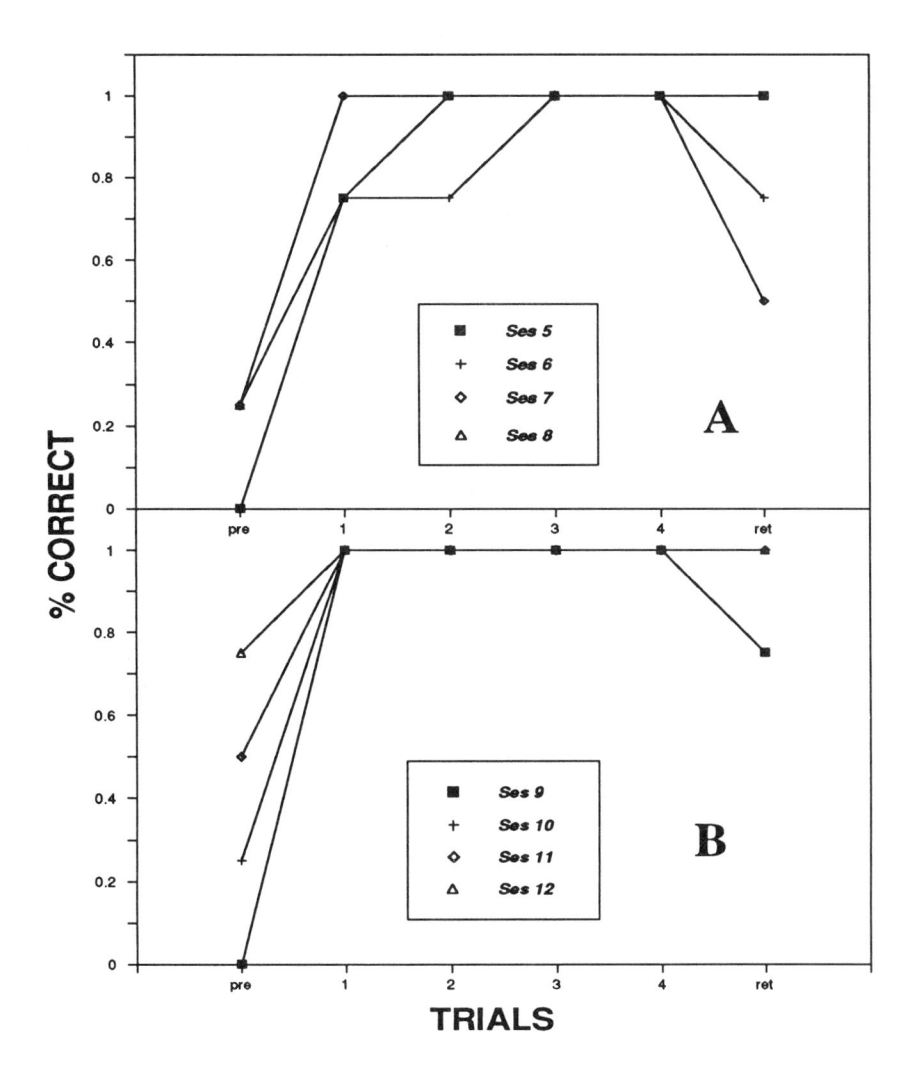

*Figure 4. Each curve shows performance in successive reading probe trials. **Pre** indicates performance in the pre-test; **1, 2, 3,** and **4** indicate performance in the successive probe trials within a session, and **ret** indicates retention assessed at the beginning of the following step. Curves in Panel A shows performance of Subject DB in four successive steps teaching words with the difficulty "nh." Panel B shows performance of Subject NC in four successive steps teaching words with the difficulty "r (followed by a vowel, in the middle of a word)".*

(unless the subject scored 100% correct in the pre-test in two successive sessions). Thus, in the sixth step four different words that also contained nh were taught; and so on, until four steps had been conducted, each one teaching four different words containing nh. After these four steps had been completed, we proceeded to another difficulty, and so on. Each step had 48 trials, conducted in a single session. If the subject was not able to name all the training words in the post-test, the step was repeated in the next session.

Figure 4A presents subject DB's acquisition of naming the training words within four successive steps. In all of them, the traineing words shared the same difficulty (nh, in this case). Each curve in this figure presents within-session results: each point shows average percent correct for the four words trained in each step.

The squares show the results for the first step with nh. The leftmost point (labeled "pre") represents scores in the pre-test. In this case, the subject did not name any of the words to be trained. The point labeled "1" in the x-axis represents the score in the naming probes given after

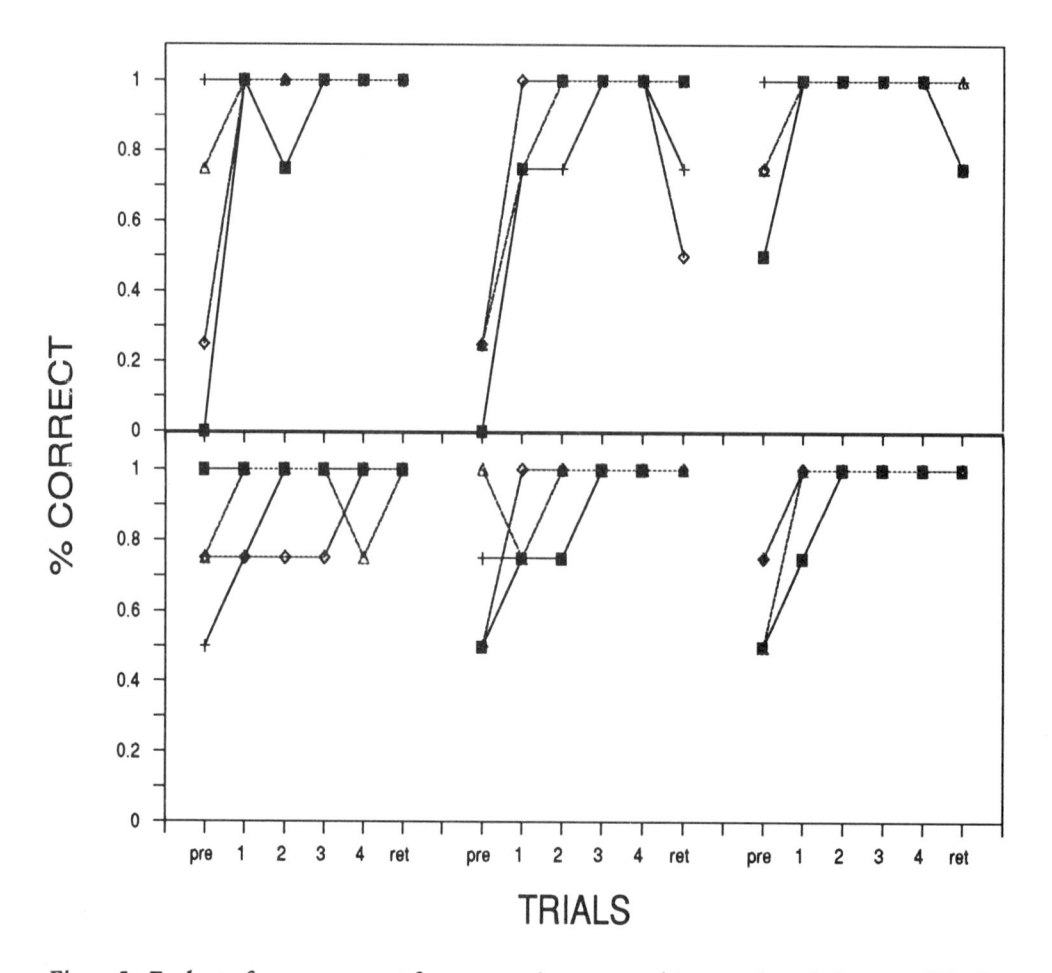

Figure 5. Each set of curves represent four consecutive steps teaching words with the same difficulty. For each difficulty, the squares show results for the first step, the plus signals show results for the second step, the triangles represent performance in the third step, and the diamonds represent performance in the fourth step.

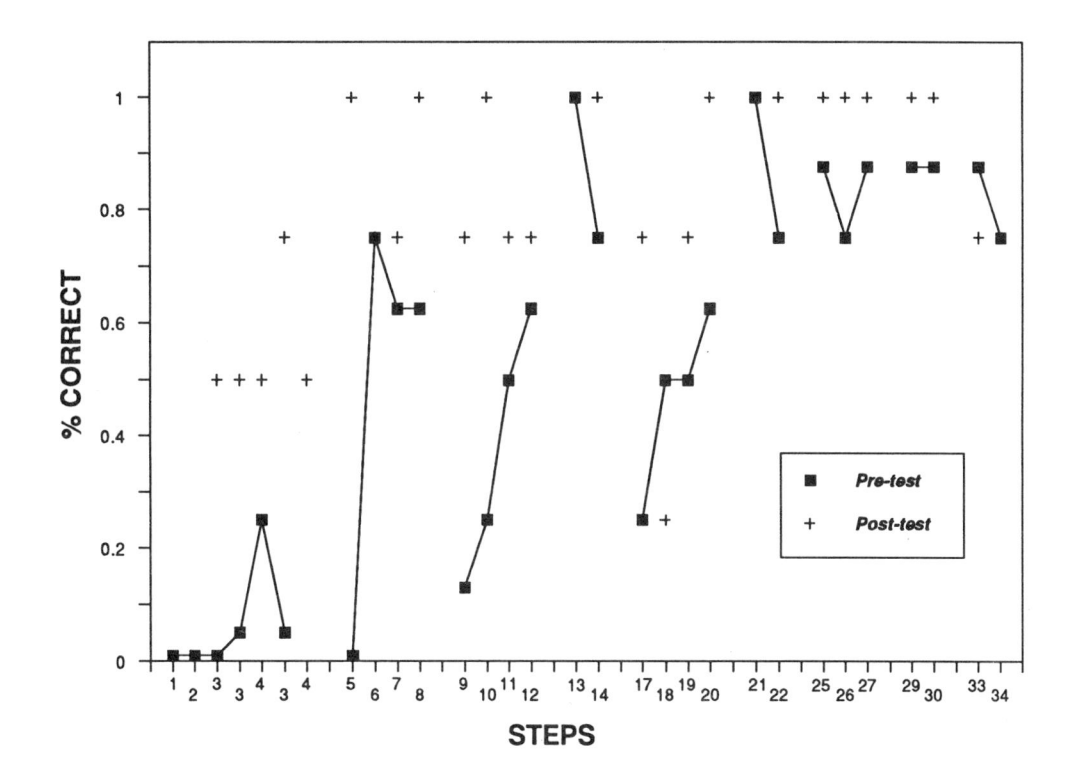

Figure 6. Performance of Subject NC in generalization probes of Experiment 2. Squares show pre-test scores, and plus signals show post-test scores.

one exclusion trial had been conducted with each training word. We see that after a single exclusion trial with each word, the subject named correctly 75% of the words, three out of four. In the second naming probe, after the second exclusion trial had been conducted with each word, the subject read 100% of the words, and this score was maintained in the succeeding probes. The rightmost point (labeled "ret") represents retention scores, assessed in the pretest of the following step. The other curves correspond to the following steps, in which other words, also containing nh were trained. We see similar trends, but much faster acquisition. As successive steps were conducted, with training words sharing the same difficulty, we also notice that scores in the pre-tests increase. This indicates an increasing generalization: After learning to read some words containing a particular difficulty, the subject becomes more able to read new words that also contain this same difficulty. This trend is particularly noticeable in Figure 4B, which shows performance of subject NC in four successive steps in which words containing another difficulty were trained. Here, acquisition is virtually immediate: scores rise to 100% after a single exclusion trial with each word. Scores in the pre-tests increase gradually over successive steps, indicating a gradual increase in generalization.

Figure 5 presents results plotted in this fashion for the whole training with subject DB. Each new difficulty that is trained represents a systematic replication of these acquisition effects.

Figure 6 shows accuracy of naming generalization words, in the pre-tests (squares) and post-tests (plus signs). The figure shows results for a representative subject (NC). Pre-test scores are linked to make more visible the increase in these scores along the training of each particular difficulty (the same effect that could be noticed in Figure 4B). Also, scores increase within session: in the pre-tests, the subject could not read some words. He is then exposed to exclusion training that enables him to learn other words, containing the same difficulty. And after this, he is able to read the very same words he could not read before.

Another thing we see in this figure is that the subject's scores in pre and post-tests exhibit a general increasing trend as training progresses. How can we account for these results? Could we consider reading as a general class, and as we reinforce some members of this class, other members come to be learned more easily? (see Lee & Pegler, 1982).

We think that our results are significant regarding to four important points.

First, the studies we have presented support the account of reading and stimulus equivalence that has been developed by Sidman and his collaborators. The establishment of the receptive relation between spoken word (as a sample) and written word (as comparison stimulus), produces the emergence of textual behavior (naming the written word) and reading comprehension. Reading comprehension is documented by the formation of stimulus classes including spoken and printed words, and pictures.

This is not new, of course (e.g.: Mackay, 1985; Mackay & Sidman, 1984; Sidman & Cresson, 1973). However, in the present study we were able to follow the course of development of emergent textual behavior, even in a trial by trial basis: Our results show that the emergent relations develop after very few receptive pairings. Often a single pairing between spoken and printed word is sufficient for the development of textual behavior, as our second experiment shows.

The second point is about reading generalization: a reading repertoire consisting purely of whole-word units would be very limited: proficient reading usually requires the development of a repertoire of minimal units. The minimal units are the building blocks that can generate a variety of textual responses, without the necessity of teaching each response directly. This is what we call reading generalization in this study.

A repertoire of minimal units may, of course, be directly taught. However, as Skinner points out in *Verbal Behavior,* "A basic repertoire at approximately the level of the single letter or speech sound may develop slowly when only larger units are reinforced, but as in echoic behavior it nevertheless appears without special guidance" (Skinner, 1957, p. 67).

In Experiment 1, subjects failed to read untrained words for several sessions; eventually they started reading untrained words, and then continued doing so in all subsequent steps. This may indicate a change in the functional unit: these were initially whole words, but later smaller units acquired control. This control by minimal units may have been facilitated by the degree of phonetical regularity of the Portuguese written language.

Experiment 2 studied systematically the acquisition of control by different specific minimal units. The results show that at least two variables are important: first, generalization is a function of amount of training with each specific unit. A second variable is suggested by the general increase in pre-test scores toward the end of the experiment: the amount of training with reading in general may affect the speed of generalization. As Lee & Pegler (1982) point out, reading in general may be considered a response class, and reinforcing some units of this class may affect other units.

However, a few subjects with very poor initial repertoires did not show generalization. This suggests that other variables may be involved in reading generalization. It is possible that the training provided in this study allowed the acquisition of several prerequisite behaviors, such as looking at the stimuli, listening to the spoken words, etc. One such behavior may be the fractioning of spoken and written words into syllables: it has been suggested that discrimination of the sound units embedded in a word is a major obstacle to learning alphabetic writing (Rozin, 1978).

For subjects that do not have this repertoire (that is, subjects that hear the word as a whole unit, without discriminating its component sounds) it may be necessary to teach it directly for generalization to occur. But if they have this repertoire at least partially developed, they may eventually match parts of the written word with the corresponding parts of the spoken word. One of our colleagues observed a subject explicitly doing that in a replication of Experiment 1 with pre-schoolers.

The third point is about the use of social reinforcement. In Experiments 1A and 2 this was the only kind of programmed reinforcement: praising and telling the subject that he or she was correct. This social reinforcement was effective. Tokens and trinkets were used in Experiment 1B, and there is no indication that this material reinforcement was more effective. This is contrary to the findings of Staats, Staats, Schutz & Wolfe (1962), who found social reinforcement ineffective. The discrepancy may be due to the protracted history of academic failure of the subjects in the present study. It is possible that such a history could increase the reinforcing value of "being correct": it is reasonable to suppose that this was the first time in their lives that these subjects met an academic situation in which they could achieve success. However, one of our colleagues, Ligia Melchiori, has replicated this study with pre-schoolers who do not have this history of failure: this indicates that social reinforcement may be more generally effective.

The fourth point is about the exclusion procedure. This procedure could constitute an important element of a successful program to teach children to read. The success in teaching students like ours is striking. It is known that students with these characteristics tend to exhibit repeated failures and become candidates for classes of special education. According to the teachers' report, these were the prospects for most of our subjects.

Our exclusion procedure is similar to the previous studies of Dixon (1977), McIlvane and Stoddard (1981), and others. However, the stimuli are far more complex: printed letters and words contain many relevant dimensions and different words contain many common features. The subjects had a long experience with those stimuli, in the context of an educational history marked by repeated failure. This history could interfere with acquisition of the relevant performances, since it is known that error histories can generate behaviors that compete with relevant learning (e.g.: Sidman & Stoddard, 1966; Stoddard & Sidman, 1967).

Exclusion was not, however, the only relevant feature of our teaching procedure: it is possible that an individualized teaching situation, with frequent reinforcement and gradual progress, could shape the complex repertoire achieved by our subjects. It remains to be assessed to what extent exclusion per se contributed to a rapid expansion of the reading repertoire.

We would like to acknowledge the support of our research program by CNPq (Grant number 402744/87, to D. G. de Souza), and FAPESP (Grant number 88-2444-0, to J. C. de Rose). The authors had scholarships from CNPq. We are grateful to Nivaldo Nale for his help in conducting this research, to Murray Sidman for invaluable critical comments on this research program, and to Steven Hayes and William Dube for their contribution to the final version of this chapter.

Footnotes

1. Data collection and analysis for this subject was completed after this chapter had been submitted, which prevented further presentation and discussion of these findings. We have now added C'B trials to our standard program, in order to study the role of this matching performance in promoting reading generalization. Note that results for this subject are similar to NJ's results in Experiment 1A. It is possible that, for some subjects, "receptive" generalization is a prerequisite for producing the names of novel words.

2. This experiment was conducted by D. G. de Souza, J. C. de Rose, and M. A. C. Liborio.

References

Dixon, L. S., (1977). The nature of control by spoken words over visual stimulus selection. *Journal of the Experimental Analysis of Behavior, 27,* 433-442.

Lee, V. L., & Pegler, A. M. (1982). Effects on spelling of training children to read. *Journal of the Experimental Analysis of Behavior, 37,* 311-322.

McIlvane, W. J., & Stoddard, L. T., (1981). Acquisition of matching-to-sample performances in severe retardation: Learning by exclusion. *Journal of Mental Deficiency Research, 25,* 33-48.

Mackay, H. A. (1985). Stimulus equivalence in rudimentary reading and spelling. *Analysis and Intervention in Developmental Disabilities. 5,* 373-387.

Mackay, H. A., & Sidman, M. (1984). Teaching new behavior via equivalence relations. In P. H. Brooks, R. Sperber, & C. McCauley (Eds.), *Learning and cognition in the mentally retarded* (pp. 493-513). Hillsdale, N.J.: Erlbaum.

Matos, M. A., & D'Oliveira, M. M. H., (1989, January). *Equivalence relations and reading behavior.* Paper presented at the III International Institute on Verbal Relations, Aguas de Lindoia, SP, Brazil.

Rozin, P. (1978). The acquisition of basic alphabetic principles: A structural approach. In A. C. Catania & T. A. Brigham (Eds.), *Handbook of applied behavior analysis: Social and instructional processes* (pp. 410-453). New York: Irvington.

Sidman, M., & Cresson, O. (1973). Reading and crossmodal transfer of stimulus equivalences in severe retardation. *American Journal of Mental Deficiency, 77,* 515-523.

Sidman, M., & Stoddard, L. T. (1966). Programming perception and learning for retarded children. In N. R. Ellis (Ed.), *International Review of Research in Mental Retardation.* Vol. 2 (pp. 151-208). New York: Academic Press.

Sidman, M., & Tailby, W. (1982). Conditional discrimination vs. matching to sample: An expansion of the testing paradigm. *Journal of the Experimental Analysis of Behavior, 37,* 5-22.

Skinner, B. F. (1957). *Verbal Behavior.* New York: Prentice Hall.

Staats, A. W., Staats, C. K., Schutz, R. E., & Wolfe, M. (1962). The conditioning of textual responses using "extrinsic reinforcers". *Journal of the Experimental Analysis of Behavior, 5,* 33-40.

Stoddard, L. T., & Sidman, M. (1967). The effects of errors on children's performance of a circle-ellipse discrimination. *Journal of the Experimental Analysis of Behavior, 10,* 261-270.

Chapter 5

Equivalence Relations and Reading

Maria Amelia Matos and Maria Martha Hubner d'Oliveira
Universidade de Sao Paulo

Studies of the conditions under which equivalence relations emerge have contributed to the understanding of thought and language (Mackay & Sidman, 1984; Sidman, 1971, 1977, 1986; Sideman & Cresson, 1973; Sidman, Kirk, & Willson-Morris, 1985). Since Sidman (1971) described the basic procedures involved in equivalence relations, this area of research has become of key importance for behavior analytic researchers.

The present chapter is concerned with the conditions under which new verbal classes may emerge. We see it as a possible contribution both to the study of verbal control by small units and to the teaching and understanding of reading.

In the study we will present we took advantage of some features of the Portuguese language. First of all, the Portuguese language has, for the majority of its words, an almost exact correspondence between the written and the spoken forms of such words. The cultivated form of the Portuguese language has the same graphic and phonetic structure. That is, with few exceptions, its phonemes correspond to its graphemes. Because of this consistency, within the Portugese language it is almost always true that upon seeing a word never before heard, one would still pronounce it correctly and having heard a word never before seen in its written form one could infer its proper spelling. There are exceptions, of course. For example, the letters r and s change their pronunciation depending upon whether they occur in the beginning or in the middle of a word, after a consonant or after a vowel, on so on. However, we will not be dealing with such rarities at the present.

The second feature we made use of is the fact that, like many other languages, Portuguese is not an ideographic language. In Japanese for example, even though it is a syllabic language with a very nice correspondence between written and spoken syllables, the meaning of the words change depending upon which alphabet is being used. Thus the word "hana" might refer to "nose" or "flower" depending on the alphabet in use. However, in Portuguese meaning is arbitrary and associated to a particular combination of syllables and letters in a particular order; not to the word as a whole written in a particular way. A given syllable and its specific sound or a given letter and its specific sound may appear in several different words. In Portuguese, written syllables (or letters) are stable stimuli for textual behavior, but not for meaning. The same is true for spoken syllables (or letters) regarding dictation taking behavior.

In his book *Verbal Behavior* (1957), Skinner proposed that the acquisition of verbal control by larger units occurred simultaneously with the acquisition of control by smaller units. If that is true, then children, upon learning how to read a few words, would come under the control of these words oral and graphic components. The question we asked in this study pertained to these matters. Would the acquisition of reading through equivalence relations, allow the acquisition of control by smaller units? Could such control be identified?

The rationale was a simple one. Based on the described characteristics of the Portuguese language we would choose a few words whose elements could be combined and recombined to form different words. We could then teach reading comprehension of the original set of words to pre-school children, via equivalence relations. Afterwards, the new set of words, produced through recombinations, would be tested and control by smaller units, if any, would be identified. Table 1 shows the original and the derived set of words used in this study, as well as the possible source of control in each case.

Table 1 - Trained and Derived Words Used in the Study

Original Words	Possible Sources of Control	Derived Words
BOLA (ball)	Letter (O and A) discrimination. Letter substitution.	BALA (candy)
BOCA (mouth)	Syllable (BO and CA) discrimination. Syllable inversion.	CABO (handle)
BOLA (ball) BOTA (boot)	Syllable (BO, LA, TA) discrimination. Combination of syllables from two different words.	LATA (can)

Both the original and the derived words were common ones, drawn from the everyday vocabulary of small children. The two syllable words had no consonant or vowel groupings, and no ambiguous graphic or vocal characteristics. If control by small units could be established through equivalence relations, we might be able to detect it in the derived forms shown in the right of Table 1. The word BALA would show letter discrimination control, the remaining words would show syllable control within and across different words. Thus, the reading of the new words that were not trained and that could only be read if derived from trained words would indicate a change in the functional units that controlled the textual behavior in this study. The identification of such controls and their sources could be an important step towards both an effective understanding and technology of reading.

Behind this rationale there was an assumption as to the effect of the transfer of equivalence relations themselves. That is, in our view reading the new words could only be accomplished if two processes occurred: A change in the functional units controlling textual behavior and a transfer of control through equivalence relations (i.e.; where AB and AC training resulted in not only BC/CB pairings, as described in the literature, but also B'C'/C'B' pairings). Let us call A, B, and C the original stimuli, where;

A are words spoken to the subject,
B are pictures corresponding to the a words, and,
C are printed words, corresponding to the A words.

Let us then call A', B' and C; the derived or new stimuli, where:

A' are words spoken by the subject,
B' are pictures corresponding to the A' words, and,
C' are printed words, corresponding to the A' words.

The apostrophe is used to indicate that the new written and spoken words are related to the previous ones via their structural properties.

Under these circumstances: (a) if illiterate subjects have the pre-requisites AB and A'B', that is, oral naming of pictures (if not, they can be taught), and (b) if they can learn the relation AC, that is, receptive reading of printed words, and (c) if through equivalence tests they show BC and CB relations, as well as B'C' and C'B' relations, (d) then one would expect a transfer of equivalence control from ABC relations to A'B'C' relations.

Our contention is that if the relations B'C'/C'B' emerge (that is, if subjects read the new verbal forms with comprehension, as indicated by matching new pictures to new printed words, and vice-versa), they only could have been established if somehow C'A' relations were present. Thus, we are suggesting the following:

1. Illiterate subjects have or will learn AB and A'B' relations.
2. S's will learn AC relations through arbitrary matching.
3. S's will show BC/CB relations in equivalence tests.
4. S's will show B'C'/C'B' relations in new tests.
5. Under conditions 1 through 4, C'A' relations may be inferred.

In our view, the only way A'C' relations could develop would be through the transposition expressed by the following relation:
"If AB as per training or pre-requisite, and A'B' idem, and if AC as per training: then, A'C'," or, "if A'B' as in AB, then A'C' as in AC."

Upon a C'B' performance one could explain it by a C'A'B' sequence, where A' (covert textual behavior) would have been primed by C', due to smaller units control; and A'B' would have been pre-requisites. However, upon a B'C' performance a slightly different process might be occurring. The B'A'C' sequence could have happened by A' (covert oral naming) being primed by B' (through A'B' pre-requisites), and A'C' pairings would occur through equivalence relations transfer primed by small units control.

The Study

The study was conducted with four small children, aged 4 to 5 years old. They attended pre-school but had no training whatsoever with reading or writing material. They were not familiar with letters or syllables. The subjects were from normal middle class homes, the eldest being from a low middle class income family. The parents of the eldest child were the only ones who hadn't completed grade school.

Stimuli were spoken words and printed words, and black and white drawings. Words were spoken by the experimenter in a neutral tone at a medium-low volume. Words were printed in capital letters with 0.2 cm wide lines and 1.0 x 1.0 cm overall dimensions. Drawings occupied an area of 4.0 to 9.0 sq. centimeters. Stimuli were presented within five white circles with the center one containing the samples, and the surrounding ones containing the comparison stimuli.

Procedure followed the standard Sidman paradigm (Sidman, 1971; Sidman and Tailby, 1982). Reinforcers were oral praises and tokens, to be exchanged for jelly bean type candies. Reinforcement probabilities during training changed gradually, from phase to phase, from 1.00 to .30. Tests were conducted under extinction. The criterion to move from one phase to the next was a score of 90.0% correct responses within the last 24 trials. Visual stimuli were xeroxed on a white sheet of paper and presented in transparent plastic envelopes. A total of eight sessions were conducted with each session lasting 20 to 30 minutes and being spaced 15 days apart.

Phase I - Pre-Training.

Pre-training was conducted to familiarize the children with the experimental setting (a small room with pictures on the wall, a shelf with toys, and a small table with two chairs), and to train them on the matching procedure. The children were first trained on color identity matching (three colors) and then, after reaching criterion, trained on arbitrary matching (auditory-visual matching, with the same colors).

The pre-training data are shown in Table 2. The identity matching training was the longest phase of the experiment, because the youngest children made more errors and required more trials (four times as many) than the older children. In the last step of color identity matching (with three comparison stimuli), Subject 4:3 (4 years and 3 months of age) developed a position preference which could not be attributed to either color or reinforcer allocations. It ceased only when the experimenter went back to the one stimulus comparison step and, after the correct response, asked, "What did you do?". The subject would point first to the sample and then to the comparison stimulus and say, "Green goes with green", (or whatever color was present). The prompt was repeated six times and from then on the child did not make an error in this phase.

Table 2 - Trials to Criterion and Proportion of Errors during Phase I Pre-Training for Color-Color and Oral Name-Color matching

Subjects Age	Color-Color Matching Trials to Criterion	Proportion of Errors	Oral Name-Color Matching Trials to Criterion	Proportion of Errors
4:1	143	20	24	0
4:3	186*	39	24	0
5:2	41	0	24	0
5:11	41	2	24	0

*Oral intervention (see text).

Phase II - Reflexivity Test.

Since equivalence relations involve identity relations (reflexivity), functional relations (symmetry) and equivalence relations proper (transitivity), a generalized identity matching test was used in this phase. Drawings (stimuli set B) of a mouth (BOCA), a boot (BOTA) and of a ball (BOLA) were presented and the children had to match these stimuli with themselves. The printed Portuguese words (set stimuli C) mouth (BOCA), boot (BOTA) and ball (BOLA), were similarly tested.

As is shown in Table 3, subjects had some degree of difficulty on this task, particularly with the C set of stimuli (printed words). Again, younger children had more difficulty than older children. It was observed that they usually pointed only to the first or the last letter of both the

Table 3 - Trials to Criterion and Proportion of Errors during Phase II Generalized Identity Matching (Reflexivity) Using Two Types of Stimuli

Subjects Age	Drawing-Drawing Matching Trials to Criterion	Proportion of Errors	Printed Word - Printed Word Matching Trials to Criterion	Proportion of Errors
4:1	48	13	99	35
4:3	48	0	72	60
5:2	24	0	24	0
5:11	24	29	24	8

Equivalence and Reading

sample and comparison words (C trials). Since reflexivity is considered a prerequisite to equivalence relations (Sidman, 1971), the experimenter intervened and asked the children to underline the whole word with their fingers saying "Draw a line with your finger, like this" as they demonstrated. No more errors were observed.

Phase III - AB Training.

Even though pre-tests showed that all children were able to pair the names of the pictures (as spoken by the E to them), AB training was conducted under the usual matching procedure. There were no errors.

Phase IV - AC Training.

As expected no child was able to pair the names of the printed words, as spoken by experimenter, to the actual printed words, as shown in the pre-tests. Not only was AC training needed, but it had to be conducted with a fading technique. Initially, only two words were used (BOTA, BOCA) under a two comparison stimuli procedure (step 1); when criterion was reached, another pair of words was used (BOLA, BOCA) under the same conditions (step 2); and, finally, a third pair (BOTA, BOLA) was used (step 3). Only then were all three words used (but only two as comparison stimuli at the time) in a mixed order (step 4). This phase ended with all three words being presented simultaneously (step 5) as comparisons.

Table 4 presents the total number of trials necessary to reach criterion on each step of this phase plus the total percentage of errors on each step. All children reached criterion, but the oldest ones showed a higher degree of difficulty (more errors and more trials to criterion) than the young ones. After the first step (BOTA, BOCA) the younger children showed practically no errors, but the older subjects continued to err. After more than 100 trials, subject 5:2 was still unable to reach criterion and an intervention was needed. On a BOTA sample trial, upon the choice of a BOCA comparison, the experimenter asked, "What is the difference?". The child pointed the letter T in BOTA and said "This one has a T, as in Terreo". (Terreo meaning ground floor, as in the elevator of the building he lived in). From then on the errors decreased sharply.

Table 4 - Trials to Criterion (TTL) and Proportion of Errors (P) during Phase IV Oral Names as Samples and Printed Words as Comparisons (see text).

Subjects Age	Step 1 TTC	P	Step 2 TTC	P	Step 3 TTC	P	Step 4 TTC	P	Step 5 TTC	P
4:1	84	.24	24	0	24	0	24	0	24	0
4:3	102	.36	24	0	24	.08	24	0	24	0
5:2	160*	.27	96	.37	24	.04	24	.08	24	.05
5:11	24	0	24	.04	72	.39	22	.05	24	.09

*Oral intervention (see text).

Phase V - AB and AC Training.

AB and AC trials were presented in a mixed order to see if the nature of the trials could affect the previous training, but all children showed 100 percent correct responses.

Phase VA - Equivalence Tests.

Table 5 shows the results of transitivity and symmetry tests. The BC and CB relations, not known and not taught, were tested under extinction and emerged perfectly for three subjects. Subject 5:11 showed a 50 percent error rate on the first set of CB trials, which happened to occur at the end of a very long session (Phase IV and V). Upon repeating the CB trials at the next session, no errors occurred. The emergence of equivalence relations during testing is often reported in the literature, but has never been fully explained (Devany, Hayes, & Nelson, 1986; Lazar, Davis-Lang & Sanchez, 1984, Sidman, Kirk & Willson-Morris, 1985; Sidman, Willson-Morris & Kirk, 1986; Spradlin, Cotter & Baxley, 1973). The response matrix (Sidman, Kirk & Willson-Morris, 1985), for Subject 5:11 during CB trials can be seen on Table 6. A strong preference for BOCA as a comparison is shown, especially when BOLA is presented as the sample. It was with BOLA as the sample that most errors occurred. (Incidentally, we had the opportunity to test this child again 39 days after the experiment was complete. Two whole sets of 18 AB/AC, trials and CB/BC trials were tested, with 100 percent correct responses.)

Table 5 - Total Trials and Proportion of "Errors" during Phase VI Equivalence Tests

Subjects Age	CB Trials Trials to Criterion	Proportion of Errors	BC Trials Trials to Criterion	Proportion of Errors	CB/BC Mixed Trials Trials to Criterion	Proportion of Errors
4:1	12	0	12	0	12	0
4:3	12	0	12	0	12	0
5:2	12	0	12	0	12	0
5:11	24*	.25	12	0	12	0

*Two sessions (see text).

Table 6 - Response Matrix for Subject 5:11 during the First Session of Phase VI Equivalence Tests (CB trials only)

SAMPLES	COMPARISONS BOCA	BOLA	BOTA
BOCA	3	0	1
BOLA	2	1	1
BOTA	1	1	2

Phase VII - New Verbal Forms.

After the equivalence tests the subjects were tested again on BC and CB type trials. The new verbal forms (See Table 1), derived from the previous ones, were presented as printed words (set stimuli C'). Besides, drawings of a wrapped candy (BALA), of the handle of a knife (CABO), and of a can (LATA), were presented as set stimuli B'. Subjects were exposed first to 12 C'B' trials, then to 12 B'C' trials, and then to 12 C'B' and B'C; mixed trials. Table 7 shows the results as percentage of errors. With three alternatives to choose from, a 67 percent error rate represents chance responding. With this in mind, all samples except for the printed sample LATA controlled correct choices by the subjects to some degree. Thus it seems that there is some evidence of transfer from the previous equivalence training (Phases I through VI), possibly primed by control from some components of the original verbal forms used in that training.

Table 7 - Proportion of Errors during Phase VIII - New Verbal Forms
Samples are indicated (N = 12)

S's age	C'B' Trials BALA	CABO	LATA	B'C' Trials BALA	CABO	LATA
4:1	.20	.25	.75	.50	.17	0
4:3	.40	.75	.75	0	0	.25
5:2	0	0	.75	1.00	.17	.50
5:11	0	.50	.50	0	0	0

The data are not extremely strong, but they do encourage further research in this area. They could mean that, by testing (and training if necessary) AB and A'B' relations, and also by training AC relations, one could obtain, with careful stimulus selection, BC, CB, B'C', and C'B' relations. The implications for the teaching of reading can not be disregarded: by naming six pictures and giving receptive reading training with three printed words, one could obtain reading comprehension with six words.

There are several ways through which the C'B'/B'C' performances might be improved. Increasing the number of trials might help. There are several studies suggesting that equivalence performance improves with the continuation of testing (Lazar, Davis-Hang & Sanchez, 1984; Sidman, Kirk & Willson-Morris, 1985; Sidman, Willson-Morris & Kirk, 1986; Spradlin, Cotter & Baxley, 1973). Another improvement might be to change the order of testing trials. Many more errors are seen on C'B' trials than on B'C" trials. It has been suggested by Prof. Catania (personal communication) that some sort of oral naming mediation might be responsible for this difference. Upon seeing the drawing of an object the children might say its name, which then acts as a prime to identify the printed name. No child except 5:3 was ever observed actually to say the names of the drawings aloud. Upon seeing the picture of the can for the first time Subject 5:3 said, "Ah that's easy, I have to find the can!" If mediation by oral names is involved, then changing the order of the testing trials (i.e. present B'C' trials first and then C'B' trials) might improve the results.

There is some evidence supporting these two suggestions. First, in the final 12 mixed C'B'/B'C' trials our results showed a significant decrease in the number of errors. However due to technical problems the records were lost before the final processing, and the exact results can not be shown. Other evidence comes from the 39th day retest with Subject 5:11. After AB, AC, CB, BC retest trials, Subject 5:11 was also retested with C'B' and B'C' trials. Results showed perfect retention for B'C' trials, 100 percent correct responses for all stimuli. For C'B' trials the results were: 0.67 correct responses for BALA, 0.83 correct responses for CABO, and 1.00 correct for LATA.

We had expected that the differences in performances with each new stimulus would show the degree of control exercised by the different units of the verbal forms (letters and/or syllables). However data from Table 7 show that there is some interaction between the different stimuli and their presentation format (drawings or printed words). Presenting a picture and then its name (in written form) is easier than presenting a written word and then its picture. In addition, each set of stimuli presents a different internal hierarchy of difficulties (as measured by the number of errors) depending whether the stimuli are presented in printed or drawn format. Thus with printed samples. LATA is the most difficult stimulus, followed by CABO and the BALA. However, with drawn samples, BALA is the most difficult one, followed by LATA and the CABO.

This hierarchy changes from subject to subject.

Table 8 allows us a closer look at the sources of control affecting responding. It provides the response distribution among the comparison stimuli available with each sample. Perfect behavioral control, (both from equivalence transfer and letter/syllable discriminations) would be indicated by a string of 1.00 scores on the diagonal line of each matrix. Any preference for a give stimulus would be indicated by a P score larger than 0.33. In this analysis both the response distribution and the P score have to be taken into account (Sidman, Kirk & Willson-Morris, 1985).

Table 8 - Response Matrix during Phase VII - New Verbal

	C'B' Trials				B'C' Trials		
Comparisons :	BALA	CABO	LATA		BALA	CABO	LATA
Samples				Subject 4:1			
BALA	.80	0	.20		.50	0	.50
CABO	0	.75	.25		.17	.83	0
LATA	.50	.25	.25		0	0	1.00
Mean	.43	.33	.23		.22	.28	.50
				Subject 4:3			
BALA	.60	.20	.20		1.00	0	0
CABO	.25	.25	.50		0	1.00	0
LATA	.25	.50	.25		0	.25	.75
Mean	.37	.32	.32		.33	.42	.25
				Subject 5:2			
BALA	1.00	0	0		0	0	1.00
CABO	0	1.00	0		.17	.83	0
LATA	.25	.50	.25		0	.50	.50
Mean	.42	.50	.08		.06	.44	.50
				Subject 5:11			
BALA	1.00	0	0		1.00	0	0
CABO	.25	.50	.25		0	1.00	0
LATA	0	.50	.50		0	0	1.00
Mean	.42	.33	.25		.33	.33	.33

Subject 4:1 had good scores, except on the printed sample LATA (C'B' trials) which produced a large amount of BALA responding, and on the drawn sample BALA (B'C' trials) which produced a large amount of LATA responses. To a lesser extent, the printed sample BALA also produced LATA responding. Thus, the source of control for both samples, seems to be the syllable LA, regardless of its position.

Subject 4:1 had very good scores on B'C' trials but seemed to be responding haphazardly on C'B' trials. Even so, on C'B' trials, BALA seemed to have a slightly better control of BALA; CABO of LATA; and LATA of CABO. On B'C' trials the few errors occur on LATA/CABO. Thus, the errors are constant, which indicates some sort of systematic control, even though it can not be traced to the smaller units which compose the words used in the present study.

Diagonal scores for Subject 5:2 on C'B' trials (1.00 on BALA and CABO) are marred by P scores. His B'C' scores are very poor. On C'B' trials he showed a very strong preference for BALA and CABO responding and, on B'C' trials, he shows a similar preference for CABO and LATA responding.

Like Subject 4:3, Subject 5:11 has very good scores on B'C' trials: 100 percent correct responding on both the first test and the retest the 39 days later. However C'B' trials only improved with retest 0.67 correct for BALA, 0.83 for CABO, and 1.00 for LATA (P scores were 0.28, 0.39, and 0.33, respectively). These C'B' results showed some CABO responding interference on LATA samples on the first test, and on BALA samples on the retest.

It seems that the new verbal form LATA, which demanded syllable discrimination across two different words, and changes in the syllable LA position was the one which produced the most interference. This interference occurred particularly when LATA was a printed sample, and it came mostly from CABO responding, but also from a few BALA responses. BALA samples also allowed for some degree of interference from LATA, particularly when BALA was a drawn sample, CABO samples allowed the least amount of interference, both from BALA and LATA.

No reflexivity test was made with B' and C' stimuli, since it could affect C'B' and B'C' responding (possibly improving its results) and in this study a major interest was to detect control by small verbal units. However, in further studies of this kind, reflexivity tests should be included to check the relative difficulty of matching each programmed stimulus to itself, as opposed to its functional match.

Phase VIII - Oral Naming Tests.

The last phase of this study consisted of presenting all visual stimuli to the subjects and asking them, "What is this?". Each one of the six drawings and six printed words was presented three times, in a mixed order. No feedback was given. Some subjects uttered a single word, some more. Table 9 represents the results obtained with the original set of stimuli. Responses are presented in their order of appearance.

Table 9 - Phase VIII - Oral Naming Tests with the Original Set of Stimuli

S's Age	BOLA Draw	BOLA Print	BOCA Draw	BOCA Print	BOTA Draw	BOTA Print
4:1	BOLA	BOLA	BOCA	BOCA	BOTA	BOTA
	BOLA	BOLA	BOCA	BOCA	BOTA	BOTA
	BOLA	BOLA	BOCA	BOCA	BOTA	BOTA
4:3	BOLA	BOLA	BOCA	BOCA	BOTA	BOTA
	BOLA	BOLA	BOCA	BOCA	BOTA	BOTA
	BOLA	BOLA	BOCA	BOCA	BOTA	BOTA
5:2	BOLA	BOLO/BOLA	BOCA	LABIO/BOCA	BOTA	BOTA
	BOLA	BOLO	BOCA	BOCA	BOTA	BOTA
	BOLA	BOLA	BOCA	BOCA	BOTA	BOTA
5:11	BOLA	BALA	BOCA	BALA	BOTA	FACA
	BOLA	BALA	BOCA	BALA	BOTA	BALA
	BOLA	BALA/BOLA/ FACA/BOLA	BOCA	BALA	BOTA	BALA

Oral naming of the drawings was perfect for all subjects, however, on the printed words it showed some variation. Oral naming of printed words by the young subjects was perfect, but the older ones exhibited interference from parallel repertoires. Subject 5:2, facing the word BOLA, said BOLO and then corrected himself. A few days before, at somebody's birthday party at school, he had asked the teacher how to spell BOLO (cake), and was very proud of his learning. Of course this responding also shows partial control by small verbal units, since the first three letters of both words are the same. His second "error" was to say LABIO (lips) before correcting for BOCA (mouth), when presented with this last word.

The analysis of Subject 5:11 is more difficult. He correctly named all the drawings and incorrectly named all the printed words. He was the sole subject not to present perfect equivalence scores on the first day he was tested (see Table 5). But, he presented perfect scores on a retest 39 days after the oral naming session. Could the incorrect oral naming for printed words, sandwiched between two perfect equivalence sessions, mean that equivalence does not bear upon textual behavior? This conclusion seems unlikely, particularly since the interference came mostly from BALA, a new word which holds some structural similarities to the ones being presented: BOLA (B LA), BOCA (B A), and BOTA (B A). Could it mean that oral naming is not a necessary condition for equivalence development? This is difficult to answer since we do not know the role of the less than perfect scores on the first equivalence test (Table 5) vis a vis his oral naming. Another puzzle is the role of FACA (knife), another new word, which the subject used to name both the picture of the handle (CABO) of a knife and its printed (CABO) word.

Table 10, which is relevant to these questions, shows the results of oral naming of the new derived verbal forms. Again, results are shown in the order they occurred. The experimental control of the situation over the subjects was such that, when faced with new words, upon erring, they did not invent names for them, rather they used the old words, usually the ones from which the new ones derived. Also, as before, oral naming for pictures is better than for printed words. The naming of the drawings did not always refer to the exact word programmed, but often involved a synonym or functionally (culturally induced) related word. The drawing of a BALA (a very popular wrapped sugar candy) produced the name BOMBOM (a smaller and less common wrapped chocolate candy). The drawing of a CABO (the handle of a table knife) produced the name FACA (knife). And finally, the drawing of a LATA (a tinned can, half open) produced the name ESPINAFRE (spinach, or rather, the spinach can shown on the popular Popeye cartoons). Even though these names were consistently used, they did not produce good C'B'/B'C' pairings, which questions the role of naming mediation.

As expected, the printed words did not show as much influence from culturally induced naming, as compared to control by the smaller units which composed such words. Thus, the word BALA produced, half of the times, the name BALA and, half of the times, the word BOLA, that is, B LA control. The word CABO produced the original word BOCA 25% of the time, and the functionally related FACA on 58%. However, FACA also partakes the syllable CA with CABO. The word LATA produced the name LATA on .25 of the times, and BOTA (syllable TA control) .50.

These data suggest why control by small units was not perfect, and also how to improve it. It seems possible that incorrect/synonym type of oral naming might have interfered with the acquisition of small units control (and thus with the development of textual behavior by new verbal form, never trained). If so, introducing an AB' or B'B' training prior to C'B' testing might avoid these synonym type deviations and improve both equivalence transfer and/or small units control.

To assess further control by smaller units, subjects were presented with a syllable reading test. Each subject was presented with each printed syllable three times in random order. Subject 4:1

Equivalence and Reading

said "Nao sei" (I don't know) for each syllable. Subject 4:3 responded by giving whole words that contained that syllable. When the syllable was an old one (BO,LA,CA,TA) he usually responded with an old word. When the syllable was a new one (BA) the child first gave an old word and then said repeatedly that she didn't know. Subject 5:2 could not be tested. Subject 5:11 said "zero" for the BO syllable, and "A" for the LA, CA, TA, BA syllables. Thus, even though no child could name the syllables, some were controlled by them in the syllable reading test.

The main conclusions that can be made from this study are:

1) Equivalence training with verbal stimuli produces some measure of control by the components of such stimuli (letters/syllables).

2) Correct oral naming of the pictures to which the words refer may be important for the development of the above mentioned control, but not for the development of equivalence relations.

3) If the oral naming of the printed words is exact it facilitates the development of textual behavior, even for new words.

4) If oral naming, both of pictures and printed words, is imprecise, the control by small verbal units may develop, but it is incomplete.

Table 10 - Phase VIII - Oral Naming Tests with the New Verbal Forms

S's Age	BALA Draw	Print	CABO Draw	Print	LATA Draw	Print
4:1	BOMBOM	BOLA	FACA	FACA	ESPINAFRE	BOTA
	BOMBOM	BOLA	FACA	FACA	ESPINAFRE	BOTA
	BOMBOM	BOLA	FACA	FACA	ESPINAFRE	BOTA
4:3	BALA	BOLA	FACA	FACA	LATA	BOLA
	BALA	BOLA	FACA	FACA	LATA	BOLA
	BALA	BOLA	FACA	FACA	LATA	BOLA
5:2	BALA	BOLA	FACA	BOCA	ESPINAFRE	BOTA
	BALA	N SEI/ BALA*	FACA	BOCA/ N SEI	ESPINAFRE	BOTA
	BALA	N SEI/ BALA*	FACA	BOCA/ N SEI	ESPINAFRE	BOTA
5:11	BALA	BALA	FACA	FACA	LATA	LATA
	BALA	BALA	FACA	FACA	LATA	LATA
	BALA	BALA	FACA	FACA	LATA	LATA

* "I don't know. Candy."

Both equivalence classes and control by small units have been suggested as relevant to reading. The present study, while very preliminary, shows that these two phenomena are indeed related and that togther they may contribute to the greater understanding of reading behavior.

References

Devany, J. M., Hayes, S. C., & Nelson, R. O. (1986). Equivalence class formation in language-able and language-disabled children. *Journal of the Experimental Analysis of Behavior, 46,* 243-257.

Lazer, B. M., Davis-Lang, D. & Sanchez, L. (1984). The formation of verbal stimuls equivalences in children. *Journal of the Experimental Analysis of Behavior, 41,* 251-266.

Mackay, H. A. & Sidman, M. (1984). Teaching new behavior via equivalence realtions. In P. H. Brooke, S. Sperber & C. McCauley (Eds.), *Learning and cognition in the mentally retarded,* (pp. 493-513). Hillsdale, N.J.: Erlbaum.

Sidman, M. (1971). Reading and auditory-visual equivalences. *Journal of Speech and Hearing Research, 14,* 5-13.

Sidman, M. (1977). Teaching some basic prerequisites for reading. In P. Mittler (Ed.), *Research to practice in mental retardation. Vol. 2 Education and Training.* (pp. 353-360). Baltimore, MD: University Park Press.

Sidman, M. (1986). Functional analysis of emergent verbal classes. In T. Thompson and M. D. Zeiler (Eds.), *Analysis and integration of behavioral units.* (pp. 213-245). Hillsdale, N. J.: Erlbaum.

Sidman, M. & Cresson, O. JR. (1973). Reading and cross model transfer of stimulus equivalences in severe retardation. *American Journal of Mental Deficiency, 77,* 515-523.

Sidman, M., Kirk, B., & Willson-Morris, M. (1985). Six-member stimulus classes generated by conditional discrimnation procedures. *Journal of the Experimental Analysis of Behavior, 43,* 21-42.

Sidman, M. & Tailby, W. (1982). Conditional discrimination vs. matching-to-sample: and expansion of the testing paradigm. *Journal of the Experimental Analysis of Behavior, 37,* 5-22.

Sidman, M., Willson-Morris, M., & Kirk, B. (1986). Matching-to-sample procedures and the development of equivalence relations: The role of naming. *Analysis and Intervention in Developmental Disabilities, 6,* 1-20.

Skinner, B. F. (1957). *Verbal behavior.* New York: Appleton-Century-Crofts.

Spradlin, J. E., Cotter, V. W., and Baxley, N. (1973). Establishing a conditional discrimination without direct training: a study of transfer with retarded adolescents. *American Journal of Mental Deficiency, 77,* 556-566.

Part 2
Derived Stimulus Relations: Theoretical Analyses

Chapter 6

Equivalence as Process

Linda J. Hayes
University of Nevada

Defining equivalence as a set of relations among stimuli, available as an outcome of their participation in a particular set of conditional discrimination training procedures (Sidman and Tailby, 1982) has facilitated our understanding of this phenomenon by insuring that everyone contributing to its understanding is contributing to the understanding of the same *it*. With very few exceptions (e.g., Vaughan, 1989), the study of equivalence has not been hampered by obligations to incorporate or otherwise consider findings pertinent to only *related* phenomena. As a result, we know a great deal about equivalence. We know a lot about the conditions under which it will show up (e.g., Siguraddottir, Green & Saunders, 1990; Saunders, Saunders, Kirby & Spradlin, 1988; Spradlin & Saunders, 1986.) We know how to build very large classes of it (e.g., Sidman, Kirk and Willson-Morris, 1974.) We've shown it with different stimulus modes (e.g., Hayes, Tilley and Hayes, 1988; Lazar, Davis-Lang and Sanchez, 1984.) We know who can do it and who can't (e.g., Devaney, Hayes, and Nelson, 1986; Lipkens, Kop and Matthijs, 1988; Sidman, Rauzin, Lazar, Cunningham, Tailby and Carrigan, 1982.) We know how to transfer stimulus functions through it (e.g., Hayes, Devaney, Kohlenberg, Brownstein and Shelby, 1987.) We've shown it to be subject to contextual control (e.g., Kennedy and Laitinen, 1988; Hayes, Kohlenberg and Hayes, 1991; Bush, Sidman, & de Rose, 1989) and how it is related to other class concepts (e.g., Hayes, Thompson & Hayes, 1989; Sidman, Wynne, Maguire, & Barnes, 1989.) Indeed, we've learned a great deal about it in a relatively brief period of study and our progress must be attributed, in large part, to the operational features of its definition. Yet despite the progress we have made toward its understanding I have still the sense that we aren't any closer to knowing what the *it* is we're understanding. And further, that more work of the sort we have been doing will not bring us any closer to the *it* of it.

The problem – at least one of the problems – is that what we are measuring in our investigations of it isn't it. We're measuring percent correct comparison selections – the proportion of choices among comparisons, given particular samples, that are correct. I'm not arguing that there is anything wrong with "percent correct" as a measure; nor even that percent correct can never be taken to be synonymous with the events one is actually interested in. I am arguing that percent correct comparisons selected is not equivalence; and so long as we continue to act as if it were, we will come no closer to an understanding of just what equivalence is.

Perspectives on Analysis

The real issue here is one of perspective on analysis. Analyses are always made from particular points of vantage and these may be said to characterize the analysis as to its nature and purpose. Defining equivalence in terms of a particular set of findings in the context of a match to sample procedure is indicative of what we may call an "observer" perspective.

An Observer Perspective

An observer perspective is characteristic of analyses in which the goals of analysis are prediction and control. In such cases, the subject of analysis is always constructed as a class of events capable of repetition by means of the occurrences of its members. Class concepts are required by such analyses in as much as unique events cannot be predicted or controlled (Hayes, in press a). An operant is a class of this sort.

In the context of equivalence, it is equivalencing that is conceptualized as capable of repetition and is thereby subject to prediction and control. Research on equivalence from this perspective is understandably concerned with such issues as the conditions under which equivalence occurs: It is among these conditions that the controlling variables are to be found, and in them the means of predicting occurrences. An analysis made from the standpoint of the observer is an attempt to describe when or under what conditions *similar* events have occurred or are likely to occur.

An Event Perspective

The perspective of the observer, as outlined here, is so common in our field that there may not appear to be any alternatives to it. There are other perspectives, though, among them the perspective of the events themselves. An event perspective does not imply, as the name suggests, that the events are "speaking for themselves". Obviously, an observer is involved in making analyses from an event perspective. The difference is one of observers' goals. In the event perspective case, the observers' goals are more on the order of description and explanation (the latter conceptualized as an elaborate case of the former), rather than prediction and control. From this perspective, events of all sorts are conceptualized as unique configurations of factors, each factor having the status of "participant", and each configuration existing in each present moment. An analysis made from the standpoint of the events themselves is an attempt to describe what is occurring now, not when or under what conditions a *similar* event may have occurred or be likely to occur (Hayes, in press a, b).

The Event Perspective of Interbehavioral Psychology

Some further orientation as to how events and their sources are conceptualized from the event perspective of interbehavioral psychology will be useful at this point. From the standpoint of interbehaviorism, a psychological event is conceptualized as an evolving function, fixed at any moment as both a point in its own evolution as well as its entirety up to that point. A psychological act, in other words, is an *historical act*. It is a history of responding with respect to stimulating in an environmental as well as an organismic context.

The organism is conceptualized as the *source* of responding. The implication here is that the organism is distinguishable from its responding and further that it is the responding and not the organism that constitutes the focus of analysis in the psychological domain from an interbehavioral perspective. It is further the organism as a *whole* and not its parts that is the source of psychological activity. The emphasis on the whole organism in this context may be taken to mean that any given psychological act is conceptualized as a complex act involving multiple response systems. In other words, for example, a rat never merely "presses a bar." He presses the bar while also looking at it. He may also be sniffing the food tray, imagining food, and salivating. And any number of other activities might be included in what it is a rat is doing when he presses a bar at a given moment. The same is of course true of human organisms, although to an even greater extent due to the involvement of language.

Stimulus objects likewise are conceptualized as *sources* of stimulating, implying that stimulus objects and their functions are distinguishable; and that it is the latter that constitute the focus in the psychological arena. A stimulus object may be a source of multiple functions. That is, for example, a bell may stimulate both hearing and salivating actions.

The relations obtaining between the responding of organisms and the stimulating of objects are what the interbehaviorist refers to as functions. Implied by this term is no sense of potency or productivity or dependency. A function is rather an interdependent relation of simultaneously operating factors (Kantor, 1950.) From the event perspective of interbehaviorism, then, psychological events ever changing, exceedingly complex *functions*, set, further, in a very elaborate field of other participating factors.

With that introduction, I would like to offer some suggestions as to what equivalence *is*. In doing so I will take the position that equivalence is not a strictly human phenomenon. I am, of course, aware of the controversy surrounding this issue. The arguments here boil down to assuming or not assuming continuity between the human species and the rest of the animal kingdom. Those who argue in favor of continuity (e.g., Sidman, 1986) do so out of respect for the nondualistic tradition of behavioral psychology, despite an absence of supporting evidence. Those who deny continuity on this issue (e.g., Hayes, 1987) do so in awe of its apparent significance in understanding human civilization. By taking the position that equivalence is not a strictly human phenomenon, I am *not* predicting that nonlinguistic or nonhuman organisms will eventually be found to select the correct comparisons in standard equivalence tests. I rather doubt that this will happen. I don't believe that it matters one way or the other, though, as I don't consider selecting correct comparisons to *be* equivalence. From an *event* standpoint, equivalence is something else, something common to both humans and animals; and it is this something that I plan to address in this chapter.

Let us move on at this point to the specific events of equivalence and how they might be conceptualized from an event perspective.

Equivalence

Above all, equivalence is a matter of association and throughout the history of psychology, there have been articulated only two irreducible, a priori, principles of association: Similarity of form and proximity or contiguity of occurrence. In other words, when these principles are invoked to explain shared functions among stimuli, they are not themselves explained in terms of other principles. No further explanation for shared functions among stimuli is deemed necessary – nor is any typically offered – than an appeal to their formal similarity (as in stimulus generalization) or to their spatio-temporal proximity (as in classical conditioning). In deference to this intellectual history, I will appeal to these principles of association, or more technically speaking, to these *conditions* of association in making an analysis of reflexivity, symmetry and equivalence from the standpoint of the events sustaining these relations.

Reflexivity

From a procedural standpoint, reflexivity is defined as selecting a comparison identical to a sample without prior training involving these particular stimuli.

Reflexivity is a special case of stimulus generalization. Animals show stimulus generalization, hence we might assume that they would also show reflexivity. Animals can be taught to select a particular comparison that is identical to a particular sample over repeated trials with those particular stimuli. There is some disagreement as to whether or not they are able to do so with respect to novel stimuli, however (see McIlvanne, this volume.) The more conservative position here is to assume that animals do not show generalized identity matching or reflexivity. What this implies to me, at least, is that similar or identical stimuli *do* share functions by virtue of this relation, but that the selection function of the comparison stimulus is not being *actualized* in the match to sample situations in which generalized identity matching fails to occur. The alternative is to assume that the act of seeing X on one occasion is in no way alike the act of seeing X on another occasion. Does not the fox act with respect to this rabbit as he did to that one, and the one before that, and the one before that? The distinction I am making here is between relexivity as an event, and reflexivity as the measure of an event.

What is *not* implied here is any concept of "sameness" that can be held responsible for or may be otherwise involved in the animal's selection of a comparison identical to a novel sample, should this occur. Neither does my analysis imply anything about what the animal knows or doesn't know as to what is "expected" of him in the generalized identity matching situation. If the animal selects the identical comparison in this situation it is because something about the setting in which this occurs actualizes this function of the comparison. For example, requiring an observing response to the sample may constitute a sufficient context for this to happen, as it establishes the required function for the comparison. Alternatively, if the animal does not select the identical comparison, it is because something about the setting actualizes this function of another stimulus.

It is clear, though, that animals act with respect to similar stimuli in similar ways; and having them do so sequentially and in the *form* of selecting the correct comparison from an array, as is required in a generalized identity matching test, is simply a matter of arranging the testing conditions in such a way as to have them do so.

Form and Function. Before going on to the case of symmetry, I would like to comment on the issue of formal similarity. I mentioned earlier that similarity has always been regarded an a priori principle of association, meaning that formally similar stimuli are also functionally similar and the explanation for shared function is shared form. This argument raises a question: How are form and function differentiated?

In attempting to differentiate form and function we say that stimuli have both direct and indirect functions, their direct functions having their sources in the natural properties of stimulus objects, their indirect functions having been attributed to those objects in a cultural or social context. For example, a piece of polished marble may feel smooth and cool to the touch and it may be heavy and difficult to lift. These we might call its direct functions, having their sources in the natural material properties of the object. Calling the object "a piece of polished marble", on the other hand, is one of its indirect functions, attributed to this object in a social context.

We would then say that a piece of polished marble and a piece of polished granite are formally similar, that is, they share natural properties; and, *for this reason*, they are functionally similar. They both feel smooth and cool and heavy.

This logic is troublesome, however, in that form as a *reason* for function -- as a *cause* of it -- seems superfluous. When we say that stimuli are the same are we doing so on the basis of something other than the fact that we respond to them in the same ways? In other words, is not form *derived* from function? It seems to me that the distinction we make between the natural and attributed properties of stimuli are really issues of the degree to which the functional properties of stimuli are subject to changes in contextual conditions. Some of our actions with respect to stimuli are relatively stable, which is to say, they occur in a large number of different contextual circumstances; while others occur only under very specific conditions. The more stable the function, the more likely we are to say it has its source in the formal properties of the stimulus object. It is clear, however, that even the most stable functions are subject to some degree of contextual change. For example, cool water feels warm after one's hand has been immersed in icy water. Various well known illusions supply other examples.

The point of all this is to suggest that perhaps *form and function are really the same thing*. And perhaps this is why formal similarity has been regarded as an a priori condition of association throughout the history of psychology: Association is measured in shared function and shared form is derived from, or defined by, shared function. To go on to claim shared form to be the *cause* of shared function is a verbal device serving to thwart further explanation – as is the purpose

Equivalence as Process

of an a priori in science. This suggestion bears on the difference between reflexivity and symmetry, to which we now turn.

Symmetry

While reflexivity is understood as shared function as a product of shared form, symmetry means shared function in the absence of shared form. Given this description, symmetry cannot be explained by appeal to the a priori principle of formal similarity. Instead, we may attempt to explain the symmetrical relations involved in equivalence by appeal to the companion process of spatio-temporal proximity or contiguity.

Some of the functions of a stimulus object develop over the course of an organism's interactions with that object; other functions develop over the course of an organism's interaction with other stimuli in spatio-temporal proximity with that object. We may call the former stimulus functions direct, the latter indirect to emphasize the circumstances of their origin.

For example, if I see your face in a context in which I also hear your voice, I may, on a subsequent occasion, see your face when only your voice is present as when I imagine your face while speaking to you over the phone; or, similarly, I may hear your voice when only your face is present, as when I imagine the sound of your voice while looking at your picture. In this example, seeing your face when only your voice is present may be understood as an indirect function of your voice; while hearing your voice when only your face is present may be understood as an indirect function of your face as a stimulus.

The acquisition of indirect stimulus functions of stimuli by virtue of their spatio-temporal proximity is illustrated in deliberate classical conditioning preparations. When the dog salivates to the bell, we can say that the bell has acquired an indirect function by virtue of its proximity to food. This process is illustrated in the diagram below.

Respondent Conditioning

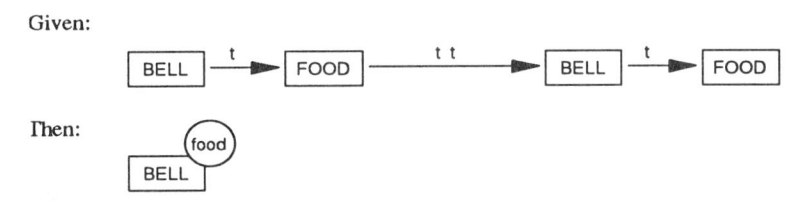

Given: BELL →t FOOD —t t→ BELL →t FOOD

Then: BELL (food)

In this diagram, as well as those to follow, the following conventions apply: A boxed symbol, such as FOOD, stands for "unconditioned" responding occurring with respect to stimulation having its source in food; it does not stand for the object food. Such responding might include salivating to food, seeing food, smelling food, tasting food, and so on. A boxed symbol may be understood as a *direct* stimulus-response function.

Similarly, a boxed letter, such as A, stands for "unconditioned" responding occurring with respect to the letter, specifically, seeing it. The letters are used in subsequent figures in place of nonrepresentative figures for ease of description.

An encircled symbol, such as food, stands for "conditioned" responding occurring through the operation of a substitute stimulus, such as a bell. Encircled symbols are always attached to boxed symbols indicating that they operate through these other stimuli. An encircled symbol may be understood as an *indirect* stimulus-response function.

The occurrence of an indirect function necessarily occurs in a context in which a direct function is ongoing. That is to say, salivating to food through the operation of a bell occurs in a context in which hearing a bell is also ongoing.

Finally, in the accompanying diagrams, t stands for the passage of time, with more time indicated by multiple expressions of t.

Returning to the example of classical conditioning illustrated above, we note certain boundaries to its operation. Specifically, it is generally agreed (Catania, 1984, pp. 197-198) that the acquisition of stimulus functions by virtue of the proximity of their occurrence is sensitive to temporal order. That is, the stimulus occurring first in the proximal relation acquires functions of the stimulus occurring second, but not the other way around. (See Spetch, Wilkie, and Pinel, 1981, p. 163 for arguments to the contrary.) The dog salivates to the bell, but he doesn't hear the food, as shown below.

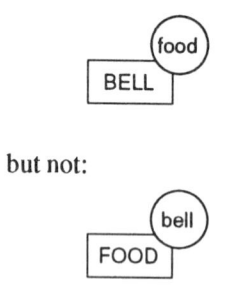

$$\boxed{\text{BELL}}\,(\text{food})$$

but not:

$$\boxed{\text{FOOD}}\,(\text{bell})$$

In actual fact, evidence for the ineffectiveness of the backward conditioning procedure consists of the absence of salivation to the bell when the bell follows the food. What the animal hears upon encountering the food has not been the subject of research in this area. We may assume, however, that if some of the functions of food are not available with respect to stimuli following it in time, then some of the functions of the bell may also be unavailable to stimuli subsequent to it.

At first glance, this unidirectional feature of classical conditioning would seem to disqualify it as a potential explanation for the symmetrical relations observed in equivalence preparations. A symmetrical relation is a bidirectional relation. Upon closer examination, though, classical conditioning can account for derived symmetry in the match to sample paradigm. Bear in mind that while symmetry is a bidirectional relation, the acquisition of stimulus functions in only one direction is derived. Acquisition in the other direction is directly trained. Hence, a unidirectional process such as classical conditioning may account for the derived relation.

Let me explain. Assume that, in the accompanying diagram, A1 is the sample, and B1 is the correct comparison for one conditional discrimination, while C1 is the correct comparison for the other. The solid arrows indicate the relations trained. Assume also that the training procedure is such that the sample always precedes the comparison.

Conditional Discrimination

Given:

A1 → B1   B2

and

A1 → C1   C2

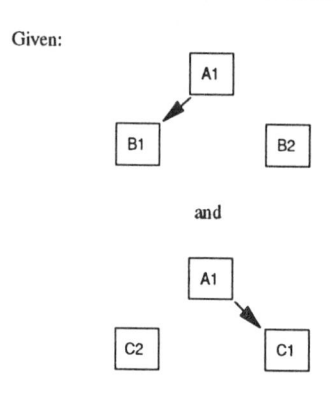

Equivalence as Process

By virtue of this training we may assume that A1 acquires indirect stimulus functions of both B1 and C1, but not vice versa. Just as the bell acquires functions of the food, but not the food functions of the bell, we have no reason as yet to assume that B1 and C1 have acquired indirect functions of A1.

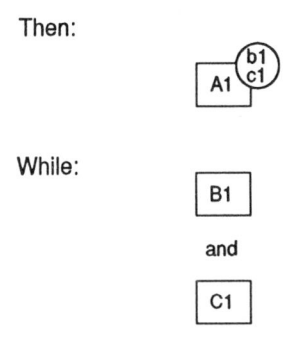

Then:

While:

B1

and

C1

In the derived symmetry testing situation, B1 and C1 become the samples, while A1 becomes the correct comparison, as shown below.

Test for Derived Symmetry

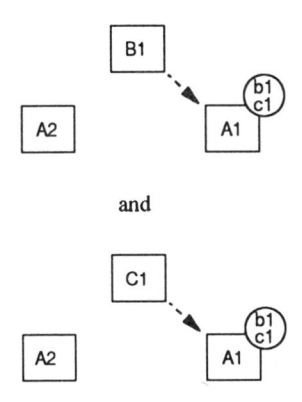

and

If, as just argued, A1 has previously acquired indirect stimulus functions of B1 such that some of the responses previously occurring with respect to B1 may now occur with respect to A1, selecting A1 during the derived symmetry test may amount to a type of identity matching based on indirect stimulus functions. That is, derived symmetry may be a case of indirect relexivity.

Equivalence

When we attempt to apply this analysis to the equivalence relation itself, we find it wanting however. In these cases, the comparisons B1 and C1 must be assumed to have acquired functions of the A1 sample during the original discrimination training trials in order to account for the correct selection of C1 given B1, or B1 given C1. This result assumes the stimulus functions are acquired by virtue of the proximal relations of stimuli *without regard to their temporal order.* That is, it assumes that the acquisition of functions occurs in both directions and classical conditioning research suggests that this is not, in fact, the case.

To solve this problem, it will be helpful to review how psychological events are conceptualized from the event perspective of interbehavioral psychology. As discussed earlier, a psychological act is an act of a whole organism, which is to say it is constituted of multiple response systems. The rat, I argued, never merely presses the bar. Further, a psychological act is conceptualized as an evolving function of stimulating and responding such that at any and each point in its evolution, all previous points are held to be entailed. Its past, thereby, is said *to be* its present. What this means is that whatever one does with respect to a stimulus at this present moment is a continuation of one's previous interactions with that stimulus.

If we apply the evolving function concept to the case of equivalence, we come up with the following account. During conditional discrimination training, A1 acquired indirect functions of B1 and C1 by virtue of classical conditioning, as previously discussed. This means that action with respect to B1 – such as seeing B1 – is occurring in the presence of A1 alone. Presumably seeing B1 in its absence, as an indirect function of A1, is different from seeing B1 in its presence – the difference being the conjoint action with respect to A1 occurring in the former case. In other words, "imagining" B1 is not exactly the same as "seeing" B1 because "imagining" B1 occurs in a situation in which seeing A1 is also occurring. This event, namely the simultaneous operation of direct and indirect functions bearing formal similarity, may constitute the conditions necessary for the acquisition of indirect functions by B1. The same applies in the case of C1.

Let me illustrate this account, first in a classical conditioning context, and then in the context of an equivalence test.

The accompanying diagram illustrates a case where salivating to food is occurring in a context in which the dog is also hearing a bell. There is no issue of temporal sequence to contend with in this situation: These events are occurring simultaneously as acts of a whole organism. Salivating to food while hearing a bell is nonetheless formally similar to salivating to food while not hearing a bell.

Given:

is similar to

Similarity of form, as discussed earlier, is another way of saying similarity of function. Further, similarity is necessarily bidirectional. As such, some of the functions available in the first circumstance may also be assumed to be available in the second. More specifically, hearing the bell may occur in the presence of the food alone.

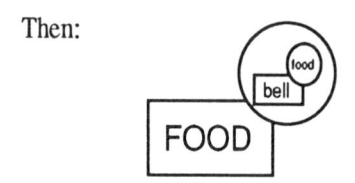

Then:

Equivalence as Process

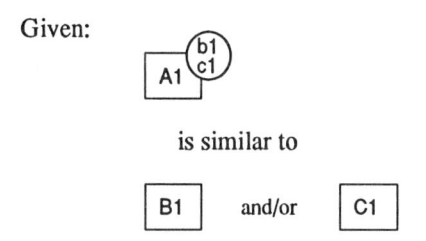

Given:

[diagram: A1 with b1, c1 inside circle] is similar to [B1] and/or [C1]

Applying this analysis to the case of equivalence, we may suppose that responding with respect to A1 (assuming that A1 has acquired indirect functions of B1 and C1 as previously discussed) is similar to responding with respect to B1 and with respect to C1.

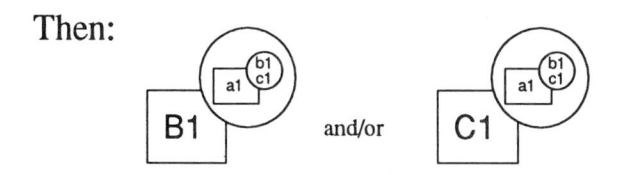

Then: [diagram: B1 with a1, b1, c1] and/or [diagram: C1 with a1, b1, c1]

Assuming further that functional similarity is derived from or defined by formal similarity, and that similarity is necessarily bidirectional, we may suppose that responding with respect to A1 is present in one's interactions with B1 and with C1. In the test situation, then, because responding with respect to A1 is present in one's interaction with B1 and C1, the selection of B1, given C1, and C1 given B1, may be understood, again, as a form of indirect reflexivity.

Test for Equivalence

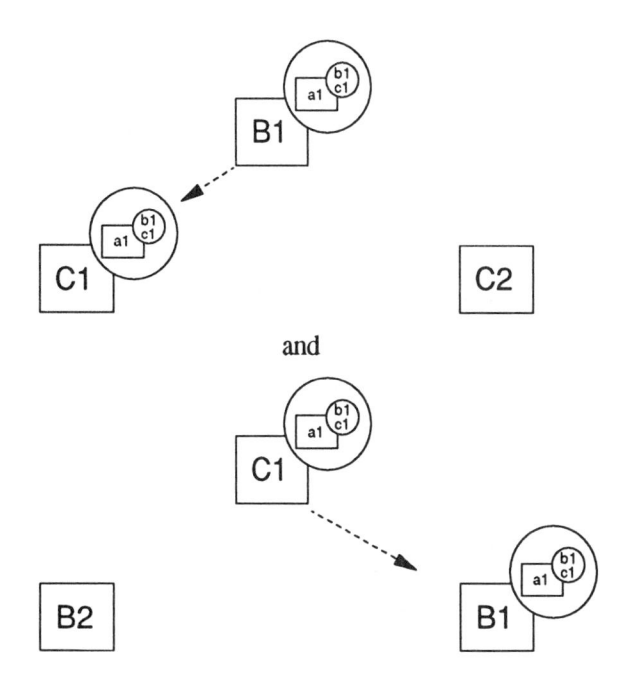

[diagram: B1 with a1, b1, c1 → C1 with a1, b1, c1; C2]

and

[diagram: C1 with a1, b1, c1 → B1 with a1, b1, c1; B2]

Proximity and Function. Conceptualizing psychological events as evolving functions in ever-present time has implications for the a priori principle of proximity as an explanation for the acquisition of stimulus functions. More specifically, if there exists only the present event, then there are no relations of temporal proximity among events to appeal to in accounting for its functions. Likewise, if there exists only the present event, then there are no relations of spatial proximity to other events; and stimulus functions cannot be explained by appeal to such relations. Events appearing to occur before or after this event are actually *of* this event. Events appearing to occur next to this event likewise are aspects of this event. Time and space are of this function; they are not the *reasons* for it. Perhaps this is why proximity has been regarded as an a priori condition of association throughout the history of psychology: It has not been possible to distinguish proximity from function. Recall that this same argument was made of the difference between form and function.

Summary and Conclusion

In summary, I have attempted to describe equivalence as a set of events – as a *what* not a *how*. These events I have interpreted as the actualization of functions by a setting or a context – direct functions in the case of reflexivity and indirect functions in the case of symmetry and equivalence. The establishment of indirect functions was articulated in terms of the principles of formal similarity and spatio-temporal proximity or contiguity. I also suggested that, from an event standpoint, these principles or conditions of association are reducible to the very functions they are said to account for.In making this analysis, I have relied on a conceptualization of psychological events that is historical, contextual, and takes the whole organism to be the source of action.

Having made this analysis does not solve all of our difficulties in this area, however. For example, how do we account for the absence of equivalence in animal subjects' data? If equivalence is the sort of thing I have been describing, why don't animals show it? I would like to comment on this issue as a way of concluding. My intention in doing so is to point to the utility of analysis from an event perspective.

Failure to Find Equivalence in Animal Data

Let us begin to address this question by reiterating our original purpose in dealing with these issues in this way. I argued that "percent correct comparisons selected" was not equivalence per se, but rather a task-specific, readily observable measure of behavior indicative of equivalence. Consequently, the common finding that animal subjects fail to select correct comparisons is not proof of the absence of equivalence. It might as easily suggest that the act of selecting correct comparisons is different from and does not automatically follow from the act of equivalencing.

The question in this case, then, is not why animals don't show equivalence. We have no evidence one way or the other on this issue. The question is rather why selecting correct comparisons does not *follow* from equivalence in animal subjects. In our language, why this function of comparison stimuli is not actualized in the test situation for animal subjects?

The answer to this question and all such questions is to be found in the setting in which such acts are expected to occur. If the animal does not select the correct comparison, it is because something in the setting actualizes this function of another stimulus. What might this be? Perhaps it is a similarity between the test situation and the setting prevailing in early phases of conditional discrimination training. Early phases of conditional discrimination training are characterized by relatively little reinforcement, and the selection of comparison stimuli is based on various irrelevant conditions such as their spatial position and formal properties. The equivalence test -- conducted in extinction and involving novel stimulus arrangements -- is rather like the setting prevailing in the early phases of conditional discrimination training. As such, the test setting may actualize the same irrelevant functions of the comparison stimuli (i.e., their position or formal properties) as were operating in training. Bear in mind that from selections based on formal properties and position have been selected the correct matches, which is to say, selections based on these things have been reinforced in training. I am not arguing that this is in fact the explanation for animal subjects' failures to select correct matches in equivalence tests. This is an empirical matter. The analysis is intended rather as an example of the *kind* of variable that might be operating in such situations.

There has been some discussion about the relation between language and equivalence (Lowe, 1986; Hayes, 1987). My arguments speak to this issue, as follows: Equivalence may *not* be a peculiarly human phenomenon. Its demonstration in the standard preparation is not likely to be made by animal subjects, however because animals do not have language. This does not mean that equivalence per se depends on language, nor does it mean that language and equivalence are the same thing. On the contrary, based on the present analysis it is not equivalence, but the acts taken to measure it that require language. That is, it could be that animals don't show equivalence because they do not possess the repertoire by which to benefit from the instructional and motivational aspects of the test situation. They don't select the correct comparisons because they haven't a repertoire by which to be aware of the demands of the situation. In common sense terms, they don't show equivalence because they don't understand the request to do so and because historical continuities of action, as discussed above, make other acts more probable.

The present analysis does suggest, however, that it might be possible to construct a history so extensive as to allow for the sort of molar generalization of strategy on the part of nonlinguistic organisms that would permit a demonstration of equivalence. The relevant history would not involve direct training of symmetry and equivalence, though, as is sometimes suggested (e.g., Hayes, 1989). Without language, equivalence involving other stimuli is not helpful. Further, a history potentially productive of equivalence in animals would not involve the use of more familiar species-specific stimuli – as is sometimes argued. Such stimuli have too many extraneous functions. On the contrary, the present analysis suggests that equivalence is a matter of indirect reflexivity and, as such, extensive training on reflexive relations might serve to bring about indirect reflexive responding, followed by selection, in an otherwise ambiguous equivalence test. In doing so, the performance commonly regarded as equivalence might be demonstrated in animals.

The value of such a demonstration, were it to be made, would be the pragmatic one of fostering a distinction between events and what are merely their measures or descriptions. It has been to clarify this distinction and to sample its fruits that the present chapter was written.

References

Bush, K. M., Sidman, M., & de Rose, T., (1989). Contextual control of emergent equivalence relations. *Journal of the Experimental Analysis of Behavior, 51,* 29-45.

Catania, A. C. (1984) *Learning.* Englewood Cliffs, NJ: Prentice Hall.

Devaney, J. M., Hayes, S. C., & Nelson, R. O. (1986). Equivalence class formation in language-able and language-disabled children. *Journal of the Experimental Analysis of Behavior, 46,* 243-257.

Hayes, L. J. (in press a). The psychological present. *The Behavior Analyst.*

Hayes, L. J. (in press b). Minimizing incompatibilities among postulates and practices. In E. Ribes & L. Hayes (Eds.), *Interbehavioral psychology.* Reno, NV: Context Press.

Hayes, L. J., Tilley, K. L., & Hayes, S. C. (1988). Extending equivalence class membership to gustatory stimuli. *Psychological Record, 38,* 473-482.

Hayes, L. J., Thompson, S., & Hayes, S. C. (1989). Stimulus equivalence and rule following.

Journal of the Experimental Analysis of Behavior, 52, 275-291.

Hayes, S. C. (1987). Upward and downward continuity: It's time to change our strategic assumptions. *Behavior Analysis, 22,* 3-6.

Hayes, S. C. (1989). Nonhumans have not yet shown equivalence. *Journal of the Experimental Analysis of Behavior, 51,* 385-392.

Hayes, S. C., Devaney, J. M., Kohlenberg, B. S., Brownstein, A. J., & Shelby, J. (1987). Stimulus equivalence and the symbolic control of behavior. *Mexican Journal of Behavior Analysis, 13,* 361-374.

Hayes, S. C., Kohlenberg, B. S., & Hayes, L. J. (1991). The transfer of specific and general consequential functions through simple and conditional equivalence classes. *Journal of the Experimental Analysis of Behavior, 56,* 119-137.

Kennedy, C. H., & Laitinen, R. (1988). Second-order conditional control of symmetric and transitive stimulus relations: The influence of order effects. *The Psychological Record, 33,* 437-446.

Lazar, R., Davis-Lang, D., & Sanchez, L. (1984). The formation of visual stimulus equivalences in children. *Journal of the Experimental Analysis of Behavior, 41,* 251-266.

Lipkens, R., Kop, P. F. M., & Matthijs, W. (1988). A test of symmetry and transitivity in the conditional discrimination performances of pigeons. *Journal of the Experimental Analysis of Behavior, 49,* 395-409.

Lowe, C. F. (1986). *The role of verbal behavior in the emergence of equivalence classes.* Paper presented at the Association for Behavior Analysis, Milwaukee.

Saunders, R. R., Saunders, K. J., Kirby, K. C. & Spradlin, J. E. (1988). The merger and development of equivalence classes by unreinforced conditional selections of comparison stimuli. *Journal of the Experimental Analysis of Behavior, 49,* 95-115.

Sidman, M. (1986). Functional analysis of emergent verbal classes. In T. Thompson & M. D. Zeiler (Eds.) *Units of analysis and integration of behavior.* Hillsdale, NJ: Erlbaum.

Sidman, M., Kirk, B. & Willson-Morris, M. (1974). Six-member classes generated by conditional-discrimination procedures. *Journal of the Experimental Analysis of Behavior, 43,* 21-42.

Sidman, M., Wynne, C. K., Maguire, R. W., & Barnes, T. (1989). Functional classes and equivalence relations. *Journal of the Experimental Analysis of Behavior, 52,* 261-274.

Sidman, M., Rauzin, R., Lazar, R., Cunningham, S., Tailby, W., & Carrigan, P. (1982). A search for symmetry in the conditional discriminations of rhesus monkeys, baboons, and children. *Journal of the Experimental Analysis of Behavior, 37,* 23-44.

Sidman, M. & Tailby, W. (1982). Conditional discrimination versus matching to sample: An expansion of the testing paradigm. *Journal of the Experimental Analysis of Behavior, 37,* 5-22.

Siguraddottir, Z. G., Green, G. & Saunders, R. R. (1990). Equivalence classes generated by sequence training. *Journal of the Experimental Analysis of Behavior, 53,* 47-63.

Spetch, M. L., Wilkie, D. M., & Pinel, J. P. J. (1981). Backward conditioning: A reevaluation of the empirical evidence. *Psychological Bulletin, 89,* 163-175.

Spradlin, J. E., & Saunders, R. R. (1986). The development of stimulus classes using match to sample procedures: Sample classification versus comparison classification. *Analysis and Intervention in Developmental Disabilities, 6,* 41-58.

Vaughan, W. (1988). Formation of equivalence sets in pigeons. *Journal of Experimental Psychology: Animal Behavior Processes, 14,* 36-42.

Chapter 7

Verbal Relations, Time, and Suicide

Steven C. Hayes
University of Nevada

The single most remarkable fact about human existence is how hard it is to be happy. Many humans – including virtually all of those now reading these words – have everything that all the rest of the living creatures on the planet need for happiness: warmth, shelter, food, mobility, social stimulation, and so on. And yet every day scores of people load a gun, put the barrel into their mouths, and pull the trigger. This chapter is about why.

Two Kinds of Knowing

The word "know" in English is an interesting one because of its multiple meanings and complex etymology. The word covers the ground formerly occupied by at least two verbs (as is still true today in other Teutonic and Romantic languages): the Latin *gnoscere* or "know by the senses" and the Latin *scire* or "know by the mind."

This division appears in many parts of our culture and our discipline, from the mind/body division to the empirical/rational division. Behavior analysts typically reject the "scire"-side of these polarities as mentalistic. If the "mental" side is interpreted by behavior analysts, usually the main theme of the interpretation includes both the rejection of dualism and the rejection of anything fundamentally different at the level of psychological process. It is worth looking again, however, at possible differences in the psychological processes involved in these two kinds of knowing. I do not think that "knowing" need be a technical term in psychology, but it is useful to examine this division seriously and the language of "knowing" is helpful in that regard.

Knowing by the senses is not a problem for behavior analysts: it is the very essence of their approach. We may describe this kind of knowing as behavior that is established by direct contingency control. The tricky issue is "knowing by the mind." What behavioral functions are established by processes other than direct contact with the contingencies and forms of generalization around this contact produced by formal properties of events (e.g., stimulus generalization)?

The Second Kind of Knowing: Arbitrarily Applicable Relational Responding

We have recently argued that there is a fundamental difference at the level of psychological process between verbal and non-verbal stimulus functions: verbal functions involve arbitrarily applicable relational responding, or relational frames. The relational frame conception of language (Hayes & Hayes, 1989; Hayes, 1991) draws upon two rather simple ideas. First, there are times when organisms learn overarching classes of behaviors that have virtually unlimited numbers of members. The behavior analytic account of generalized imitation provides an example (e.g., Gewirtz & Stengle, 1968). While imitation may begin with some small repertoire that is evolutionarily established, we seem to go on to acquire a general class of "do-what-other-people-do-behavior" as an operant. Thus, when a child is shown some new behavior to imitate, the action of imitating that behavior is "new" only in a limited sense. The class itself – the behavioral relation – is not new. "Do-what-other-people-do-behavior" has an extensive history that has organized it as a class of action. The specific topography is the only truly new aspect of the performance. The relational frame view takes the position that the action of relating two arbitrary stimuli itself has a history. When a subject shows equivalence, for example, the specific stimuli are the only truly new aspects of the performance. A relational frame is an overarching class of instumental behavior.

Second, a relational frame account views the core action in language as one of relating two stimuli (as a historically situated overarching behavioral class) based on contextual cues to do so, not solely on the formal properties of the relatae. There should be nothing too extraordinary for behaviorists about the idea of learned stimulus relations. A variety of experimental findings (for example, transposition, Reese, 1968) show that humans and infrahumans can learn to respond to *formal* or *non-arbitrary* relations between stimuli. What the relational frame account supposes in addition is that relating as an action can become abstracted and brought under contextual control. Because the action is under contextual control it is *arbitrarily applicable*. What I mean by "arbitrarily applicable" is that it is readily capable of modification via social convention.

Take the case of a young child learning the name of an object. A child is oriented toward several objects, such as the child's many toys spread out on the floor. One is pointed out and the parent asks "what's that?" At first parents do not expect a response and after a pause, they say the name (e.g., "is that your ball?"). If the child shows any sign of acknowledgment (e.g., a smile when the name is given), the child is rewarded (e.g., "That's right. What a smart girl you are! That's your ball!"). At other times the parent may deliberately say an incorrect name (e.g., while orienting toward daddy, saying "is that your brother, Charlie?"). If the child shows any sign of rejection (e.g., shaking "no" or laughing with derision), child is again rewarded. Later only actual vocalizations are rewarded. Incorrect responses result in additional prompting of the name.

Eventually, the child learns "see object, say name" (object -> name.) But the child is also asked "Where is (name)." Orientation toward the named object is also rewarded with tickles, play, or verbal consequences ("That's right! That's the (name)"). We can say that the child learns "hear name, see and point to object" (name -> object.) This is a kind of trained symmetrical responding. Furthermore, training in this responding occurs only when certain cues are present (e.g., phrases like "what's that?" or the juxtaposition of objects and words).

The relational frame conception makes the simple assumption that with enough instances of such training the child begins to learn to derive name -> object given only object -> name and vice versa. In short, with enough instances of directly trained bi-directional responding in a given context, derived responding may emerge with respect to novel stimuli in that context.

We need not be confused about the fact that the actions are not strictly symmetrical, since, for example, in one case we are dealing with hearing and the other with saying. The child has learned to hear-and-say in extensive imitative training. Were that not the case, we indeed would not expect the child to derive one performance from another. Suppose in a new situation with a verbally competent child I say "truck!" and promptly pull out a truck from behind my back. We may say that I have trained this relation: "hear 'truck', see truck." Now I find that the child calls a truck a "truck." Strict symmetry would lead to the derived relation "see truck, hear 'truck'" not "see truck, say 'truck'." This would present a problem except that the child has already learned to imitate and thus can "hear word, say word." For this reason, the child can say what she hears to herself. Similar analyses seem readily available for other aspects of elementary language performance that are not strictly interpretable in terms of derived relations.

Arbitrarily applicable relational responding has the properties of mutual entailment, combinatorial entailment, and transfer of functions. We have dealt with these matters in detail elsewhere (e.g., Hayes & Hayes, 1989; Hayes, 1991) but a brief review is in order. Mutual entailment means that if there is a trained or specified relation between A and B in a given context, then there is a derived relation between B and A in that context (it may be thought of as the generic case of symmetry). Combinatorial entailment means that if there are trained relations between A and B and between B and C, then there are derived relations between both A and C, and C and A (it may be thought of as the generic case of transitivity).

Transfer of functions is a more subtle issue. By transfer of functions I mean that if an event A has a psychological function, and there is a derived relation between A and B, under certain conditions B may acquire a new psychological function based on the function of A and the derived relation between A and B. Whether a transfer of function will be seen in given instance is a matter of contextual control, but all arbitrarily applicable relations enable such transfer under some conditions. The transfer of functions concept is not an arbitrary or purely pragmatic aspect of the definition of relational frames, although it may at first appear to be so. By their very nature, mutual entailment and combinatorial entailment involve a transfer of functions in a limited sense. For example, in an equivalence class the function of a sample as a conditional stimulus transfers to a comparison or there would be no "equivalence class." Entailment processes therefore *are* a kind of transfer of functions. Relational frames simply are names for patterns of the mutual transformation of stimulus functions of stimuli. It is useful to distinguish transfer of functions from entailment processes (even though both are a kind of transfer of function) because entailment defines a kind of minimal unit upon which more and more elaborate transfers of functions can be based.

The term "relational frame" was coined to designate the various kinds of arbitrarily applicable relational responding (Hayes & Hayes, 1989). A relational frame is a type of responding that shows the contextually controlled qualities of mutual entailment, combinatorial entailment, and transfer of functions; is due to a history of relational responding relevant to the contextual cues involved; and is not based on direct non-relational training with regard to the particular stimuli of interest, nor solely on their form. Relational frames are situated actions of whole organisms, not structures or entities. Whenever we speak of a "relational frame" we are speaking of an organism who, given the proper historical and situational context, is framing events relationally. The concept refers to a verb. The noun form "relational frame" is dangerous, but it is too useful given the structure of our language to abandon. It is helpful in this regard that "frame" can also be thought of as a verb ("I've been framed!").

Does this Kind of Knowing Involve a New Behavioral Process?

Consider the following example: a young child is scratched while playing with a cat. Later for the first time the child learns that "gato" goes with cats. Now the child's grandmother peers around a corner and says "oh, a gato!" and the child cries. The question is this: why did the child cry?

We would argue that there is an equivalence relation between "gato" and cats. Cats have an eliciting function for the child via direct experience ("knowing by the senses"). "Gato" also has an eliciting function, but not via direct experience. Rather, this function transferred through the underlying equivalence class ("knowing by the mind").

Is such a transfer really a different process psychologically, or can it be reduced to direct contingency processes?. At least two resolutions have been suggested. On the one had, equivalence may be a primitive process (e.g., Sidman 1986; 1990). If this is true, equivalence and the transfer of functions it permits instantiates a new behavioral principle by definition. Conversely, equivalence and other derived stimulus relations may be learned, as in the relational frame conception. In this case, neither equivalence per se nor higher-order concepts such as relational frames involve new behavioral principles because the processes appealed to are known. But the transfer of functions through such relations instantiates a new behavioral principle, because these functions are based on a learned process.

When, as in the example earlier, the child cries upon hearing "gato" we cannot say that "gato" is a CS because it does not have the history of a CS. Its function is only CS-like, based on a transfer of control through a derived stimulus relation. Note, however, that while in behavior analytic accounts the control exerted by any given CS is learned, classical conditioning per se is not learned. In the case of relational frames, the transfer of stimulus functions is based on a learned process and this is why it is new. Behavior analysts have always distinguished between stimulus functions on the basis of history and current context. For example, conditioned and unconditioned reinforcers are distinguished on the basis of the particular histories that give rise to each. If the CS-like functions of "gato" are based on a learned pattern of the derivation of stimulus relations, then this is a new kind of behavioral control – a second and distinct kind of "knowing" at the level of psychological process.

Thus either of these interpretations lead to the same end. There *is* a fundamental distinction between these two sources of behavioral control – these two forms of "knowing." For analytic purposes I will continue to refer to "knowing" in the present chapter, but I confess that "knowing by the mind" is both awkward and jarring for a behaviorist. Thus, in the rest of the chapter I will call knowing in the *gnoscere* sense "experiential knowing" and knowing in the *scire* sense "verbal knowing." This is consistent for us since, as mentioned above, we have defined verbal activity as activity based on arbitrarily applicable relational responding (Hayes & Hayes, 1989).

For those behaviorists who chafe at the very word "knowing," it should be obvious that neither type of knowing need be thought of as a mental event. We are talking about the organization of behavior. "Know how" is doing. "Know that" is also doing. "Knowing about" something is behaving with regard to something. My point is simply to distinguish two broad classes of psychological activity, and the language of "knowing" seems useful for that purpose.

Knowing About Time

What is Time?

Time is a measure of change. Clocks are devices based on regular change: the change produced by water or sand passing through a hole, or the change of a shadow on the ground. As modern clocks have become more sophisticated, more and more orderly processes of change have been used as the basis of clocks – electrical cycles, or atomic decay – but it is still true that all clocks measure is change.

We do not actually experience time. We experience what time is a measure of: change. Change is an evolutionary process. It is the transition from one totality to another; but the second totality now stands on, evolved from, or in a sense includes the first. For that reason, time can only go forward. If the totality of the universe is at point x and then at point y, we may say that "time has passed." But it is not possible to revert to point x because the change would then be from point x to y to x. The second x cannot be the first, unless there would be a way not to include the history of the change from x to y in the change to the second x. That history *must* be included because it is the basis for there being "change" in the first place. Without the x to y change, we could not change to x. In other words, event y is actually event *(x)y*. If we were to revert to x we would have to revert from event *(x)y* and the second "event x" would in actuality be event *(xy)x*. Furthermore, the change from *(x)y* to *(xy)x* would in fact be a change. The measure of change is time. Therefore, time would not reverse – there would simply be more time.

I am speaking abstractly, but the point is a simple one. Imagine a middle aged man who wishes on his 45th birthday to have time be reversed, so that mistakes of the past might be avoided. He wants to go back to his 18th birthday, and relive his life from that point. We will call his 18th birthday point x and his 45th birthday point y. The changes from x to y can be measured against a regular standard of change – we can say, for example, that he is now "27 years older." Point y *includes*, or stated another way *is*, the change from x to y. If the person changed again "back to point x," the new "point x" would necessarily include the change from x to y and back again, and thus it would not be the first point x. The man would be older still, not 18. Ironically, if this were not true there would be no reason for the man to be interested in his fantasy because otherwise the mistakes of the past could not be avoided. If the process of evolutionary change could be cancelled and the *original* x could be reached it would be no different the second time around because nothing of condition y (or, more properly, of the change from x to y) would be retained. The man would be 18 again and literally know nothing that the 45 year old man learned later.

Stated another way, change has only one direction, from now to now. No one has ever changed from now to not now (e.g., then), and if it did happen there would be no way to experience it, since any experience is an experience of now. Change can occur more or less quickly in a relative sense; it may even stop (e.g., in the timeless nothingness before the big bang). It cannot "change back" because there is no back side to change. A change "back" is still change. And change can be measured. And onward "time" flows.

Experiential Time

What, then does a non-verbal organism know about time? In other words, how is behavior organized with regard to time? A non-verbal organism knows what it has experienced directly, and generalizations based on the form of these experienced events. Experiential knowing about time refers to a direct history with change, and behavioral organization based on this. First there was an observed green light, then a peck on a key, then food eaten. Later, there was an observed green light, then a peck on a key, then food eaten. Still later, there was an observed green light, then a peck on a key, then food eaten. A bird exposed to such a set of experiences has experienced an orderly process of change from one act to another. Each builds on the other (in an important sense, it is not the same light each time, for example) but the formal similarities organize these events into a process of change. When the bird now observes the green light, it is a light that reliably predicts that a peck on a key will lead to food eaten. Change-to-food is part of the light and part of the peck made to it. The "see light-peck key-eat food" relation is a temporal relationship (a change relationship) that has been directly experienced by the bird. Behavior is organized with regard to this temporal relationship (and such organization is what we mean here by "knowing").

We may say it this way: for a non-verbal organism time is an issue of *the past as the future in the present*. That is, based on a history of change (the "past"), the animal is responding in the present to present events cuing change to other events. It is not the literal future that is part of the psychology of the animal – it is the past *as* the future. As with all psychological events, the event is happening in the present or it is not happening at all. Experiential time is thus behavior organized with regard to the past as the future in the present.

Verbal Time

Now we come to the second kind of knowing: verbal knowing. What does it mean to know about time verbally? The essence of verbal relations, we have argued, is arbitrarily applicable relational responding. Thus, we must ask "what kind of derived relations are involved in time?"

Temporal relations are part of a class of relations that have to do with change, such as cause-effect, if ... then, or before-after. These relations satisfy the criteria for arbitrarily applicable relational responding. If we are told that "right after A comes B," we "know" (i.e., we derive) that "right before B comes A." Similarly, if we are taught directly that "right after A comes B" and "right after B comes C," we can derive that "shortly after A comes C" or that "shortly before C comes A." If B has functions (for example, if B is an intense shock), other stimuli may have functions based on their derived relations with B. For example, A may now elicit great arousal, while C may lead to calm.

The verbal relation of time is arbitrarily applicable: it is brought to bear by contextual cues, not simply by the form of the relatae. So, for example, a person can be told "after life comes heaven," or "after smoking comes cancer," or "after investing comes wealth." These change relations need not be directly experienced for the human to respond with regard to such relations. The relatedness of life and heaven, for example, is *constructed* – it is an instantiation of a particular relational frame involving temporal sequence.

Framing relationally is an act with a history, as we have argued. But the history is not with regard to the relatae so much as it is with regard to the relating. Thus, although verbal events are also experientially based in a sense, they produce a kind of behavioral organization – a kind of knowing – that is different than that based on direct experience. We can say it this way: verbal time is behavior organized with regard to *the past as the constructed future in the present*. That is, based on a history of deriving temporal sequences among events (the "past"), the organism is responding in the present by constructing a sequential relation between at least two events. Again, it is not the literal future that is part of the psychology of the verbal animal – it is the past *as* the future but in this case the future is constructed by arbitrarily applicable relational responding. As with all psychological events, the event is happening in the present or it is not happening at all.

The behavior of verbal organisms instantiates both experiential and verbal knowing. But verbal relations are difficult to fence off into one area of life. Precisely because they are arbitrarily applicable, this repertoire of verbal construction tends to occur in most contexts. Thus, a normal human adult experiencing a temporal (change) relation directly will very often also construct a version of that relation verbally.

I should note that while verbal relations are arbitrarily applicable that does not mean that they are arbitrarily applied. For example, a scientist may construct a temporal relation in which the presence of that relation is virtually 100% based on the non-arbitrary properties of the described events. But the self-same verbal processes that allow the scientist to describe temporal sequences also allow the construction of, say, imaginary mathematical universes that bear no relation what exists. The act is of a sort that is arbitrarily applicable, but its application in a given instance may be anything but arbitrary. Indeed, good science often has this property of non-arbitrary construction. I mention this because when we are dealing with both experiential and verbal time, it is all too easy to miss the verbal component since it is not arbitrarily applied. A person who describes an experienced contingency to herself may still act in ways that appear to be very like what a rat or pigeon does in the same circumstance, but the psychological processes involved differ to a degree. The person is deriving a temporal relation in addition to experiencing one; the rat or pigeon, so far as we know, is not. These differences in behavioral processes do not disappear no matter how similar the behavioral outcomes might happen to be in a given circumstance.

Suicide

Although it is talked about in various ways, there is general agreement among suicidologists that suicide involves the purposeful taking of ones own life (e.g., Douglas, 1967; Shneidman, 1985). Two facts are shockingly evident with regard to suicide: 1. it is ubiquitous in human societies, and 2. it is arguably absent in all other living organisms.

Suicide rates vary among human cultures, usually between 1/100,000 and 100/100,000 (Lester, 1972). The rate in the United States is about 12.6/100,000, increasing across the age range until it peaks at about 27.9/100,000 between ages 75-84 (Shneidman, 1985). There are apparently no well-studied human societies in which suicide is absent. Conversely, it is difficult to find clear examples of suicide in non-humans. Several exceptions have been suggested to this generalization. The Norwegian lemming is the usual ready example. Lemmings migrate at least twice a year, and their patterns of mass movement lead at times to large numbers of deaths by drowning when water is encountered. Their mass movements appear in part to be triggered by population density. When a lemming falls into the water, it attempts to get out.

Suicide does not involve mere death, however. As a definitional matter it involves psychological activities that are oriented toward personal death as a consequence of that activity. This is part of what is meant by suicide being "purposeful." Thus, we must deal with the issue of purpose.

Psychological purpose, for a non-verbal organism, has to do with the directly experienced consequences of action. A bird pecking a key "in order to get food" is engaging in a purposeful action in the sense that the organism's history of the temporal sequence between key pecking and food now participates in the action of pecking, and the bird is acting with respect to a consequence. Indeed, that is what we mean when we say that "pecking is an operant class reinforced by food." It is also why we say "in order to get food" – we are literally speaking of the temporal order among these events. Not all behaviors are purposeful in this sense because not all behaviors involve consequential control. The jerk of a knee when struck is not purposeful, for example, while all operant behavior is purposeful. I am not using purpose here as a cause, but merely as a quality of some kinds of behavior.

How, then, could a non-verbal organism commit suicide? It could do so only if death could be a consequence that participated in an action of self-destruction for a non-verbal organism. When it is only experiential time that is at issue, it is not possible for the organism's actual history of a temporal sequence between and action and personal death to now participate in that action. Death cannot function as a reinforcer. Thus, to the extent that we mean purposeful behavior when we say "suicide" it is hard to see how a non-verbal organism could commit suicide. It is certainly possible to shape more and more careless behavior that would result in death. But how could one shape suicide?

Anyone would admit that it is not possible for death to be a psychologically important consequence based on a direct experience of ones own death, but this does not totally resolve the issue. It is known that animals can learn to discriminate dead and alive animals (Schaefer, 1967). Couldn't a non-verbal organism learn about death by observing it in others and extending that experience to oneself?

I believe that the answer is no, and for several reasons. Generalization of this kind must occur along some formal dimension. An animal might have a direct history with, say, an orange light and thus respond differently based on that history when, say, a red light is seen. But this kind of stimulus generalization occurs along the formal dimension of color. Death does not share formal properties with life. I cannot see the stimulus dimension along which knowledge about death would generalize to oneself.

Second, even if the animal could relate the death of others to oneself what would establish this as a reinforcer? Why would death have consequential properties?

Suicide as a Verbal Action

When the motivational conditions involved in suicide are analyzed, more than half of actual or attempted suicides involve an attempt to flee from aversive situations (Loo, 1986; Smith &

Bloom, 1985). These aversive situations include especially aversive states of mind such as guilt and anxiety (Bancroft, Skrimshire & Simkins, 1976; Baumeister, 1990). Persons who commit suicide evaluate themselves quite negatively, believing themselves to be worthless, inadequate, rejected, or blameworthy (Maris, 1981; Rosen, 1976; Rothberg & Jones, 1987).

In directly experienced escape and avoidance conditioning paradigms, the organism must be exposed to an aversive event (either directly or via cues associated with such an event), and the withdrawal or prevention of that event made contingent upon some action. The reinforcer in escape or avoidance conditioning is the reduced probability of the aversive event relative to its probability before responding.

Suicide cannot fit such a pattern of direct escape conditioning for two reasons: the reduced probability of an aversive event relative to its probability before responding cannot have been directly experienced and, further, suicide occurs even when the action of taking ones own life produces direct exposure to aversive events long before death occurs (e.g., self-strangulation, wrist cutting, and so on). Suicide does not seem to be an issue of directly experienced escape and avoidance conditioning. It is quite possible, however, to construct the consequences of death verbally.

Verbal purpose. There is a second kind of purpose that is made possible by the construction of temporal relations. Take an example: a person goes to college "in order to a degree." Naturally, going to school involves many behaviors that have been directly reinforced (studying, taking tests) but this observation must not lead us to ignore the degree itself. The person herself may say ""I am going to school to get a degree." We cannot rule out the relevance of this goal by fiat. I believe that working to get a degree is purposeful action in the sense that: 1) the person's history with regard to the construction of temporal sequences has been brought to bear on college and degrees, and 2) the action of going to college involves (at least in part) the constructed consequence. Psychological purpose, in a verbal sense, that has to do with the constructed consequences of action. When we say "in order to get a degree" -- we are still speaking of the temporal order among these events (as we were before when we were speaking of non-verbal purpose) but now the order need not be experienced directly. It can be totally derived. Thus, verbal organisms can have purposes that have never been directly experienced by anyone. For example, the Wright brothers purposefully built machines to fly, even though this had never been done before.

Personal death is not something that has been directly experienced: it is a verbal concept that has many stimulus functions based on the many relations it sustains with other events. For example, death might be associated verbally with heaven, or an absence of suffering. We have an enormous amount of verbal training with regard to death, and while much of it presents death as fearsome or negative, much of it does not. As viewed by Hamlet, for example, death is devoutly to be wished so long as it means an end to "the thousand heart aches that flesh is heir to."

A person can construct an if ... then relation between death and many other events.
"When I die:
My suffering will stop.
The world will be better off.
They will know how much they've wronged me.
It will be a relief."

And so on. These various verbal events ("relief," "suffering" and the like) have psychological functions via their participation in relational networks with other events. "Relief," for example, is in an equivalence relation with feelings associated with directly experienced contingencies in which aversive events have been removed. The sentence *If death then relief* is a kind of substitute contingency: a verbal formula in which *death* as a verbal concept is placed into a temporal sequential relation with *relief* as a verbal concept. If *relief* has acquired positive functions in the manner described above, then -- for a person in considerable psychological pain – the formula *If death then relief* will transfer these positive functions to *death*. But the person can also construct relations between certain actions and death -- *If I jump then I will die*. The source for these constructions include directly experienced but also verbally constructed events with others (e.g., seeing someone jump to his death), and indirectly constructed relations of this kind (e.g., reading about a person who jumped to her death). The verbal concept of death readily enables this verbal knowing to be associated with oneself, verbally conceived (*If I jump then I will die*). In this manner humans can construct rules of the sort: *If I jump, then I will find relief*. I believe that such activity is a necessary component of self-destruction when it is defined as a purposeful act. If so, then suicide is a kind of rule-governed behavior. Suicide is a verbal action.

Verbal Time and the Existential Dilemma

It is interesting that the sin that lead Adam and Eve out of the Garden of Eden was eating from the Tree of Knowledge. The "knowledge" that was on that tree was not experiential knowing – Adam and Eve had that already. It is verbal knowing that removes our ignorance casts us out of innocence.

Verbal behavior is a two-edged sword. Its relation to suicide is multifacted. Arbitrarily applicable relational responding enables verbal purpose – action with regard to constructed futures that need not ever have been experienced. Humans can attempt to eliminate disease, war, or hunger from the face of the earth. They can fly to the planets, or discover the atom. Life can become, as it were, meaningful. It can be about something.

Arbitrarily applicable relational responding also enables verbal comparisons that need not be based on experience: I want to get better. I want more. I have my own standards. I have my beliefs.

Unfortunately perhaps, the self-same action that enables us to act with regard to constructed positive futures allows us to construct futures in which we will not be here, or in which all that we have worked for will be as dust. We can realize that the universe will eventually collapse into an infinitely dense but timeless mass, only to explode again. We can deal with our own death and that of all other living things. Life can become, as it were, meaningless. It can be about nothing.

And our verbal comparisons can serve not as a goad to acheivement, but as a mocking torment, revealing our utter failure. I want to get better, but I am not doing so. I want more of what I will never have. I have my own standards, and I am not living up to them. I have my own beliefs, and it all amounts to nothing.

If language is a force for adaption, suicide and meaninglessness is the unavoidable dark side of the force. Verbal behavior enables us to be warm, sheltered, fed, informed, and mobile. It also enables us to load a gun, put the barrel into our mouth, and *find relief*.

References

Bancroft, J., Skrimshire, A., & Simkins, S. (1976). The reasons people give for taking overdoses. *British Journal of Psychiatry, 128,* 538-548.

Baumeister, R. F. (1990). Suicide as escape from self. *Psychological Review, 97,* 90-113.

Douglas, J. D. (1967). *The social meanings of suicide.* Princeton: Princeton University Press.

Gewirtz, J. L. & Stengle, K. G. (1968). Learning of generalized imitation as the basis for identification. *Psychological Review, 5,* 374-397.

Hayes, S. C. (1991). A relational control theory of stimulus equivalence. In L. J. Hayes & P. N. Chase (Eds.), *Dialogues on verbal behavior* (pp. 19-40). Reno, NV: Context Press.

Hayes, S. C. & Hayes, L. J. (1989). The verbal action of the listener as a basis for rule-governance. In S. C. Hayes (Ed.), *Rule-governed behavior: Cognition, contingencies, and instructional control.* (pp. 153-190). New York: Plenum.

Lester, D. (1972). Why people kill themselves. Springfield, IL: Charles C. Thomas.

Loo, R. (1986). Suicide among police in federal force. *Suicide and Life-Threatening Behavior, 16,* 379-388.

Maris, R. (1981). *Pathways to suicide: A survey of self-destructive behaviors.* Baltimore: Johns Hopkins University Press.

Reese, H. W. (1968). *The perception of stimulus relations: Discrimination learning and transposition.* New York: Academic Press.

Rosen, D. H. (1976). Suicide behaviors: Psychotherapeutic implications of egocide. *Suicide and Life-Threatening Behavior, 6,* 209-215.

Rothberg, J. M. & Jones, F. D. (1987). Suicide in the U. S. Army: Epidemiological and periodic aspects. *Suicide and Life-Threatening Behavior, 17,* 119-132.

Schaefer, H. H. (1967). Can a mouse commit suicide? In E. S. Shneidman (ed.), *Essays in self-destruction* (pp. 494-509). New York: Science House.

Shneidman, E. S. (1985). *Definition of suicide.* New York: Wiley.

Sidman, M. (1986). Functional analyses of emergent verbal classes. In T. Thompson & M. D. Zeiler (Eds.), *Analysis and integration of behavioral units* (pp. 213-245). Hillsdale, New Jersey: Erlbaum.

Sidman, M. (1990). Equivalence relations: Where do they come from? In D. E. Blackman & H. Lejeune (Eds.), *Behaviour analysis in theory and practice: Contributions and controversies* (pp. 93-114). Hillsdale, N.J.: Erlbaum.

Smith, G. W. & Bloom, I. (1985). A study in the personal meaning of suicide in the context of Baechler's typology. *Suicide and Life-Threatening Behavior, 15,* 3-13.

Part 3
Rules and Verbal Formulae

Chapter 8

Rules as Nonverbal Entities

Hayne W. Reese
West Virginia University

In a survey of behavior analysts, Place (1987) found that about two-thirds agreed that rules are necessarily verbal, though with the proviso that some rules are expressed by signs or gestures instead of words and lack the internal structure of a formula or sentence (Item 2 in Place's survey). In contrast, many cognitivists believe that rules can be nonverbal in the sense that they are not expressed by words, signs, gestures, or any other verbal vehicle. The purpose of the present paper is to examine the cognitive position.

A study reported by Steele and Hayes at the 1987 meeting of the Association for Behavior Analysis provides a preview of the cognitive position. The study dealt with stimulus equivalence as a basis for generative grammar, and involved second-order discriminative stimuli for complex stimulus-equivalence classes. The procedures used in the study were based on logical analysis of the relations to be learned, and the logic was so complex that according to Steele, he and Hayes made several logical errors in the course of designing the study. In spite of this complexity, most of the research participants, who were college students, exhibited perfect or virtually perfect stimulus equivalence. Furthermore, when questioned at the end of the study, the successful participants did not give accurate descriptions of the procedures. An inference that rules were learned seems unproblematic; however, the study provides no basis for an inference that the rules were verbal but does provide at least two bases for an inference that they were nonverbal: The complex rules to be learned posed no great difficulty for the participants even though the verbal expression of the rules in logical terms and in self-reports was extremely difficult.

In the rest of the paper, I will discuss first the question of whether rule-governance is "special" or is reducible to contingency-shaping, then I will discuss various forms and functions of rules, then what is meant by "knowing a rule," and finally the senses in which rules can be nonverbal entities.

Is Rule-Governance "Special"?

The issue considered first is whether rule-governance is "special": Does rule-governance differ from contingency-shaping? The specific issues are why rules are obeyed, whether any rules are optional, and how their effects differ from the effects of contingencies.

Why Obey Rules?

Most cognitive psychologists have ignored the question of why rules are followed, and most behaviorists who have considered the question have given the pat answer that rules are followed because following them is reinforced (without specifying the reinforcer) or because following rules has a history of reinforcement (without empirically demonstrating the reality of the purported history). The question is important and deserves empirical as well as theoretical attention. Work by Malott (e.g., 1982, 1986) illustrates what needs to be done. Work by Hayes and colleagues (e.g., Zettle & Hayes, 1982) on "pliance" may also be relevant.

Role of consequences. Skinner (1982) suggested that "most students study to avoid the consequence of not studying" (p. 4). However, Malott (1982) has argued that more immediate consequences are needed. Malott analyzed rules that appear to be "weak" because the specified consequence is far in the future. In addition to studying, examples include doing homework assignments and flossing teeth. Rules that specify the discriminative stimulus, the behavior, and the consequence may be more effective than our usual rules, which often specify these components only vaguely or not at all; but even when a consequence is specified in the rule, the actual reinforcer for rule-following may not be the consequence that is specified. Malott suggested that rule-following is an escape procedure. An implication is that the functional consequence is not the one specified in the rule, such as the good grades that will result from studying and doing homework assignments or the sound teeth that will result from flossing, or the bad grades that will result from not studying and not doing homework assignments or the cavities and tooth loss that will result from not flossing. Rather, the functional consequence may be a negative reinforcer; rule-following terminates self-blame, guilt, anxiety, or some other private event and thereby is reinforced.

Riegler, Kohler, and Baer (1985) suggested that rules are obeyed because of "the development of a behavior class describable as *compliance with instructions*" (p. 3), which reflects generalization (1) from rules paired with reinforcement for compliance, to rules not previously paired with reinforcement for compliance; (2) from rule-staters and instruction- givers who reinforce compliance, to rule-staters and instruction-givers who have not previously reinforced compliance; and (3) from self-produced rules paired with reinforcement for compliance, to self-produced rules not previously paired with reinforcement for compliance. As Riegler et al. pointed out, this conceptualization suggests that the analysis of rule- governed behavior might be furthered by use of paradigms from the areas of compliance training, correspondence training (between saying and doing), and self-instruction training.

The question of interest to a behavior analyst is whether training in compliance, correspondence, and self-instruction produces generalized compliance. If it does, the question of interest to a cognitive psychologist is *why* it does: What cognitive activities can plausibly be affected by the training and can plausibly lead to generalized compliance?

Are any rules optional? Skinner (1978) said that if human behavior is controlled by reinforcement and punishment rather than by free will, then it will be so controlled regardless of whether the human believes in the principles of reinforcement and punishment or believes in free will. Alternatively, however, if human behavior is controlled by free will rather than by reinforcement and punishment, then it will be so controlled whatever the human believes. The issue is about rules that are sometimes followed and sometimes not followed. Why is such a rule sometimes followed and sometimes not followed? In every relevant scientific theory, the choice is assumed to be determined rather than a matter of free will. It is determined by the context in which the choice occurs, including the history of the individual and the present internal and external circumstances. A rule is optional only in the sense that present knowledge does not permit accurate prediction and effective control of when the rule is followed.

Are Rule-Governance and Contingency-Shaping Different?

A distinction is made between rule-governance and contingency-shaping, obviously, but the precise nature of the distinction has been unclear. In fact, Schnaitter (1977) suggested that rule-governance is really contingency-shaping (see also Bentall, Lowe, & Beasty, 1985); and Brownstein and Shull (1985) argued that "rule-governed" is not a technical term and does not imply the existence of any behavior analytic principles different from those involved in contingency-shaping. In Place's (1987) survey, 73% of the respondents agreed that "all behavior including rule-governed behavior is contingency-shaped" (Item 7).

One explanation of rule-governance is that "We tend to follow [rules] because previous behavior in response to similar verbal stimuli has been reinforced" (Skinner, 1969, p. 148; the bracketed word "rules" is substituted for Skinner's word "advice"). Or, without the unsupported assumption of stimulus similarity, one might say that we tend to follow rules because we have been reinforced for following rules in the past. This explanation is very abstract, because it requires defining "following rules" as an operant behavior. Such an operant can have no topography of its own (Baron & Galizio, 1983); it is a behavior class that includes all of a person's behaviors that have been or will be rule-governed. It is everything, and therefore it is nothing– it is all behaviors, not any one behavior. The conception of rule-governance as an operant behavior, or as any other kind of behavior, is therefore unsatisfying.

Rule-governed and contingency-shaped behavior. All behaviors that are regular are rule-governed, either in the sense of control by a normative rule or in the sense of instantiation of a normal rule. (The distinction between *normative* and *normal* rules is discussed later.) To avoid this trivialization of the adjective, I will use "rule-governed" to refer to the first sense and "contingency-shaped" to refer to the second sense. (I am ignoring innate behavior, which is rule-governed in the second sense but determined by genetic factors rather than by contingencies.) Rule-governed behavior and contingency-shaped behavior are different operants:

> Rule-governed behavior is . . . never exactly like the behavior shaped by contingencies. . . . When operant experiments with human subjects are simplified by instructing the subjects in the operation of the equipment . . ., the resulting behavior may resemble that which follows exposure to the contingencies and may be studied in its stead for certain purposes, but the controlling variables are different, and the behaviors will not necessarily change in the same way in response to other variables. (Skinner, 1969, pp. 150-151)

(For further discussion of differences between rule-governed and contingency-shaped behavior, see Skinner, 1969, chap. 6.)

Luria (1981) described a phenomenon that can be interpreted to reflect rule-governed versus contingency-shaped speech:

> For some people word meaning does not evolve on the basis of contextualized speech (i.e., in live communication), but consists of acquiring the dictionary meanings of individual words. In those instances, there may be considerable difficulty in comprehending the meanings of words in actual communication. Perhaps the most striking instance of this phenomenon is word comprehension by deaf-mute individuals for whom word meaning does not evolve as a result of participating in live communication. A deaf-mute child learns word meaning by acquiring individual words. . . . Similar phenomena occur in the learning of a foreign language, a process that begins not with contextual speech, but with the dictionary meaning of individual words. (p. 176)

Hineline (1983) made the same point: "A native speaker of German is not following the rules of a grammar book as is the language student who is following those rules" (p. 184). Speech acquired through "live communication" is contingency-shaped; speech acquired through the dictionary is rule-governed.

Baron and Galizio (1983) and Hayes, Brownstein, Haas, and Greenway (1986) made a similar point in noting that schedule sensitivity can be mimicked by following a rule, but that the rule-governed behavior will generally be insensitive to changes in the schedule. (I can imagine, however, a complex rule that could produce behavior that mimicked sensitivity to schedule changes, provided the schedule changes are signaled in some way.)

Skinner (1977a) has argued:

Behavior that consists of following rules is inferior to behavior shaped by the contingencies described by the rules. Thus, we may learn to operate a piece of equipment by following instructions, but we operate it skillfully only when our behavior has been shaped by its effect on the equipment. The instructions are soon forgotten. (p. 86; p. 12 in 1978 reprint; italics deleted)

This argument provides support for the familiar "learn by doing" dictum.

Instructed and shaped rules. In a learning situation, the relation between rules and performance should be interactive in the sense of Mao Zedong's (1937/1965) practice-theory-practice dialectic. Practice, in the sense of behaving, experimenting, and so on, leads to theory, in the sense of rules, knowledge, and so on, which in turn leads to changed behaving, experimenting, etc., which leads to changed rules, knowledge, etc.–and on and on. In other words, rules are abstracted or induced from practice and then they change the practice, and the changed practice leads to changes in the rules, etc.

In the practice-theory-practice dialectic, the development of rules is contingency-shaped. The rule-governed behavior exhibited in the practice is not perfectly adaptive, and the feedback functions as a contingency that shapes modifications that improve the adaptiveness of the rule. Because rule-governed behavior is inferior to contingency-shaped behavior, and because rules that govern behavior are themselves behaviors, one might expect rule-governed *rules* to be less effective than contingency-shaped rules. Catania, Matthews, and Shimoff (1982) confirmed this expectation: Shaped verbal rules controlled nonverbal behavior more reliably than did instructed rules. Thus, the "learn by doing" dictum is supported with respect to rules as well as with respect to other behaviors.

A cognitivist might hypothesize that a person is more likely to believe shaped rules, because they are discovered rather than taught. Discovery, according to cognitivists, yields understanding, and instruction yields mere information. Understanding is retained; information is forgotten. (This distinction was also made by St. Augustine [*De Diversis Quaestionibus,* Quaestio IX], St. Thomas Aquinas [*Summa Theologica,* Pt. 1, Question 84, Article 6], Piaget [e.g., Aebli, 1979, Furth & Wachs, 1974, chap. 1; Pulaski, 1971, chap. 18], and others.)

In addition to the general superiority of shaped rules over instructed rules, shaped rules in a psychological experiment might be superior because the research participants are suspicious of instructed rules. In the study by Catania et al. (1982), the participant might well have thought that the experimenter must have been using deception in saying, for example, "Write 'press fast' for the left button and write 'press slowly' for the right button." The participants might therefore have inferred that the schedules were the same for both buttons.

Any given instructed rule may or may not accord with reality, that is, it may or may not be an accurate description of natural contingencies. However, the received opinion among cognitivists is that the effectiveness of an instructed rule in controlling behavior depends less on its being accurate than on its being believed to be accurate. As Thomas and Thomas (1928) said, "If men define situations as real, they are real in their consequences" (p. 572). (Thomas's editor commented that this sentence is "one of the most quoted in the literature on social relations" [Thomas, 1951, footnote 14, p. 81]. The same point was made by Karl Marx, Sigmund Freud, and others, according to Merton [1968, p. 475], and also by Anaxagoras: "There is also recorded a saying of Anaxagoras to some of his disciples, that things would be for them as they judged them to be" [Aristotle, *Metaphysics,* Bk. 4, chap. 5, 1009b 25-26; 1933, p. 187].)

These considerations lead to the following conclusions: (1) Rule-governed behavior is not the same as contingency-shaped behavior. (2) Rule-governance and contingency-shaping are processes. (3) Rule-governance emerges from contingency-shaping. (4) Once rule-governance has emerged, it is no longer reducible to contingency-shaping.

Forms and Functions of Rules

Several taxonomies of rules have been proposed, but the one presented here has the advantage of simplicity, being based on dichotomous classes.

Normal and Normative Rules

As a noun, *rule* has two general meanings that are relevant for present purposes: a generality and a prescription. A generality is a *normal* rule, referring to what is; a prescription is a *normative* rule, referring to what should be (Reese & Fremouw, 1984). A normative rule can be a prescription, specifying the way one ought to proceed, or it can be practical advice, specifying a way to succeed. In Skinner's (1957) terms, the former is a mand and the latter has the form of a tact but is actually a mand. In Zettle and Hayes's (1982) terms, the former is a ply and the latter is a track (a ply specifies appropriate behavior and a track specifies "the way the world is arranged"– p. 81).

The following doggerel is an example of a practical normative rule (mand in tact-form; track), referring to effective operation of a forge bellows.

Up high, down low,
Up quick, down slow—
And that's the way to blow. (Skinner, 1969, p. 139)

Although this rule tacts effective operation of the bellows, it is an implicit mand when presented by a blacksmith to an apprentice.

A normative rule is *functional* if it sometimes affects behavior, and *nonfunctional* if it does not affect behavior (Reese & Fremouw, 1984). According to this view, normative rules—prescriptions—are behaviors or cognitive activities of a speaker. When they affect the behavior of a listener (who may be the same person as the speaker), they are functional; otherwise, they are nonfunctional.

The phrase "nonfunctional rule" is self-contradictory if part of the definition of a rule is that it is functional. However, in Place's (1987) survey two-thirds of the respondents agreed that a rule "controls, or is *capable* of controlling" behavior (Item 1, emphasis added). Perhaps any sentence or formula is *capable* of controlling behavior and therefore can be a rule whether or not it currently controls behavior. Furthermore, Hayes (1987) distinguished between understanding a rule and following a rule, and thereby implied that a rule does not necessarily control behavior.

If a functional normative rule is always exhibited in behavior, it can be designated as a *normal rule*. A nonfunctional normative rule can be *normal* only as verbal behavior. An important research question for behavior analysts is how a nonfunctional normative rule is maintained, and for cognitivists, why it is maintained. However, these questions are not addressed in this paper; I will therefore use "normative rule" hereafter to refer only to functional normative rules.

Locus of Rules

Skinner (1977b) said that the processes of association, abstraction, and the like are in the experiment, not in the research participant. Rules are also in the design of the experiment, and may or may not be in the research participant. For example, Nissen (1953) discussed an "if-then" mechanism that could explain performance in conditional-discrimination and other stimulus-patterning tasks (e.g., if *red*, then choose *square*; if *green*, then choose *circle*). However, the if-then relation is in the task, not necessarily in the research participant.

In the conditional-discrimination task, two-dimensional stimuli are presented and the correct choice is determined by the conjunction of two conditional rules:

(If A, then B) and (if a, then b)

where A and a refer to the presence of alternative values on one dimension and B and b refer to the choice of alternative values on another dimension. Children as young as 5 years of age can solve the conditional-discrimination task (e.g., Doan & Cooper, 1971), but children do not fully understand the verbal if-then rule until teen age (O'Brien & Overton, 1982), perhaps late teen age (Overton, Byrnes, & O'Brien, 1985). Evidently, young children can respond in accordance with a conditional regularity—a normal rule—before they understand a verbal description of conditional regularities. The verbal if-then rule therefore seems to be not in the young child but in the experimenter.

Rules as Guides

A normal rule is a regularity—a generality or norm. When a regularity is discovered, it can be described and its description is also called a rule. This is, in fact, the usual textbook definition of *rule*. Confusion might be avoided if the description of a regularity were called a *law* (Bergmann, 1957, p. 136), but *law* also has a juridical sense. "Obeying" a natural law is a matter of fact; obeying a juridical law is a matter of choice, or at least it is often considered to be. The phrase "normal rule," therefore, refers both to regularities in nature and to descriptions of regularities in nature.

In the sense of a regularity in nature, a normal rule is unproblematic. It occurs; it is exhibited. It is not a guide, because behaving consistently with it is a matter of fact, not of choice. Persons and objects have no options with respect to rules defined as regularities of nature; these rules are followed inexorably. (If the instances of their being followed are probabilistic, they are still "followed inexorably" in the sense intended here, because the probabilistic nature of their instantiation is a matter of deficiency in our ability to predict rather than of indeterminacy or free choice.) A normal rule may be verbalized or unverbalized. In the verbal form, a normal rule is a description of a purported regularity in nature; in the nonverbal form, it *is* the regularity in nature. Like the regularity itself, a verbal normal rule is not a guide; it is only a description of a regularity. The regularity as such will occur whether or not it is described accurately, in fact, whether or not it is described at all.

The argument so far is that behavior is not controlled by a rule of the normal type, whether the rule is verbal or nonverbal. However, behavior can be controlled by a description, whether or not the description is accurate. When a description has this function, it has become a normative rule. Normative rules—moral, practical, and juridical—are guides that are optional in the sense that they can be followed or ignored (Skinner, 1969, p. 148). Why they are followed or ignored is therefore a problem, which I discussed earlier in the paper.

According to Searle (1976), "the rules of language are not like the laws of physics, for the rules must do more than describe what happens, they must play a role in guiding behavior" (p. 1120). Chomsky (1980) agreed: "The rules of grammar are mentally represented and used in thought and behavior" (p. 129). (However, Chomsky disagreed with Searle on some other points.) Actually, the rules of language might be like the laws of physics, that is, descriptions of regularities in nature—in this case regularities in language. Speakers exhibit regularities in language use, and linguists describe these regularities. The relevant rules are normal: Rules as regularities are exhibited in language use, and rules as descriptions are induced by linguists. The issue is whether the regularities are guided by normative rules (which presumably resemble the normal descriptive rules). Even mature speakers cannot state all the rules of grammar that linguists infer they use (Searle, 1976; Slobin, 1979, p. 5). Therefore, at least some of the rules are normal rather than normative; or put more weakly, at least some of the rules can be normal and need not be assumed to be normative. The Steele and Hayes (1991) report is directly relevant here.

Of course, once a normative rule has been formulated, it can control behavior. As Skinner (1969) said, "one may upon occasion speak grammatically by applying rules" (p. 162). Furthermore, even young children are amused by word play in which the rules of language are violated

(Shultz & Robillard, 1980). If a rule is deliberately violated, it must be normative—a normal rule cannot be deliberately violated (otherwise, it would not be a *normal* rule). Therefore, even young children must understand some normative rules of language. However, their understanding may be vague or intuitive (Shultz & Robillard, 1980) rather than verbally formulated. Furthermore, their ordinary language may reflect normal rules rather than normative ones.

In summary, a normal descriptive rule can control behavior if it becomes a normative rule, but in this guise it is a *verbal* rule because it was already a verbal description.

Rules as Dispositions

Dispositional concepts are defined by if-then statements (Bergmann, 1957, p. 60; Fodor, 1981). Examples are brittleness and testiness:

Brittleness means that if an object that has this property is hit, then the object shatters.

Testiness means that if a person who has this property is provoked even slightly, then the person becomes angry.

A brittle object does not express brittleness unless it is hit, that is, it does not shatter unless hit; and a testy person does not express testiness--become angry—unless provoked. The distinction between the disposition and the action is the same as Aristotle's distinction between *hexis* and *energeia* (or *entelecheia*): *Hexis* is a potentiality that could be actualized but is not presently actualized, that is, it is not presently expressed in action; *energeia* is present actualization, or action (Aristotle, *Nichomachean Ethics*, Bk. 1, chap. 8; 1926, pp. 38, 39). The distinction is also the same as that between competence and performance when competence means ability or capacity rather than effectiveness or fitness. A disposition, then, is competence to perform in a specified way; performance is the actualization or application of competence.

"**Normal**" **dispositions.** As a regularity in nature, a rule is the concatenation of two (or more) sets of events and their interrelation(s), for example, one set of events regularly antecedent to another set of events. Concretely, as a regularity in nature the law of falling bodies refers to the antecedent event of removing whatever has been holding a body in place and the subsequent event of the body's falling. The formula $s = 1/2\ gt^2$ is a description of this regularity; it is not the regularity. As Skinner (1969) said, this formula "does not govern the behavior of falling bodies, it governs those who correctly predict the position of falling bodies at given times" (p. 141; see also Moore, 1981). In the terms used herein, the formula is a normal rule of the descriptive type when it is used to describe the rule-as-regularity of falling bodies; and when it governs those making predictions, it is a normative rule.

A normal rule interpreted as a disposition is "obeyed" inexorably; when the antecedent set is sufficiently complete, it is regularly followed by the subsequent set and the rule can be said to be an actualization. When the antecedent set is not sufficiently complete, the subsequent set does not occur and the rule can be said to be a disposition instead of an actualization. The connection between the rule as a disposition and the rule as an actualization depends entirely on the physical completeness of the antecedent set of events. For example, the rules relating patterns of key pecking to schedules of reinforcement are regularities. The scallop in the rate of behavior controlled by a fixed interval schedule and the high rate of behavior controlled by a variable ratio schedule are not caused by the respective rules; they are part of these rules. The actual key pecking–the actualization–is not *controlled* or *governed* by the rule; it is an *instantiation* of the rule. Rules of this type–whether in the guise of a potentiality or the guise of an actualization–are nonverbal, but the issue of control or capability of control is not relevant. That is, such a nonverbal rule is a disposition or potential to behave or is actual behavior, but *control* refers to the relation between the potentiality and the actualization, and only in a teleological system can a potentiality be said to *cause* (control) behavior. (Even then, the teleological cause is a potentiality not in the sense of *hexis* but in the sense of *telos*, but this distinction is not addressed in this paper.)

"Normative" dispositions. Normative dispositions refer to normative rules—moral, practical, and juridical rules, and rules as competence. A normative rule is always a disposition, because the rule itself cannot be actualized but can only *lead to* actual behavior. The actualization of the rule for operating a forge bellows, for example, is not part of this rule; it is caused or occasioned by the rule in conjunction with other setting conditions. In cognitive psychology a normative rule is a cognitive activity that can be utilized by a person to control his or her own behavior. In behavior analysis, given particular setting conditions and a particular reinforcement history, a normative rule functions as a conditional stimulus that elicits respondent behavior or it functions as a stimulus that occasions operant behavior. It could have the latter function as a discriminative stimulus or as an "establishing operation," an "establishing stimulus" (Chase & Hyten, 1985; Michael, 1982), an "augmental" (Zettle & Hayes, 1982), or a "precurrent stimulus" (e.g., Parsons, Taylor, & Joyce, 1981).

The connection between a normative disposition, or competence, and an actualization, or performance, depends on variables that are outside the rule itself. A normative rule is one element in an antecedent set (and researchers have not yet identified all the other elements in this set).

For example, consider the normative rule "If a speaker asks for something a listener can give, and the listener gives it, then the speaker will return the favor some time." Now, suppose a speaker asks a listener for a glass of water. This mand together with the normative rule may occasion the listener's giving the speaker a glass of water. However, enormous complexities are involved in the actualization of this normative rule. The listener must have a glass and water available; the rule must not be superseded by a conflicting rule, such as the listener's own rule to hoard all the available water; perhaps the listener must believe the speaker is a person who can be expected to return the favor; etc.

According to Skinner (1969, p. 160), a complete rule of the kind I am calling normative—and verbal—specifies a three-term contingency: In the presence of a specified discriminative stimulus, occurrence of a specified behavior will be consequated in a specified way. However, in Place's (1987) survey, about two-thirds of the respondents indicated that a rule might specify only two of the three terms (Item 3/4). In fact, as Skinner noted (1969, p. 158), many normative rules actually in use fail to specify one or even two of the three terms. In these cases, the discriminative and/or consequent stimuli are presumably implied, or intended to be implied. An example is "Whatsoever ye would that men should do to you, do ye even so to them" (Matthew vii 12). This rule specifies neither the occasions nor the consequences for the doing, and as Skinner noted it also leaves the doing pretty much unspecified. It is nevertheless a rule and for all I know it governs some people's behavior some of the time.

At least implicitly, a verbal normative rule states an antecedent and a consequent, and thus it is at least implicitly an if-then statement. The antecedent is a condition and an action that might be taken—the discriminative stimulus and the behavior. The consequent is the outcome that can be expected—the consequent stimulus. "If this action is taken in this situation, then this outcome should occur." Any of these components, however, may be implicit, and indeed the if-then form may be implicit. The rule for operating a forge bellows is an example: The action is specified, but the condition, the outcome, and the if-then form are all implicit. The Golden Rule is another example. These rules do not have the if-then structure on the surface, but one might say they have the deep structure of an if-then statement.

Throughout this subsection on normative dispositions, all my examples have been verbal normative rules. I will consider the issue of whether any normative rules are nonverbal later, after considering what is meant by "knowing a rule."

Knowing a Rule

The concepts of knowing and remembering have posed problems for psychologists and philosophers, perhaps in part because they feel a need to postulate a trace of some kind and a locus for the trace in order to provide a physical basis for the knowledge or memory. Skinner himself may have felt this need; he explicitly—and unnecessarily from the viewpoint of his system—postulated physiological traces of reinforcement histories (e.g., 1974, pp. 213-215). This aspect of the problem of knowing a rule is closely relevant to the present topic because verbal rules are clearly embodied in a concrete vehicle—words, signs, or gestures—and nonverbal rules seem to be disembodied and to have no concrete existence. Only instantiations or actualizations of nonverbal rules seem to have concrete existence. However, space in the present paper does not permit discussing everything that is relevant, and I will limit my discussion to another aspect of the problem, involving distinctions between "knowing that" and "knowing how."

Knowing That Versus Knowing How

Consider the following two anecdotes:

(1) I can describe how to drive a golf ball, in the sense that I can describe the component movements (and nonmovement with respect to my head) and how they are coordinated. However, the outcomes of my actual attempts to drive the ball are unpredictable.

(2) I can transform any sentence from the active to the passive voice and vice versa. However, I cannot state a grammatical rule that covers all active/passive transformations—and evidently neither can the linguists (cf. Slobin, 1979, p. 5).

The distinction made in these two anecdotes is between knowing in a cognitive way and knowing in a behavioral way. The former is called "knowing that" and the latter is called "knowing how"; or the former is "knowing about things" and the latter is "knowing how to do things" (Parrott, 1983); or "describing contingencies" versus "performing in accordance with them" (Matthews, Catania, & Shimoff, 1985, p. 155). (These and other distinctions are summarized in Table 1.)

"Knowing that" refers to verbally expressed facts or information; "knowing how" refers to behavior. Hineline (1983) equated "knowing that" with tacting and "knowing how" with behaving. In cognitive psychology, "knowing that" refers to "declarative knowledge," and "knowing how" refers to "procedural knowledge" or "cognitive skill" (Anderson, 1980, p. 223; Anderson, 1982; Cohen, 1984). The postulation of a memory trace is strongly tempting in the case of "knowing that," but not in the case of "knowing how" (Coulter, 1983, p. 78; Skinner, 1969, p. 170).

Rule Knowledge

In one sense, knowing a rule is "knowing that," and one can "know how" without "knowing that" (Miller, 1981, p. 3). That is, one can exhibit a regularity in performance (knowing how) without being able to describe the regularity (knowing that; knowing the rule).

Table 1
Knowing That and Knowing How

Knowing that	Knowing how
Cognitive knowing	Behavioral knowing
Knowing about things	Knowing how to do things
Describing contingencies	Performing in accordance with contingencies
Facts, information	Behavior
Tacting	Behaving
Declarative knowledge	Procedural knowledge, cognitive skill
Knowing a rule	Knowing a rule (behaving consistently with a rule)
Description of a regularity in performance	Regularity in performance
Stating a rule	Exhibiting know-how
Effects of discriminative stimuli (?)	Effects of contingencies
Symbolic representation of a learned capability	Learned capability
Information capability	Performance capability
Being able to state a rule	Behaving consistently with a rule
Normative disposition or rule	Normal disposition or rule
Not causal	Not causal

In another sense, knowing a rule is "knowing how." A normal rule is a regularity in nature, and knowing a rule of this kind can mean behaving consistently with the rule (Gagne, 1970, p. 57). However, in this case behaving consistently with the rule is not a *result* of knowing the rule, because "knowing the rule" in this sense is not itself any kind of behavior–it is only a descriptive phrase.

"Stating a rule" is also a descriptive phrase, but it is defined independently of behaving consistently with the rule. Stating a rule is verbal behavior, and it can affect other behavior. The stated rule is not the regularity in nature, however; it is a description of the regularity. Gagne (1974) expressed this position in distinguishing between performance capability and information capability:

> The statement of a rule is merely the representation of it–the rule itself is a learned capability of an individual learner.... The capability of doing something must be carefully distinguished from *stating* something, which is the information capability [i.e., a concept]. (p. 61)

Skinner (1969) expressed a similar distinction:

Discriminative stimuli which improve the efficiency of behavior under given contingencies of reinforcement . . . must not be confused with the contingencies themselves, nor their effects with the effects of those contingencies. (p. 124)

The kind of confusion Skinner referred to is reflected in Chomsky's statement, "The child who learns a language has in some sense constructed the grammar for himself" (quoted in Skinner, 1969, p. 124, from Chomsky, 1959, p. 57). Skinner commented that this statement "is as misleading as to say that a dog which has learned to catch a ball has in some sense constructed the relevant part of the science of mechanics" (p. 124).

In short, knowing a rule means either being able to state the rule (knowing that) or being able to behave consistently with the rule (knowing how). ("Being able" is used here so that the statement refers to dispositions as well as actualizations. Cognitive abilities or capacities are not implied.) Knowing a rule in the first sense (being able to state it) cannot by itself cause behavior; it can be at most only a normative disposition to behave. Likewise, knowing a rule in the second sense (behaving consistently with it) cannot cause behavior, because knowing a rule in this sense is only an assertion that a normal disposition has been actualized. Nevertheless, rules can be legitimately conceptualized as causes: A normative rule (knowing that) can cause behavior by being applied, and a normal rule (knowing how) can cause behavior by being instantiated. However, conceptualizing rules as causes hides the need to understand how "being applied" and "being instantiated" are accomplished.

Can Rules be Nonverbal?

The question of whether rules can be nonverbal is now easy to answer. First, a normal rule in the sense of a regularity is always nonverbal, but behavior that is consistent with such a rule is not called rule-governed. Second, a normal rule in the sense of a description of a regularity is always verbal, but this kind of rule does not control the regularity. Third, however, a normal rule in the sense of a description of a regularity can control behavior, but then it is properly called a normative rule. This kind of normative rule is always verbal. Fourth, a disposition to behave— a competence or potentiality—can be nonverbal. However, such a disposition can be as readily interpreted as contingency-shaped as rule- governed.

I will end this paper with two illustrations of the last point: First, I can transform any active sentence into a grammatically correct passive sentence even though I cannot state a grammatical rule that covers all such transformations. Doing such transformations is interpretable as behavior shaped by the verbal community in which I learned language, and nothing is gained by assuming the existence of some unverbalized transformation rule. Second, returning to the Steele and Hayes (1991) paper, I would argue that relational frames, or complex equivalence classes, are learned during language acquisition by means of contingency- shaping and that although the rules that are learned are nonverbal, they are not *normative* rules. Rather, they are normal rules that refer to certain regularities. They are hard to describe verbally, as Steele and Hayes found; but being normal regularities they should be interpreted as nonverbal rules that can be instantiated in behavior, as Steele and Hayes demonstrated, not as nonverbal rules that control behavior.

References

Aebli, H. (1979, June). *Continuity-discontinuity from the perspective of Piagetian and post-Piagetian theory*. In H. W. Reese & W. F. Overton (Chair), Continuity-discontinuity as metatheoretical and theoretical issues. Symposium conducted at the meeting of the International Society for the Study of Behavioral Development, Lund, Sweden.

Anderson, J. R. (1980). *Cognitive psychology and its implications*. San Francisco: Freeman.
Anderson, J. R. (1982). Acquisition of cognitive skill. *Psychological Review, 89*, 369-406.
Aristotle. (1926). *The Nichomachean ethics* (trans. H. Rackham). London: William Heinemann.
Aristotle. 1933). *The metaphysics: Books I-IX* (trans. H. Tredennick). London: William Heinemann.
Baron, A., & Galizio, M. (1983). Instructional control of human operant behavior. *Psychological Record, 33*, 495-520.
Bentall, R. P., Lowe, C. F., & Beasty, A. (1985). The role of verbal behavior in human learning: II. Developmental differences. *Journal of the Experimental Analysis of Behavior, 43*, 165-181.
Bergmann, G. (1957). *Philosophy of science*. Madison: University of Wisconsin Press.
Brownstein, A. J., & Shull, R. L. (1985). A rule for the use of the term, "rule-governed behavior." *The Behavior Analyst, 8*, 265-267.
Catania, A. C., Matthews, B. A., & Shimoff, E. (1982). Instructed versus shaped human behavior: Interactions with nonverbal responding. *Journal of the Experimental Analysis of Behavior, 38*, 233-248.
Chase, P. N., & Hyten, C. (1985). A historical and pedagogical note on establishing operations. *The Behavior Analyst, 8*, 121-122.
Chomsky, N. (1959). Review of Verbal behavior. By B. F. Skinner. *Language, 35*, 26-58.
Chomsky, N. (1980). *Rules and representations*. New York: Columbia University Press.
Cohen, N. J. (1984). Preserved learning capacity in amnesia: Evidence for multiple memory systems. In L. R. Squire & N. Butters (Eds.), *Neuropsychology of memory* (pp. 83-103). New York: Guilford.
Coulter, J. (1983). *Rethinking cognitive theory*. New York: St. Martin's Press.
Doan, H. McK., & Cooper, D. L. (1971). Conditional discrimination learning in children: Two relevant factors. *Child Development, 42*, 209-220.
Fodor, J. A. (1981). The mind-body problem. *Scientific American, 244(1)*, 114-123.
Furth, H. G., & Wachs, H. (1974). *Thinking goes to school: Piaget's theory in practice*. New York: Oxford University Press.
Gagne, R. M. (1970). *The conditions of learning* (2nd ed.). New York: Holt, Rinehart & Winston.
Gagne, R. M. (1974). *Essentials of learning for instruction*. Hinsdale, IL: Dryden.
Hayes, S. C. (1987, May). *Symbolic control and units of analysis*. In H. W. Reese (Chair), Abstraction and generalization. Symposium conducted at the meeting of the Association for Behavior Analysis, Nashville, TN.
Hayes, S. C., Brownstein, A. J., Haas, J. R., & Greenway, D. E. (1986). Instructions, multiple schedules, and extinction: Distinguishing rule-governed from schedule controlled behavior. *Journal of the Experimental Analysis of Behavior, 46*, 137-147.
Hineline, P. N. (1983). When we speak of knowing. *The Behavior Analyst, 6*, 183-186.
Luria, A. R. (1981). *Language and cognition* (J. V. Wertsch, Ed.). New York: Wiley.
Malott, R. W. (1982, May). *Some theoretical considerations about rule-governed behavior*. In H. W. Reese (Chair), Rule-governed behavior. Symposium conducted at the meeting of the Association for Behavior Analysis, Nashville, TN.
Malott, R. W. (1986). Self-management, rule-governed behavior, and everyday life. In H. W. Reese & L. J. Parrott (Eds.), *Behavior science: Philosophical, methodological, and empirical advances* (pp. 207-228). Hillsdale, NJ: Lawrence Erlbaum Associates.
MaoTse-tung. (1965). On practice. *In Selected works of . . .* (Vol. 1, pp. 295-309; trans. of 2nd Chinese ed.). Peking: Foreign Languages Press. (Original work dated 1937)
Matthews, B. A., Catania, A. C., & Shimoff, E. (1985). Effects of uninstructed verbal behavior on nonverbal responding: Contingency descriptions versus performance descriptions.

Journal of the Experimental Analysis of Behavior, 43, 155-164.
Merton, R. K. (1968). *Social theory and social structure: 1968 enlarged edition.* New York: Free Press.
Michael, J. (1982). Distinguishing between discriminative and motivational functions of stimuli. *Journal of the Experimental analysis of Behavior, 37,* 149-155.
Miller, G. A. (1981). *Language and speech.* San Francisco: Freeman.
Moore, J. (1981). On mentalism, methodological behaviorism, and radical behaviorism. *Behaviorism, 9,* 55-77.
Nissen, H. W. (1953). Sensory patterning versus central organization. *Journal of Psychology, 36,* 271-187.
O'Brien, D. P., & Overton, W. F. (1982). Conditional reasoning and the competence-performance issue: A developmental analysis of a training task. *Journal of Experimental Child Psychology, 34,* 274-290.
Overton, W. [F.], Byrnes, J. P., & O'Brien, D. P. (1985). Developmental and individual differences in conditional reasoning: The role of contradiction training and cognitive style. *Developmental Psychology, 21,* 692-701.
Parrott, L. J. (1983). Perspectives on knowing and knowledge. *Psychological Record, 33,* 171-184.
Parsons, J. A., Taylor, D. C., & Joyce, T. M. (1981). Precurrent self- prompting operants in children: "Remembering." *Journal of the Experimental Analysis of Behavior, 36,* 253-266.
Place, U. T. (1987, May). *What some behavior analysts think about rules and rule-governed behavior: Questionnaire responses from an unrepresentative sample.* Paper presented at the meeting of the Association for Behavior Analysis, Nashville, TN.
Pulaski, M. A. S. (1971). *Understanding Piaget: An introduction to children's cognitive development.* New York: Harper & Row.
Reese, H. W. (1989). Rules and rule-governance: Cognitive and behavioristic views. In S. C. Hayes (Ed.), *Rule-governed behavior: Cognition, contingencies, and instructional control* (pp. 3-84). New York: Plenum.
Reese, H. W., & Fremouw, W. J. (1984). Normal and normative ethics in behavioral sciences. *American Psychologist, 39,* 863-876.
Riegler, H. C., Kohler, F. W., & Baer, D. M. (1985, May). *Rule-governed behavior: A discussion of its origins, functions, and maintenance.* Paper presented at the meeting of the Association for Behavior Analysis, Nashville, TN.
Schnaitter, R. (1977). Behaviorism and ethical responsibility. In J. E. Krapfl & E. A. Vargas (Eds.), *Behaviorism and ethics* (pp. 29-42). Kalamazoo, MI: Behaviordelia.
Searle, J. (1976). The rules of the language game [review of N. Chomsky, Reflections on language]. *Times Literary Supplement,* September 10, pp. 1118-1120.
Shultz, T. R., & Robillard, J. (1980). The development of linguistic humour in children: Incongruity through rule violation. In P. E. McGhee & A. J. Chapman (Eds.), *Children's humour* (pp. 59-90). Chichester: Wiley.
Skinner, B. F. (1957). *Verbal behavior.* New York: Appleton-Century- Crofts.
Skinner, B. F. (1969). *Contingencies of reinforcement: A theoretical analysis.* New York: Appleton-Century-Crofts.
Skinner, B. F. (1974). *About behaviorism.* New York: Knopf.
Skinner, B. F. (1977a, September). Between freedom and despotism. *Psychology Today,* pp. 80-91. Reprinted as "Human behavior and democracy" in B. F. Skinner (1978), *Reflections on behaviorism and society* (pp. 3-15). Englewood Cliffs, NJ: Prentice Hall.
Skinner, B. F. (1977b). Why I am not a cognitive psychologist. *Behaviorism, 5(2),* 1-10. Reprinted in B. F. Skinner (1978), *Reflections on behaviorism and society* (pp. 97-112), Englewood Cliffs, NJ: Prentice-Hall.

Skinner, B. F. (1978). Are we free to have a future? In B. F. Skinner, *Reflections on behaviorism and society* (pp. 16-32). Englewood Cliffs, NJ: Prentice-Hall.

Skinner, B. F. (1982). Contrived reinforcement. *The Behavior Analyst, 5,* 3-8.

Slobin, D. I. (1979). *Psycholinguistics* (2nd ed.). Glenview, IL: Scott, Foresman.

Steele, D., & Hayes, S. C. (1991). Stimulus equivalence and arbitrarily applicable relational responding. *Journal of the Experimental Analysis of Behavior, 56,* 515-555.

Thomas, W. I. (1951). *Social behavior and personality: Contributions of W. I. Thomas to theory and social research* (E. H. Vokart, Ed.). New York: Social Science Research Council.

Thomas, W. I., & Thomas, D. S. (1928). *The child in america: Behavior problems and programs.* New York: Knopf.

Zettle, R. D., & Hayes, S. C. (1982). Rule-governed behavior: A potential framework for cognitive-behavioral theory. In P. C. Kendall (Ed.), *Advances in cognitive-behavioral research and therapy* (Vol. 1, pp. 73-118). New York: Academic Press.

Chapter 9

Behavioral Contingency Semantics and the Correspondence Theory of Truth

Ullin T. Place
University of Wales, Bangor

This paper falls into two parts. The first part gives an exposition of what I call "Behavioral Contingency Semantics". The second part examines one of the implications of Behavioral Contingency Semantics, namely, its commitment to a version of the Correspondence Theory of Truth.

Part 1. Behavioral Contingency Semantics

It is now generally accepted by behavior analysts that the effect of a discriminative stimulus is to orientate the behavior of an organism towards the possibility of encountering a particular contingency or type of contingency, where a contingency is defined as a state of affairs whereby, given certain antecedent conditions, behaving in a certain way will have or is liable to have a particular consequence or set of consequences. What is, perhaps, less widely accepted is that the nature of the behavior emitted by the organism, when its behavior is controlled by a discriminative stimulus, depends on the organism's current motivational attitude towards the anticipated consequences of the behavior in terms of which the contingency is defined. The operation of this principle has been demonstrated by Adams and Dickinson (1981) who showed that if a rat's lever pressing response is reinforced by the opportunity to eat a particular foodstuff and that foodstuff is then subjected to a taste aversion procedure outside of the lever-pressing situation, lever-pressing is suppressed by the contingent presentation of the devalued foodstuff despite the fact that the rat has never experienced the taste aversion procedure as a consequence for lever-pressing.

Given this account of the control exercised by discriminative stimuli over behavior, Zettle and Hayes in their 1982 paper on 'Rule-governed behavior' raise a question as to the difference between the stimulus control over behavior which is exercised by a "rule" in the sense which Skinner uses that term in his 'Operant analysis of problem solving' (Skinner, 1966/1988) and the kind of control that is exercised by discriminative stimuli which do not qualify as rules in Skinner's sense. According to Skinner, a rule is "a contingency-specifying stimulus"; though, as Zettle and Hayes point out, he does not explain what he means by the verb "to specify", either in this context or in *Verbal Behavior* (Skinner, 1957) when he speaks of the mand as verbal behavior which is reinforced when the behavior which it "specifies" is emitted by the listener.

From the fact that for Skinner both rules and mands are varieties of verbal behavior (from the standpoint of the speaker) and verbal stimuli (from the standpoint of the listener), it is safe to conclude that the verb "to specify" connotes some distinctive feature of the control exercised by verbal discriminative stimuli over the behavior of the listener. But since Skinner, on his own admission (Skinner, 1989), has had little to say hitherto about the response of the listener, we are left very much to our own devices in trying to work out what difference, if any, there is between verbal and non-verbal discriminative stimuli, between those that do and those that do not "specify" the contingency to the possibility of encountering which they orientate the responding organism.

I hold that the kind of stimulus that "specifies a contingency" is always a string of what are recognizable by a competent listener as words in a particular natural language which together constitute a sentence in that language. By linking words together in accordance with the conventions of sentence construction, a speaker is able to depict or represent to the listener a contingency the like of which the listener may never have personally experienced. It is within this context of novel sentence construction that I would place Hayes' (1991) concept of a "relational frame." Construed in this way, a relational frame is a class of relational or polyadic sentences all of which depict a relation between the same number of terms and from which the same pattern of relational inferences can be deduced. A relational frame in this sense has a place

Table 1

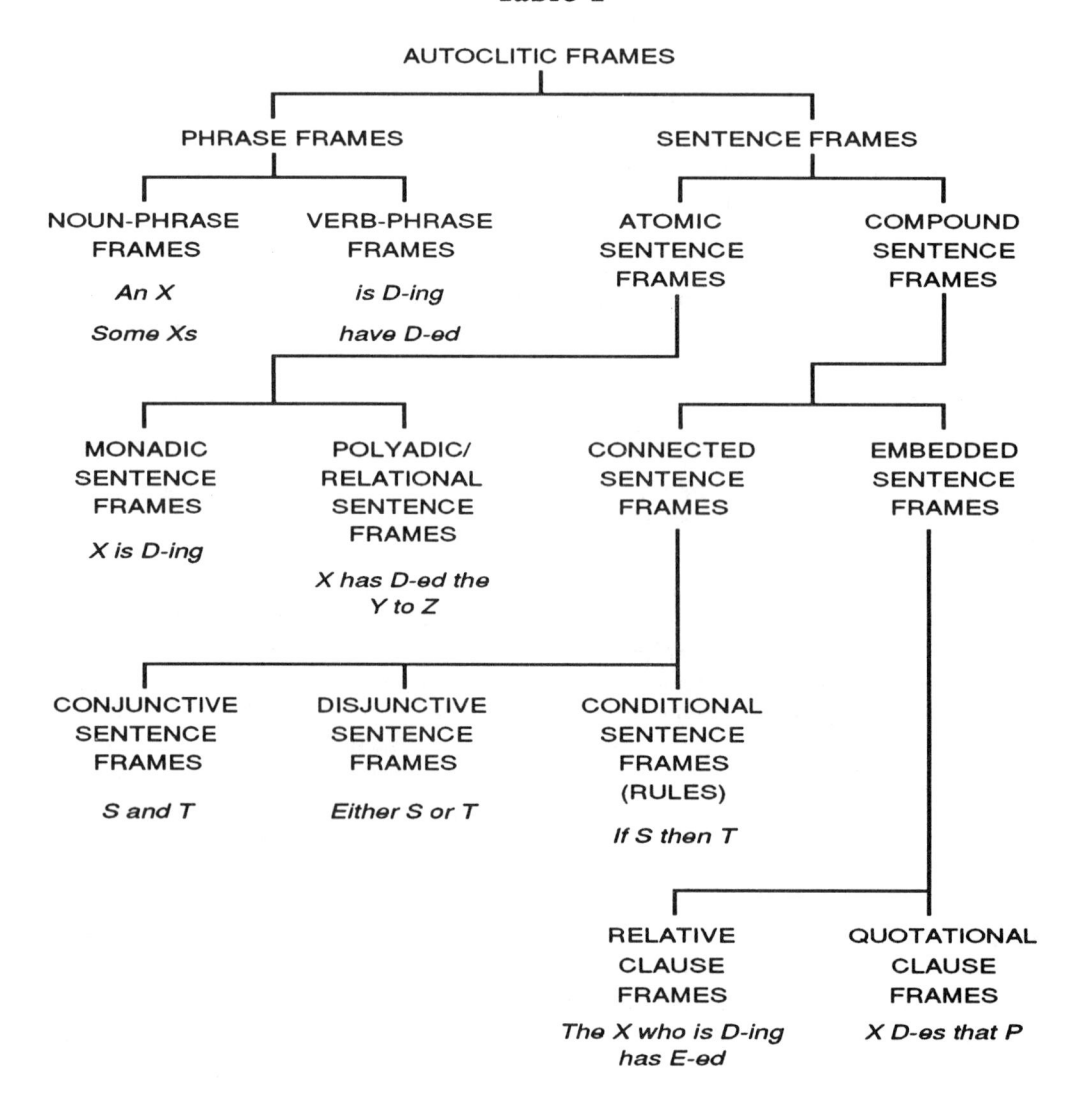

```
                              AUTOCLITIC FRAMES
                    ┌──────────────────────┴──────────────────────┐
              PHRASE FRAMES                                SENTENCE FRAMES
         ┌──────────┴──────────┐                    ┌──────────┴──────────┐
    NOUN-PHRASE           VERB-PHRASE            ATOMIC                COMPOUND
      FRAMES                FRAMES              SENTENCE               SENTENCE
                                                 FRAMES                 FRAMES
      An X                 is D-ing
      Some Xs              have D-ed
                    ┌──────────┴──────────┐              ┌──────────┴──────────┐
               MONADIC              POLYADIC/         CONNECTED            EMBEDDED
              SENTENCE             RELATIONAL         SENTENCE             SENTENCE
               FRAMES               SENTENCE           FRAMES               FRAMES
                                     FRAMES
              X is D-ing
                                  X has D-ed the
                                      Y to Z
         ┌──────────┬──────────┐                              
    CONJUNCTIVE  DISJUNCTIVE  CONDITIONAL
     SENTENCE     SENTENCE     SENTENCE
      FRAMES      FRAMES        FRAMES
                                (RULES)
     S and T    Either S or T
                               If S then T
                                               ┌──────────┴──────────┐
                                          RELATIVE              QUOTATIONAL
                                           CLAUSE                 CLAUSE
                                           FRAMES                 FRAMES
                                     The X who is D-ing       X D-es that P
                                         has E-ed
```

Table 2

Verb + Qualifying Autoclitic(s)	= Verb Phrase
Noun + Quantifying Autoclitic	= Noun Phrase
Verb Phrase + Relational Autoclitic(s) + Noun Phrase(s)	= Atomic Sentence
Atomic Sentence + Manipulative Autoclitic(s) + Atomic Sentence	= Compound Sentence

in a conditional discrimination learning task (the context in which Hayes introduces the term) only in so far as such sentences are used by the subject to formulate the contingency imposed by the experiment.[1]

In this view, relational frames are construed as a special case of the more general category of *simple or atomic sentence frame* which includes single place or monadic predicate frames like *X is bald* as well as polyadic or relational predicate frames like *X is the same as Y* or *X is the opposite of Y* etc., and these in turn as instances of the still more general category of *autoclitic frames*[2] which includes phrase frames and compound sentence frames. The proposed hierarchical organisation of the different types of autoclitic frame is set out with appropriate examples on Table 1. What I am suggesting here is that autoclitic frames of which I take relational frames to be a sub-variety need to be understood in terms of the process which is familiar to us from the work of grammarians and linguists over the centuries, and more recently from the work of Chomsky (1958, etc.) and his followers, whereby words are put together to form phrases, phrases are put together to form the simple sentences which predominate in ordinary conversation and form the clauses which go to make up the compound sentences which predominate in literary and scientific texts. Construed in this way, we can understand an autoclitic frame as an abstract structure to which a phrase or sentence must conform, if the resulting sentence is to exercise effective discriminative control over the behavior of the listener, and the autoclitic as the glue which, as it were, sticks the structure together. I have tried to set out these relationships in Table 2.[3]

Behavior analysts who are accustomed to thinking about verbal behavior in functional or, as the linguists would put it, in pragmatic terms are inclined to become impatient when these abstract structural features of language are discussed. In particular they resent the negatively prescriptive attitude traditionally adopted by the grammarian towards utterances which are functionally effective, but which break one or other of the accepted "rules" of "correct" literary speech. But underlying the niceties of correct literary speech there is a complex set of syntactic and semantic conventions to which the speaker must conform, if his or her utterances are to exercise effective discriminative (semantic) and establishing (pragmatic) control over the behavior of the listener. I use the word "convention" here rather than the word "rule", because "a rule" in Skinner's sense of that word is a verbal formula or sentence, whereas these patterns of socially reinforced behavior need not be, seldom are, and in some cases could never be formulated in words.

In order to breathe life and function into the bare bones of syntactic structure, we need to appreciate that, by conforming to the syntactic and semantic conventions of a natural language, the speaker is able to construct an infinite variety of novel sentences and, by so doing, to control the behavior of any listener, provided he or she is a member of the verbal community within which that set of conventions is reinforced, in an infinite variety of subtle ways.

There are, it is true, a number of signs, gestures and conventional utterances which perform an indispensable role in verbal communication, but which either have no discernible syntactic structure, like nodding the head and uttering *Mmhmm* as an expression of agreement or shaking the head and uttering *Uhuh* as an expression of disagreement, or which *have* a syntactic and semantic structure, but one which has become stereotyped and ossified to the point where its literal meaning has ceased to determine its function. The sentence *How d'ye do?* is a case in point. At one time this sentence was a question used to inquire about the listener's state of health. It is now, and has long been, a conventional response on the part of someone who has just been introduced to a stranger, requiring no response on the part of the listener other than participating in the proffered hand shake and, perhaps, a muttered *How d'ye do?* in return.

These non-sentential signs and stereotyped sentences perform important establishing, reinforcing and disinforcing functions in verbal interactions. What they do not do is exercise any precise discriminative stimulus control over the behavior of the listener. In particular they do not enable the speaker to instate behavior which the listener has never before emitted or convey information to the listener about contingencies which he/she has never previously encountered. In order to do *that*, the speaker must put words together in accordance with conventions which are selectively reinforced within the relevant verbal community in such a way as to form a string which constitutes a semantically coherent and syntactically complete sentence.

The fact that the listener can often anticipate the drift of the speaker's sentence before it reaches the conclusion that syntax demands in no way alters the fact that only a semantically coherent and syntactically complete sentence can be relied on to exercise effective discriminative control over the behavior of any competent listener who is a member of the verbal community constituted by speakers and interpreters of the natural language or code to which the sentence in question belongs. Moreover, only by constructing a new sentence on each occasion of utterance can the speaker exercise the kind of discriminative control over the behavior of the listener which does not rely, as do other forms of discriminative control, on a past history of an association between stimuli resembling the currently controlling discriminative stimulus and the contingency towards the possibility of encountering which the behavior of the organism is thereby alerted.

It is true, of course, that the more common "tact"[4] or "lexical" words, by which I mean the more common nouns, verbs, adjectives and adverbs, have been repeatedly associated in the listener's past history with contingencies involving the kinds of object, event or property which they are said to "connote". It is likewise true that the various sentence frames which individual sentences instantiate have been repeatedly associated in the listener's past history with recurrent patterns which are common to a wide variety of different contingencies or contingency terms. Nevertheless in most cases the particular combination of a particular sentence frame with a particular set of lexical or "tact" words which fill the gaps or "argument places" in the frame is one which has never previously occurred in the past history of the listener and, consequently, has never previously been associated in the course of that history with the contingency to the possibility of encountering which the listener is nevertheless alerted.

This ability of novel sentences to act as discriminative stimuli for the listener with respect contingencies the like of which he or she has never previously encountered is explained by means of the principle which I have referred to elsewhere (Place 1983) as "Behavioral Contingency Semantics". This is a version of Wittgenstein's (1921/1971) Picture Theory of the meaning of sentences according to which a sentence is a kind of map or plan which depicts or represents or purports to depict or represent either an actual situation which currently exists or has existed in the past or one whose future existence is either predicted or demanded from the listener.

The concept of a "situation" which I have used in this definition comes from the so-called

Behavioral Contingency Semantics

"Situation Semantics" which has been developed in recent years by the American philosophers Jon Barwise and John Perry, the most accessible account of which is to be found in their (1983) book *Situations and Attitudes*. For Barwise and Perry situations are of two kinds, *states of affairs* in which one or more properties of an entity and/or relations between two or more entities remain unchanged over a period of time and *events* in which the properties of an entity and/or the relations between entities undergo change either at a moment of time (instantaneous event) or over an extended period of time (process).

The distinctive contributions of Behavioral Contingency Semantics are the suggestions
1. that the situation or situations depicted by a sentence constitute for the listener a part, or occasionally the whole, of what Skinner (1969) calls a "three-term contingency", consisting of (a) a set of *antecedent conditions*, (b) some *behavior* called for under those conditions either from the listener or, as in the case of a narrative, from someone with whom the listener identifies, and (c) the probable or actual *consequences* of so behaving, and
2. that by constructing, in the form of a sentence, a representation of one or more terms of a contingency, the speaker provides the listener with a discriminative stimulus which alerts him or her to the possibility of encountering the contingency one or more of whose terms (antecedent, behavior or consequence) is thereby specified.

It is proposed that this sentential representation exercises stimulus control over the behavior of the listener by virtue of an isomorphism or point-to-point correspondence between the form and content of the sentence on the one hand and the form and content of the contingency or contingency term which is thereby represented or specified on the other. It should be emphasised, however, that the contingency or contingency term which a sentence specifies is not an actually existing situation. The situation or sequence of situations represented by a sentence is what Brentano (1874/1973) calls an "intentional object". In other words, it is the *kind* of situation or sequence of situations to the possibility of encountering which hearing or reading the sentence alerts the listener and towards encountering which the listener's behavior is thereby orientated. All that actually exists in such a case is the speaker's emission of the sentence and the orientation of the listener's behavior which occurs as a consequence of hearing or reading what the speaker has said. When we talk about what a sentence "represents", "specifies" or "means", all we are doing is characterising the behavioral orientation which the sentence evokes or is capable of evoking from any competent listener who is a member of the relevant verbal community by describing the kind of situation or sequence of situations which the listener is thereby alerted to encounter.

But just as there is a point to point correspondence, on this view, between the form and content of the sentence and the form and content of the contingency term or complete contingency (situation or situation sequence) that is thereby specified, so there is a point to point correspondence between the form and content of the sentence on the one hand and the form and content of an actual situation which either exists, has existed in the past or will exist in the future in the case where a declarative sentence is true or will exist in the future in a case where an imperative sentence is subsequently complied with.

In order to give substance to this notion of a double correspondence between the sentence and the situation which it specifies and between the specified situation and the actual situation, we need three things:
1. a way of analysing sentences which brings out their various components and the way they are related to one another,
2. a way of analysing contingencies and the situations of which they are composed which brings out those features of them to which the various components of the sentence correspond, and
3. an account of the way the one analysis maps onto the other.

In selecting an appropriate analysis for sentences I have made use of two reasonably well known logical principles:
1. an account of the way in which compound sentences are built up out of simple or atomic sentences, using such logical devices or "manipulative autoclitics", to use Skinner's (1957 pp.340-342) term, as conjunction *Both s and t*, disjunction *Either s or t*, the conditional *If s then t*, or the embedding of one sentence within another, either in the form of a relative clause used to make an identifying reference to some object or person or in the form of a quotation of what someone has or might say or think, and
2. Frege's (1879; 1891) analysis of the internal structure of atomic sentences in terms of the distinction between function and argument place.

For our present purposes the most important variety of compound sentence is the compound conditional sentence of the form *If s then t*. The importance of sentences of this type is that they provide us with a formal syntactic criterion both for distinguishing 'rules', in Skinner's (1966/1988) sense, from other types of sentence, and for drawing the important distinction between *prescriptive rules*, like *If the baby cries, give it a bottle*, in which the consequent is in the imperative mood, and *descriptive rules*, like *If you give the baby a bottle, it will go back to sleep*, in which the consequent is in the future tense of the indicative or declarative mood. This distinction between Prescriptive and Descriptive Rules is close to if not identical both with the distinction which Hayne Reese draws in his chapter between "Normative" and "Normal Rules" and with the distinction drawn by Zettle and Hayes (1982) between "Plies" (or, to use their spelling, "Plys") and "Tracks".

Frege's function and argument analysis which I use to analyse the internal structure of an atomic sentence, was originally conceived in order to account for sentence pairs like $2+2=4$ and $4=2+2$ or like *John loves Mary* and *Mary is loved by John* whose equivalence cannot be handled in terms of the traditional Subject-Predicate analysis which had dominated logical, grammatical and philosophical thinking since the days of Aristotle. The term "function" here is being used in its mathematical rather than its biological sense in which, for example, $2+2=4$ is an instance of the function $x+y=z$ or $z=x+y$ where the function is represented by the autoclitics $+$ and $=$ and the three argument places generated by the function are represented by the variables x, y and z which in this case are occupied by the numerals 2, 2 and 4. Likewise in *John loves Mary* the function *loves* creates two argument places occupied by the proper names *John* and *Mary* respectively.

In the fourth of my papers on Skinner's *Verbal Behavior* in *Behaviorism* (Place 1983), I illustrated the application of Frege's notion to sentences in natural language by the example of a sentence drawn from T.Whellan's *History of York and the North Riding* (1859) where, under the entry for Marton-in-the-Forest, we read *Ascitel de Bulmer purchased Marton of King Henry I*. In this sentence the function is the verb phrase *purchased*. This function generates three "substantial" or "concrete" argument places as I call them which are occupied respectively by the names or descriptions of:
1. the purchaser, in this case *Ascitel de Bulmer*,
2. the vendor, in this case *King Henry I* and
3. the property sold, in this case the village or estate of *Marton-in-the-Forest*.

In addition to these three "substantial"[6] argument places the function, which can appear either in the form *buy/purchase* or in the form *sell*, generates three additional "abstract" argument places whose filling in this particular sample sentence remains either unspecified, as in the case of the price paid (let us say that it was 25 shillings) and the place where the transaction was executed (let us suppose that it was at York) or, as in the case of the time at which the transaction took place, is indicated approximately and indirectly by the information that the vendor was the monarch

Behavioral Contingency Semantics

whose reign coincided with the early years of the 12th century (let us suppose that a more precise date for the transaction was Whitsuntide 1107).[7]

Table 3. shows the complete sentence, with all its six argument places filled, in the form of a six spoke wheel with the functional expression at the hub. Given this basic pattern, it now transpires that there are at least eight different ways of constructing this sentence each of which is derived from the others by the principles of grammatical transformation beloved of the generative grammarians, the effect of which is to alter the position of the various argument places within the sentence so as to bring the occupant of each argument place and, finally, the functional expression itself into the focus of attention by putting it into the crucial subject position at the beginning of the sentence. Thus if we begin with

1. *Ascitel de Bulmer purchased Marton of King Henry I for 25s. at York on Whitsuntide 1107*,

substituting *sold* for *purchased* we get

2. *King Henry I sold Marton to Ascitel de Bulmer for 25s. at York on Whitsuntide 1107*;

by Active to Passive transformation Version 1 yields

3. *Marton was purchased by Ascitel de Bulmer from King Henry I for 25s. at York on Whitsuntide 1107*;

likewise Version 2 yields

4. *Marton was sold by King Henry I to Ascitel de Bulmer for 25s. at York on Whitsuntide 1107*;

Table 3

bringing the price into the focus of attention gives us

5. *25s. was the price paid by Ascitel de Bulmer when he purchased Marton of King Henry I at York on Whitsuntide 1107;*

bringing the location of the transaction into focus gives

6. *York was the place where the sale of Marton by King Henry I to Ascitel de Bulmer for 25s. took place on Whitsuntide 1107;*

bringing the date of the transaction into focus yields

7. *Whitsuntide 1107 was the date when the sale of Marton by King Henry I to Ascitel de Bulmer for 25s. took place at York;*

finally we can bring the function itself into focus with

8. *The sale of Marton by King Henry I to Ascitel de Bulmer for 25s. took place at York on Whitsuntide 1107.*

Turning now to the analysis of extra-verbal reality to which this syntactic analysis of sentences corresponds, we find that this "metaphysical analysis", as we may appropriately call it, has three sources:
1. Barwise and Perry's (1983) concept of a Situation,

Table 4

Syntactic Unit		Metaphysical Unit
Prescriptive-Descriptive Rule	->	Complete three-term contingency - Antecedent, Behavior, Consequence
Prescriptive Rule	->	Antecedent and Behavior
Descriptive Rule	->	Behavior and Consequence
Function/Predicate/Verb Phrase	->	Property or relation which persists or changes
Verb Phrase with continuous aspect	->	State of affairs, property or relation which persists
Verb Phrase with non-continuous aspect	->	Event, property or relation which changes
Noun phrase in subject, direct or indirect object argument places in an atomic sentence	->	Substance/entity whose property persists or changes or which stands in a relation which persists or changes

2. Skinner's (1969) concept of the Three-term Contingency,
3. The mapping proposed by Aristotle between sentences analysed into Subject and Predicate Terms on the one hand and a Substance or enduring space-occupying entity and its Properties on the other.

We have seen that the term "situation", as used by Barwise and Perry, covers both states-of-affairs which persist without change over a period of time and events in which something changes either at or over time. Any situation in this sense can be regarded from the standpoint of a behaving organism as one of the terms of a three-term contingency. However the same situation constitutes a different contingency term for a different organism. For example, the event constituted by a baby's crying may be a consequence with respect to behavior of someone whose behavior woke the baby, behavior on the part of the baby itself and an establishing antecedent condition which calls for behavior on the part of the mother or baby sitter. When we ask what it is that persists in a state of affairs or changes in an event, we can think of it as either a property of what Aristotle calls a substance, i.e. a discrete spatio-temporally extended body or a relation between two or more such entities or between different parts of one such entity. The correspondence between this metaphysical analysis and the syntactic analysis of the sentence is given in Table 4.

Part 2. The Correspondence Theory of Truth

Having, I hope, given something of the flavour of Behavioral Contingency Semantics, I now want to turn to a discussion of the Correspondence Theory of Truth. Behavioral Contingency Semantics is committed to the Correspondence Theory of Truth by its endorsement of a correspondence between the situation which the sentence specifies and, in the case of a true declarative sentence, a situation which either has existed, exists now or will exist in the future at the time and place specified in the sentence. My reason for raising this issue is that there are a number of behavior analysts, including some of the contributors to this volume, who would subscribe to the following five propositions all of which with the possible exception of the first are, to my mind, patently false:
1. There are three principal theories of Truth, the Correspondence Theory, the Coherence Theory and the Pragmatic Theory.
2. These theories are mutually exclusive in the sense that subscribing to one theory is incompatible with subscribing to the other two.
3. Different scientific methodologies involve subscribing to a different theory of Truth.
4. The scientific methodology of Behavior Analysis involves its practitioners in subscribing to the Pragmatic Theory of Truth.

Given these premises, we can deduce:

5. The scientific methodology of Behavior Analysis is incompatible with subscribing to either the Correspondence or the Coherence Theory of Truth.

The contrasting theory of truth to which I subscribe and which I would recommend to other behavior analysts takes as its starting point the principle that truth and falsity are properties of things called "propositions". For these purposes a proposition is defined as a family of declarative sentence utterances, both actual and possible, whose members are to be found in every natural language which possesses the conceptual resources required in order to formulate an appropriate sentence. A sentence utterance belongs to the family of sentence utterances which "express the same proposition", if every member of the family
1. specifies the same situation or kind of situation,
2. has the same truth value (either "true" or "false") as every other member, and
3. uses the same or corresponding device (proper name, definite description or indexical) to make

identifying reference to each of the entities involved, their spatial location and the temporal location of the situation itself.

From a functional or pragmatic perspective to say that a proposition in this sense is true is to say that any member of the family of sentence utterances which constitute the proposition in question can be relied upon in constructing a plan of action in relation to that part or aspect of the environment to which the proposition relates; whereas any sentence which contradicts it cannot be similarly relied upon. However, sentences expressing true propositions can be relied upon in constructing and executing a plan of action, only in so far as all the sentences which make up the plan of action are similarly true. Only if they are, will the plan of action so formed accurately and completely depict the contingencies involved. Only in so far as the contingencies are accurately depicted, can the plan of action be relied upon to succeed.

A proposition can be relied upon to contribute to the construction of a complete and accurate specification of the contingencies by which an agent is confronted, only if it is true; and a proposition is true only if

1. it forms part of a system of propositions (beliefs) accepted as true within a verbal community which is coherent in the sense that no two propositions which manifestly contradict one another are tolerated within the system, i.e., the system conforms to the principle of non-contradiction which holds that if two propositions contradict one another they cannot both be true,
2. to the extent that it purports to specify a situation which either has existed in the past, exists now or will exist in the future, there is a correspondence between the situation specified and the actual situation.

It will be apparent that this definition of truth combines elements from all three of the traditional theories of Truth, the Pragmatic Theory, the Coherence Theory and the Correspondence Theory. The Pragmatic Theory is used to provide an account of the adaptive function of preferring true propositions to false ones as a basis for the individual's rule-governed behavior, and hence of the importance that is attached, within the verbal community, to discriminating between true and false propositions. But while the Pragmatic Theory can tell us why truth and its discrimination are important, what it cannot tell us is what the truth of a proposition consists in.

On the present view there is no single answer to the question, "What does the truth of a proposition consist in?" which is true for all true propositions. For this purpose true propositions need to be classified into two classes. On the one hand we have a class of propositions which are true solely by virtue of the relation between the conventions governing the sentence frames which they instantiate and those governing the linguistic expressions which occupy the argument places thus formed. For example, the sentence frame *All X's are Y's* yields a true proposition of this kind when *bachelor* is substituted for X and *unmarried man* for Y to yield the proposition *All bachelors are unmarried men*. Again the sentence frame $x + y = z$ yields a true proposition of this kind when we substitute *2* for both x and y and *4* for z, yielding the true proposition *2 + 2 = 4*. Such propositions were said by Hume to express "relations between ideas" or, as we would say nowadays, "relations between concepts". They were described by Kant as "analytic", although he would not have agreed that arithmetical propositions are analytic.[8] Propositions of this kind are also *necessary truths* in the original Aristotelian sense of a proposition which it is self-contradictory to deny. Moreover, their truth is established *a priori*, in so far as it is fixed by the pre-existing conventions of the language; and no empirical observations, other than those required to determine the reinforcement practices of the verbal community in question, are relevant to their truth. Truth in these cases is determined entirely in accordance with the principle of Coherence.

Coherence in the sense of conformity to the linguistic conventions is also a necessary condition of the truth of the other contrasting variety of true proposition which Hume described as expressing "matters of fact", and which Kant called "synthetic". In this case, however, coherence, though necessary, is not sufficient for truth. There must also be a correspondence between what is said on the one hand and some state or event in the extra-linguistic environment on the other. Such propositions are said to be *contingently* true in that there is no self-contradiction involved in supposing them to be false. They are also *empirical* in the sense that their truth can only be established by demonstrating their coherence with results of observation.

But while it is true of these factual propositions, as we may call them, both that their truth consists in a correspondence between the proposition and some actually existing situation in the extra-linguistic environment and that empirical observation is required to determine their truth, it is a grievous mistake, but one which is often made, to suppose that what is observed in such cases *is* the correspondence between what is said and the way things are in the extra-linguistic environment. What gives substance to this mistaken view is the notion that when a theoretical proposition of science is tested empirically, a prediction is made on the basis of theory as to the outcome of an experiment and this prediction is then verified or falsified, confirmed or disconfirmed, as the case may be, by its correspondence or lack of correspondence with observation statements describing the actual outcome.

Two points need making. Firstly the principle that is appealed to when theoretical predictions are said to be confirmed by the agreement with or correspondence to the actual outcome is not in fact the principle of correspondence between what is said and the actual situation which the proposition specifies, it is rather the principle of coherence in the form of the principle that all true propositions must be consistent with one another. Indeed the reason why a single observation only weakly confirms and by no means establishes the truth of the theory on which the prediction is based is that in order to establish the truth of a theory, you must be able to show that that theory and only that theory is consistent with *all* the propositions which are relevant to its truth and whose truth has been established beyond doubt on other grounds. This, I submit, is totally unintelligible on an account which supposes that correspondence with *observation* is what makes a theory true.

My second point is that the correspondence which is spoken of in the Correspondence Theory of Truth, as I understand it, is not a correspondence between theoretical sentences and observation, as this mistaken view implies, but a correspondence between both theoretical sentences and observation sentences, in so far as they purport to describe matters of fact, and the situations, the events and states of affairs, they describe. That this cannot be a matter of direct apprehension or observation becomes apparent when we consider the case of a very simple observation sentence like *This is a table* uttered, as in the present case, in the presence of the kind of situation which it specifies and to which on the Correspondence Theory it corresponds. In a case such as this we can simultaneously hear the sentence and see the situation which it describes or specifies. What we cannot either see or hear is the correspondence between them; not because it isn't there, but because it is a function of the linguistic conventions to which speakers must conform if their utterances are to be reinforced by other members of the English-speaking verbal community.

The same goes for the Spanish *Esto es una mesa* which specifies the same situation by virtue of the conventions to which utterances must conform, if they are to be reinforced by the Spanish-speaking verbal community. The correspondence between these sentences and the situation which they specify exists only by virtue of the reinforcement practices of the relevant verbal community and will continue to exist only so long as those reinforcement practices are maintained.

Although we can justifiably claim to have intuitive knowledge of the kind of situation which the English sentence *This is a table* specifies, intuitive knowledge, as Skinner points out in 'An operant analysis of problem solving', is both acquired and maintained by the contingency-shaping of the behavior involved by repeated exposure to the consequences of emitting that behavior in the appropriate context. In this case the relevant consequences are those provided by the verbal community, when the sentence is uttered in the presence of the situation which it purports to describe. It is this opportunity which it provides for the speaker's utterance to be reinforced in the presence of the situation it describes which, in my view, is the key to the importance of the observation sentence as the foundation of empirical knowledge. By uttering a sentence like *This is a table* in the presence both of an actual table and of one or preferably more fully competent members of the English-speaking verbal community, the speaker's verbal behavior will be reinforced by the other speakers present, always provided that it conforms to the syntactic and semantic conventions governing its construction and use. The speaker is thereby reassured that he or she is using his or her words and sentence frames in accordance with the accepted conventions and that the sentences he or she constructs using those words and sentence frames will have the desired effect on the behavior of any listener who is a member of the verbal community in question on relevantly similar occasions in the future.

This view of the epistemological function of observation sentences has a number of important consequences. I shall mention only a few of them. The first is a consequence which connects up with a principle which is fundamental to Behaviorism as a standpoint both in Psychology and in Philosophy, the principle of objectivity in scientific observation. This principle contrasts with the subjectivist epistemology of Ernst Mach (1885) and, following him, of the Logical Positivists who saw the observation of private sense-data as the ultimate foundation of empirical knowledge.

If the function of observation sentences is to ensure correspondence between what is said and what is described by giving the verbal community the opportunity to reinforce a sentence utterance in the presence of the situation it describes, it follows that the only kind of observation sentence that can perform this function is an observation sentence describing a *state of affairs* (events tend to disappear too quickly into the past) in the common stimulus environment of one and preferably more observers who are members of the relevant verbal community and can agree that the sentence correctly describes the state of affairs in question. There is just no way that an observation sentence describing a private event could conceivably perform this function.

That is why Comte (1830-42) was right to insist that introspective observation could never provide a basis for an empirical science, and, since in his day Psychology was defined as the science which uses introspection as its only source of empirical data, right to insist that Psychology, so defined, could never be a science. That is why J.B.Watson (1913) was right to insist that if Psychology is to be a science, its observational data must be the publicly observable behavior of living organisms. That is why Wittgenstein (1953) was right to insist that our ordinary mental concepts are used primarily to describe and explain public behavior, and that, in those cases where we *do* talk about our own private events, we can only do so by characterising an experience in terms of its "publicly observable concomitants", both on the stimulus and on the response side, in the standard or typical case.

Mention of Wittgenstein brings me to the second consequence of this view which I would like to discuss, namely, the light which it throws on that cryptic remark which he makes in paragraph 242 of *Philosophical Investigations I* (1953)

"If language is to be a means of communication there must be agreement not only in definitions but also (queer as this may sound) in judgments."

Taken at its face value, it might be supposed that what Wittgenstein is saying here is that communication is only possible if there is total agreement in judgments between speaker and listener. Clearly this cannot be right. So unless we are prepared to dismiss this statement of Wittgenstein's as an aberration, we must suppose that there are some kinds of judgment on which there must be agreement if communication is to occur and others on which there need not be agreement.

There are no doubt other judgments on which speaker and listener must agree in order for effective communication to be possible. For example, as Strawson points out in his book *Individuals* (1959), some of the basic facts of local history and geography must be agreed, if identifying reference is to be made to objects, persons and events remote in time and or place from the context of utterance. But agreement between speaker and listener on the correct description of the more salient features of their common public environment is even more fundamental than this to the process of linguistic communication. If you won't agree with my judgment that this in front of us is a table, I begin to lose my grip on how we are using words, and so, I suggest, do you.

This brings me to the third and final consequence of this view of observation sentences to which I would like to draw attention, namely, the light which it throws on the practice whereby speakers frequently emit "tact"[9] or descriptive sentences which are often unsolicited or solicited only out of politeness and which are reinforced by an expression of agreement on the part of the listener and where this expression of agreement is frequently pursued by an expression like *Right?*, *True?*, *Not so?*. Again the assurance which this agreement provides that the speaker is using his words in accordance with the standard conventions accepted within the verbal community is part, but only part, of the explanation for this phenomenon.

The other factor which would take us too far afield to explore adequately is the speaker's need, in his or her capacity as agent, to have a stock of ready-made descriptive rules or beliefs which can be called upon as required to govern his or her behavior in relation to the contingencies which they specify. In order to perform this function effectively it is important that, as far as possible, all of the beliefs in the stock be true, that they should combine to provide accurate predictions of future outcomes on which effective action can be based, and that they should include beliefs relating to as wide a variety of possible future contingencies as can be achieved.

All members of the verbal community share this need for a reliable and comprehensive stock of rules or contingency-specifying beliefs which they can use to govern both their own individual behavior and that of the group in any co-operative venture undertaken with other community members. Moreover, a rule which correctly specifies a contingency which operates in the common public environment for one member of the verbal community will do so for all. It is, therefore, in the interest of every community member to co-operate with others to ensure the construction and maintenance of a common stock of such beliefs within the community which each individual member can rely on in constructing his or her individual stock.

However, this stock of common beliefs which is maintained within the verbal community by the constant exchange of information and opinions between its members is not just a resource on which members can draw in constructing their own individual stocks, it also provides a standard against which the truth of the individual's beliefs are evaluated and to which they must conform, if their utterance is to be reinforced by an appropriate expression of agreement.

Since it is informed by the collective reinforcement history of the group going back over the centuries, this collective view is on balance more likely to be true, and hence reliable as a basis for behavior, than is that of a single individual who has only his or her own experience to go on. Nevertheless *vox populi* is not always *vox dei*. The opinions endorsed within the verbal community must eventually give way, if they can be shown to conflict with observation sentences which are consistently reinforced by the verbal community in the presence of the situation which the observation sentence describes. Though, as the history of science repeatedly demonstrates, beliefs which are deeply entrenched in the collective view will survive repeated and unambiguous disconfirmation by the empirical evidence, unless and until an alternative is found which integrates the new observations with the rest of the existing stock of beliefs without conflicting with any of those beliefs, apart from the ones it replaces.

This brings me to my final point. We have been concerned thus far with the metaphysical question of what truth consists in; not with the epistemological question about how we tell true propositions from false ones, and about the criteria we can use for this purpose. Nevertheless, certain consequences with respect to this epistemological question can be deduced from the account that has been given.

If I am right in thinking that we can never observe correspondence between a sentence and the reality it depicts, it follows that correspondence cannot be a criterion of truth; even though, if I am right, it is what the truth of a synthetic proposition consists in. That leaves us effectively with only two criteria of truth, the pragmatic criterion - what works - and the coherence criterion - what agrees. The principal application of the pragmatic criterion is in evaluating the truth value of factual-synthetic propositions; although, if I am right in thinking that arithmetical truths are analytic, the practical utility of arithmetic and other forms of mathematical reasoning is not wholly irrelevant in persuading us of the truth of at least some analytic propositions.

The coherence criterion, on the other hand, operates somewhat differently in the case of analytic propositions than in the case of synthetic ones. In the case of an analytic statement, it is a matter of relying on intuition and demonstration to show that the denial of the statement involves an inescapable contradiction sooner or later. In the case of a synthetic proposition, it is a matter demonstrating that the proposition in question is at least consistent with and preferably entails a greater number and variety of objective observation sentences than any alternative that has been suggested hitherto. These truth criteria, *pace* the Pepperians (Pepper, 1942), are not in conflict. They reinforce and supplement one another. And we need all the help we can get.

References

Adams, C. D. & Dickinson, A. (1981). Instrumental responding following reinforcer devaluation. *Quarterly Journal of Experimental Psychology, 33,* 109-112.

Barwise, J. & Perry, J. (1983). *Situations and attitudes.* Cambridge, Massachusetts: M.I.T. Press.

Brentano, F. (1874/1973). *Psychologie vom empirischen Standpunkt.* Leipzig: Duncker u. Humblot. English translation as *Psychology from an empirical standpoint.* L. L. McAlister (Ed.). London: Routledge & Kegan Paul.

Chomsky, N. (1958). *Syntactic structures.* Gravenhage: Mouton.

Comte, A. (1830-1842). *Cours de philosophie positive.* 6 vols. Paris.

Crystal, D. (1985). *A dictionary of linguistics and phonetics.* Oxford: Blackwell.

Ekwall, E. (1959). Etymological notes on English place-names. *Lunds Universitets Årsskrift. N.F.* Avd.1 Bd.53 Nr 5. (*Lund Studies in English.* XXVII.)

Farrer, W. (1915). *Early Yorkshire Charters,* Vol.II. Edinburgh: Ballantyne, Hanson & Co.

Frege, G. (1879/1960). *Begriffschrift.* English translation P. T. Geach. In P. T. Geach & M. Black (Eds.), *Translations from the philosophical writings of Gottlob Frege,* 2nd. Ed. Oxford: Blackwell.

Frege, G. (1891/1960). Function and concept. *Jenaischer Gesellschaft für Medicin und Naturwissenschaft.* English translation P. T. Geach. In P. T. Geach & M. Black (Eds.), *Translations from the philosophical writings of Gottlob Frege,* 2nd. Ed. Oxford: Blackwell, 1960.

Hayes, S. C. (1991). A relational control theory of stimulus equivalence. In L. J. Hayes and P. N. Chase (Eds.), *Dialogues on verbal behavior* (pp. 19-40). Reno, Nevada: Context Press.

Mach, E. (1885). *Contributions to the analysis of the sensations.* English translation C. M. Williams.

Chicago: Open Court, 1897.
Page, W. (1912). *The Victoria history of the County of York*, Vol.II. London: Constable.
Pepper, S. C. (1942). *World hypotheses.* Berkeley, California: University of California Press.
Place, U. T. (1983). Skinner's *Verbal Behavior* IV - How to improve Part IV, Skinner's account of syntax. *Behaviorism, 11,* 163-186.
Place, U. T. (1985). Three senses of the word "tact". *Behaviorism, 13,* 63-74
Place, U. T. (in press). Some remarks on the social relativity of truth and the analytic/synthetic distinction. *Human Studies.*
Quine, W. v. O. (1953). Two dogmas of empiricism. In *From a logical point of view.* Cambridge, Massachusetts: Harvard University Press.
Sidman, M. (1971). Reading and audio-visual equivalences. *Journal of Speech and Hearing Research, 14,* 5-13.
Sidman, M. & Tailby, W. (1982). Conditional discrimination vs. matching to sample: an expansion of the testing paradigm. *Journal of the Experimental Analysis of Behavior, 37,* 5-22.
Skinner, B. F. (1957). *Verbal behavior.* New York: Appleton-Century-Crofts.
Skinner, B. F. (1966/1988). An operant analysis of problem solving. In B. Kleinmuntz (Ed.), *Problem solving: Research, method and theory.* New York: Wiley. Reprinted with revisions and peer commentary in A. C. Catania and S. Harnad (Eds.), *The selection of behavior. The operant behaviorism of B. F. Skinner: Comments and consequences.* Cambridge: Cambridge University Press, pp. 218-236.
Skinner, B. F. (1969). *Contingencies of reinforcement.* New York: Appleton-Century-Crofts.
Skinner, B. F. (1989). The behavior of the listener. In S. C. Hayes (Ed.), *Rule-governed behavior: Cognition, contingencies and instructional control* (pp. 85-96). New York: Plenum.
Steele, D. L. & Hayes, S. C. (1991). Stimulus equivalence and arbitrarily applicable relational responding. *Journal of the Experimental Analysis of Behavior, 56,* 519-555.
Strawson, P. F. (1959). *Individuals.* London: Methuen.
Watson, J. B. (1913). Psychology as the behaviorist views it. *Psychological Review, 20,* 158-177.
Whellan, T. & Co. (1859). *History and topography of the City of York and the North Riding of Yorkshire* (Volume II). Beverley: John Green.
Wittgenstein, L. (1921/1971). Tractatus logico-philosophicus *Annalen der naturphilosophie. Tractatus Logico-Philosophicus* with second English translation by D. F. Pears & B. F. McGuinness, Second Edition, London: Routledge and Kegan Paul.
Wittgenstein, L. (1953). *Philosophical investigations.* English Translation by G. E. M. Anscombe. Oxford: Blackwell.
Zettle, R. B. & Hayes, S. C. (1982). Rule-governed behavior: A potential theoretical framework for cognitive behavior therapy. In P. C. Kendall (Ed.), *Advances in cognitive-behavioral research and therapy* (Vol.1). New York: Academic Press.

Footnotes

1. This is not Hayes' concept of a "relational frame." For him, a relational frame is a pattern of derived and mutually transformed stimulus functions, of which *stimulus equivalence,* as defined by Sidman (Sidman, 1971; Sidman & Tailby, 1982), is a special case. According to Hayes (1991; see also Steele & Hayes, 1991), patterns of spontaneous generalization are found that conform to relations other than equivalence, such as 'different from' or 'is a cause of.' Both Sidman and Hayes would reject the implications of the present analysis that such generalizations are based on a verbal construal of the relation between the stimuli.
2. Skinner's (1957, p. 336) introduction of this term accords with the standard usage of the term 'frame' in grammar. A 'frame' is defined by Crystal (1985) in his *A Dictionary of Linguistics*

and Phonetics as "the structural context within which a class of items can be used. For example, the frame *He saw _____ box* provides an environment for the use of determiners (*the, a, my,* etc.)." Crystal's example is a sentence frame. Skinner's example of an autoclitic frame (*"the boy's _____ "*) is a noun-phrase frame.

3. Skinner's "descriptive autoclitics" (Skinner, 1957, pp. 313-320) are not included in Table 2. A descriptive autoclitic, in these terms, is a quotational-clause frame in which the speaker's indentifying indexical ("I") occupies the subject position in the main clause. In this case, however, what is syntactically the embedded subordinate clause is not a quotation, as it is when the subject is in the third position. It is rather a disguised main clause in which the speaker makes an assertion and uses what is syntactically the main clause as an autoclitic device to indicate the confidence with which the assertion is made or otherwise modify its effect on the listener.

4. For this use of Skinner's term "tact," see Place (1985).

5. *s* and *tt* here are to be interpreted as sentences which may or may not have a truth value, and not, as in the propositional calculus, as propositions whose truth value is determinable independently of the truth value (if it has one) of the compound sentence as a whole.

6. *substantial* in the sense that their natural occupants are the names and descriptions of what Aristotle called "substances," or dimensionally extended "space-time worms," such as living organisms, their artifacts and other enduring entities from galaxies down to sub-atomic particles.

7. The charter putting this transaction into effect is not amongst those relating to the fee of Bulmer (to which Marton belonged) in Volume II of Farrer's *Early Yorkshire Charters* (Farrer, 1915) and must be presumed lost. Consequently, there is no means of knowing precisely when and where it took place and at what price. It seems unlikely, however, that Ascitel de Bulmer would have been qualified to act as Sheriff of York, as he did from c. 1114 until the time of his death in c. 1129, if he had not already acquired the status of tenant-in-chief with respect to the estate from which he and his descendents derived their surname. We know (Page, 1912, p. 222) that at the time of the Domesday survey (1086) the Bulmer lands were held by Nigel Fossard as tenant of the Count of Mortain. We also have evidence of a close connection between the Fossards and the de Bulmers. Ascitel de Bulmer is named in a document of the 1120's (Farrer, 1915, p. 339) as steward to Nigel's son Robert Fossard whose daughter Emma was married to Ascitel's son Bertram de Bulmer (Farrer, 1915, p. 128). This makes it tolerably certain that Ascitel was both steward and tenant with respect to the Bulmer fee to Robert's father Nigel. It suggests further that his acquisition of the tenancy-in-chief of the Bulmer fee was part of the disposal of the fee of Count William of Mortain, when it was forfeited to King Henry as a consequence of the defeat (at the battle of Tinchebrai in September 1106) of a rebellion led by the count in an attempt to unseat the king and reunite the crown of England with the Dukedom of Normandy under the Conqueror's eldest son Duke Robert. It would seem that, as a result of this forfeiture, Nigel Fossard was allowed to acquire (presumably by purchase) the tenancy-in-chief of most of the land which he had previously held as tenant of the count. However, in the case of the Bulmer fee he appears to have ceded his right of purchase to the man who was his steward and sub-tenant with respect to that part of his former estate. The name *Ascitel* (from Old Scandinavian *Asketill*) no doubt indicates a lower social status than that of the other men who were or became tenants-in-chief in Yorkshire at this time, whose names are exclusively French. It seems, however (Ekwall, 1959, pp. 11-12) that this is one of the few Scandinavian personal names introduced into England from Normandy at the time of the Conquest and may suggest that Ascitel or his father arrived in Yorkshire from Normandy as part of the Fossard household. This seems more probable than

the alternative hypothesis that he was descended from Norman (i.e., "The Norwegian") who is recorded in Domesday (Page, 1912, p. 222) as having held Marton T. R. E. (in the time of Edward the Confessor). The hypothetical date proposed for the purchase of Marton (Whitsuntide 1107) is the presumed date of a surviving document mentioned, but not reproduced, by Farrer (1915, p. v) in which King Henry informs the shiremote of Yorkshire of an exchange of land in the county between himself and another of the beneficiaries of Tinchebrai, Robert de Brus. The hypothetical price (25s.) allows for a reasonable appreciation over the thirty years which had then elapsed since the Domesday survey when Marton was valued at 16s (Page, 1912, p. 222).
8. It is widely believed by philosophers that Kant's analytic/synthetic distinction has been decisively refuted by Quine's (1953) paper 'Two dogmas of empiricism.' To my mind, Quine's arguments reflect the logician's reluctance to accept that the speaker's conformity to linguistic convention is contingency-shaped with the result that what is analytic frequently depends on the context of utterance and can only be accessed through the linguistic intuitions of verbal community members. For a more extensive discussion of this issue, see Place (in press).
9. For this, in contrast to other uses of the term, see Place (1985).

Chapter 10

Problem Solving by Algorithms and Heuristics

Hayne W. Reese
West Virginia University

The purpose of this paper is to examine two kinds of problem-solving rules—algorithms and heuristics—that cognitivists have described and studied, and to suggest that behavior analysts might find the distinction useful for a behavior analysis of rules, specifically herein the behavior analysis of problem-solving rules. The paper begins with a discussion of the cognitive and behavioral approaches, then proceeds to discussions of the two kinds of rules.

How the Cognitive Approach Can Usefully Influence the Behavioral Approach

At the First and Second International Institutes on Verbal Relations, in Bad Kreuznach, Germany, and Tequesquitengo, Mexico, respectively, I suggested several areas in which behavior analysts might profitably borrow concepts or research topics from cognitive approaches. These suggestions are summarized in this introductory section, ending with an extension to the area of problem solving.

Areas of Potential Influence

Broadly, my suggestions at the first Verbal Relations institute were that (a) "case grammars" might be useful conceptual analyses for a behavior analysis of language because case grammars are based on functional rather than structural properties of syntactical elements; (b) "semantic network" models might provide useful topics for a behavior analysis of concept formation, including stimulus equivalence, because the networks can be interpreted as behavioral chains that are not just linear but that branch in ways that might be interesting; and (c) Vygotsky's (1934/1987, chap. 4) theory that human thinking originates in social speech might be useful for a behavior analysis of thinking. (The point may need clarification: Vygotsky believed that young children and animals exhibit a kind of thinking that has no relation to speech, but he believed that thinking of a kind that might be considered truly human originates in speech.)

The last suggestion might seem unnecessary, given that Skinner (1945) had already theorized that knowledge or awareness of one's own private events originates in social speech. However, a major difference is that Vygotsky theorized that social speech becomes "internalized" and in the process becomes free of external stimulus control, and Skinner theorized that private events are like any other behaviors—completely determined by environmental events (and the individual's history of interactions with environmental events). The suggestion, then, was that behavior analysts should consider the possibility that thinking mediates between experience and behavior not in the traditional American sense of being a link in a behavioral chain but in the Vygotskian sense of being able to change the direction of a behavioral chain by transforming the experiential input. Actually, Skinner's concepts of setting conditions and precurrent behaviors have a similar role: Setting conditions affect stimulus functions and precurrent behaviors can further modify stimulus functions. However, Vygotsky attributed this role to *verbal* behavior, or more precisely, verbal behavior after it has been transformed into "verbal thinking." At the second Verbal Relations institute, I analyzed the conception of rules as nonverbal entities, and concluded that nonverbal rules are regularities in nature, and that these regularities have causes. That is, nonverbal rules do not *cause* regularities in behavior or other aspects of nature; rather, nonverbal rules *are* the regularities. Conversely, according to the analysis offered, *verbal* rules can cause regularities in behavior. This conclusion can be given a Skinnerian or a Vygotskian interpretation, which can be illustrated by considering the simplest chain:

Present Experience – Verbalized Rule – Emitted Behavior

where the dash means "is followed by" and not, as it might in stimulus-response learning theories, "elicits."

From Skinner's viewpoint, the conclusion is that verbal rules can function as links in a behavioral chain. In principle, emitting this link is completely determined by the individual's present experience and history, and therefore the behavior emitted at the end is in principle completely *predictable* from the individual's present experience and history, and the behavior emitted at the end is in principle completely *controllable* by manipulation of the individual's present experience and/or history. Therefore, in this view the prediction and control of the final behavior are not furthered by knowing anything about the nature of the verbal-rule link of the chain. An example is Baer's (1982) answer to the question of how a person extracts square roots with paper and pencil: The person was taught how to do it. Knowing this history, and perhaps other facts, allows the prediction that the person extracts square roots with paper and pencil; and nothing that might be said about the mental operations the person uses adds anything to the predictability of the behavior.

From Vygotsky's viewpoint, the verbal rule cannot be ignored because it can be the sole determinant of the final behavior. That is, if a given individual is capable of emitting more than one verbal rule about a given present experience, then the behavior that finally occurs depends on which rule the individual emits, or, even more of a problem, the individual emits more than one rule and the behavior that finally occurs depends on which rule the individual *chooses* to obey. From this point of view, behavior is caused but cannot be completely predicted or controlled. That is, failures of prediction and control of behavior can result from the laws of nature, including the nature of the mind, rather than from ignorance of the laws of nature.

Is a natural science of behavior therefore impossible from this viewpoint? No; but the goal must be to predict and control what we can and to understand our failures at prediction and control by inferring what unexpected rules the individual actually used and by searching for regularities in the use of unexpected rules. (Criteria that can make the inference persuasive are outlined in the next subsection.)

As will be seen later, both algorithms and heuristics are interpretable from either viewpoint, but heuristics are more easily interpretable from the Vygotskian than the Skinnerian viewpoint.

Criteria for Inferring Rule Use

The use of a rule is usually unobservable and therefore must be inferred. However, the number of possible inferences for a given case is usually very large and unless this number is constrained, the inferences that are generated cannot be compelling. Cognitivists have proposed two kinds of criteria to provide the needed constraint. They are summarized below without evaluation (evaluation and discussion can be found in Reese, 1989). In general, the criteria are listed in the order of increasing persuasiveness. The first three criteria can be used to infer *that* a rule was used; the last four can be used to infer *which* rule was used. However, no one criterion is persuasive by itself because each one could be satisfied by contingency-shaped behavior or by behavior that is actually controlled by a rule other than the inferred one.

1. Regularity of behavior. If problem solving or other complex behavior, such as that involved in problem solving, is highly regular, the behavior can be inferred to be rule-governed.

2. Discontinuity of behavior. If behavior changes suddenly, it can be inferred to be rule-governed.

3. Self-report of rule-governance. If a person reports using a rule for self-control of behavior, the person's behavior can be inferred to be rule-governed.

4. Awareness of using a specific rule. If a person reports using a specific rule, or otherwise indicates awareness of using that rule, use of that rule can be inferred. This inference is independent of whether or not the person's behavior is consistent with the rule, because the person could have used the rule badly. As Ryle said, one can "plan shrewdly and perform stupidly" (1949, p. 31).

5. Consistency of behavior with a specific rule. If a person's behavior is consistent with a specific rule, use of that rule can be inferred.

6. Occurrence of concomitant behavior. If use of a specific rule should generate certain concomitant behavior (such as moving the lips while working on a problem), and this concomitant behavior is observed, use of the rule can be inferred.

7. Occurrence of expected transfer. If use of a specific rule should yield transfer to certain other problems, and this transfer is observed, use of the rule can be inferred.

Kinds of Problems

Cognitivists classify problems on various dimensions, including specificity, definition of structure, and nature of the operations needed for solution.

1. Specificity: A problem is *well-specified* if its instances are narrowly constrained. For example, although medieval English arithmetists referred to algorithms for "the extraction of roots," they correctly set forth different algorithms for the extraction of square roots and cube roots: "Here folowithe the extraccioun of rotis, the first in nombre quadrates [i.e, square numbers]" (Steele, 1922, p. 46) and the second "in cubike nombres" (p. 49).

2. Definition of structure: A problem is *well-defined* or *well-structured* if the problem solver can accurately identify the relevant problem space (Anzai, 1987; Reitman, 1965, p. 151). The "problem space" consists of the initial "problem state," the terminal problem state, that is, the goal state, intermediate problem states, and operations for moving from state to state (Anderson, 1990, p. 223; Mayer, 1983, p. 169). A *problem state* is a description of the problem situation.

Sometimes, *well-defined* is used in a narrower sense, to mean that the acceptability of a solution can be determined in a specified, systematic way; that is, the conditions that are necessary and sufficient for a solution are explicitly stated (Reitman, 1965, p. 148). Problems lacking such a statement are ill-defined in both the narrow sense and the broad sense—that is, they are ill-structured—and by definition they are outside the scope of algorithms, as will be seen in the next section.

3. Nature of operations: Problems can be classified on the basis of the operations needed for solution, including (a) transforming or manipulating elements in the initial problem state; (b) rearranging the elements in the initial problem state; and (c) finding a common structure, pattern, or relation (Ellis & Hunt, 1989, pp. 217-219). Respective examples are (a) the Luchins jars problem (described later); (b) anagram puzzles; and (c) verbal analogies, such as:

Parent is to Child as Buyer is to _____.

(Seller, because Parent and Child are correlative opposites and Buyer and Seller are also correlative opposites [as defined by Aristotle in *Categories,* Chapter 10]).

Kinds of Problem-Solving Rules

According to cognitive theory, problem solving can be based on facts, algorithms, or heuristics (Mayer, 1983, p. 165). *Facts* are remembered solutions of specific problems, or as might more likely be said, remembered answers to specific questions; *algorithms* are routines that are guaranteed to solve problems of a given kind, such as the paper-and-pencil routine for extracting square roots; and *heuristics* are rules of thumb that may or may not lead to solution of a problem. Trial-and-error is a heuristic routine, because it will not be successful unless the solution is in the repertoire of "trials" and is actually tried. These three kinds of problem solving are discussed in the next three subsections, with several examples of each kind.

Facts

Problem solving is based on facts, according to cognitive theory, when the solution comes entirely from memory. For example, the following four problems are likely to be solved on the basis of facts:

1. What is the capital of France?
2. What does "remorse" mean?
3. What is 7 X 8?
4. What is the square root of 144?

As Chase pointed out in his paper in this volume, this kind of problem solving is traditionally not considered to be problem solving because the behavior is not novel. The use of memory to solve a problem might reflect a deliberate rule such as "Search memory for the answer." Such a rule would be a heuristic, as described later. The use of a heuristic is also not novel behavior, however, and therefore not all problem solving involves novel behavior. Furthermore, the four sample problems and others of the same sort do not *demand* the use of memory. Each of these problems can also be solved in other ways. One can look in an encyclopedia or atlas to find the capital of France, one can look in a dictionary for the meaning of "remorse," and one can use algorithms to find the product of 7 and 8 and the square root of 144. Algorithms are described in the next subsection.

Algorithms

The word *algorithm*, or *algorism* in medieval terminology, originally referred to rules of arithmetic when the numeration included zero. For example, in 15th century English manuscripts nine sets of rules were specified:

(a) **Numeration**, or rules for using the Arabic number system (Steele, 1922, pp. 4-5, 34, 70-71);
(b) **Addition**;
(c) **Subtraction**;
(d) **Multiplication**;
(e) **Division**;
(f) **Extraction of Roots**;
(g) **Duplation**, or doubling a number (pp. 14-16, 39);
(h) **Mediation**, or halving a number (pp. 16-20, 38-39); and
(i) **Progression**, or finding the sum of a series of numbers (pp. 45-46).

All but the first and last of these were covered by the 9th-century Arabian scholar, al-Khorezmi, who wrote several mathematical texts including an arithmetic and an algebra and from whose name the word "algorithm" was derived (Zemanek, 1981). (His name is transliterated in

Problem Solving by Algorithms and Heuristics

various ways. The one given here is the most accurate, according to Zemanek [1981]; but according to Knuth [1981] "al-Khwârizmi" is better.)

Factoring. Factoring could be added to the list of algorithms of arithmetic, but it was implicitly included in other rules. For example, the rule for multiplying two nonprime numbers, especially useful when at least one number has more than one digit, is implicitly to factor the numbers. For instance:

$$8 \times 12 = 8 \times (2 + 10) = (8 \times 2) + (8 \times 10) = 16 + 80 = 96.$$

One who does not remember that 7 X 8 is 56 could use the factoring algorithm:

$$7 \times 8 = 7(4 + 4) = (7 \times 4) + (7 \times 4) = 2(7 \times 4) = 2(28) = 56. \qquad \text{(Eq. 1)}$$

Alternatively, one could use the 12th century rule for multiplying with an abacus:

$$X \times Y = 10[Y - (10 - X)] + (10 - X)(10 - Y)$$

where X and Y are less than 10 (Steele, 1922, p. xiv). For example:

$$7 \times 8 = 10[8 - (10 - 7)] + (10 - 7)(10 - 8)$$
$$= 10[8 - 3] + (3)(2) = 10[5] + (3)(2) = 50 + 6 = 56.$$

Or one could derive a rule from the algorithm for multiplying sums:

$$(X + Y)(X + Z) = X^2 + XZ + YX + YZ.$$

For example, let $X = 10$, $Y = -3$, and $Z = -2$. Then:

$$7 \times 8 = (10 - 3)(10 - 2) = 10^2 + 10(-2) + (-3)10 + (-3)(-2)$$
$$= 100 - 20 - 30 + 6 = 56.$$

The point of this example is that the factoring algorithm is actually a family of algorithms, all of which yield the same answer, barring errors. In general, the point is that alternative algorithms are generally available for solving a given kind of problem. The best algorithm to use may depend on whether the application must be done with or without memory aids such as paper and pencil, and how likely errors are to occur with and without memory aids. I knew a man who was an expert at mentally solving an age-doubling problem. He would ask a person's age and with no hesitation after hearing it, he would say that n years ago he was twice (or half) as old as the person was, or n years from now he would be twice (or half) as old as the person would be. The algorithm is:

$$n = X - 2Y$$

where n is the number of years, X is the older person's age in years, Y is the younger person's age in years, and X is not equal to Y. The algorithm is simple, but applying it is complicated by the need to refer to the past if n is negative and the future if n is positive and to refer to "twice as old" if he was older than the person and "half as old" if he was younger than the person.

Another use of factoring. Another use of factoring is in al-Khorezmi's algorithm for solving a problem such as:

$$X^2 + 10X = 39. \tag{Eq. 2}$$

His algorithm was to complete the square, which implicitly involves factoring. In general, any square can be symbolized:

$$X^2 + 2XY + Y^2 = (X + Y)^2 \tag{Eq. 3}$$

The partial square in the example, $X^2 + 10X$, can be completed as follows. Let $10X$ equal the middle term on the left side of Eq. 3; that is:

$$10X = 2XY. \tag{Eq. 4}$$

Dividing both sides of Eq. 4 by X and then solving for Y:

$$Y = 10/2 = 5.$$

Completing the square, then, consists of adding $(5)^2$ to each side of Eq. 2:

$$X^2 + 10X + 25 = 39 + 25 = 64. \tag{Eq. 5}$$

The left side of Eq. 5 is a square and can be written as $(X + 5)^2$. Therefore, taking the square root of both sides of Eq. 5 yields:

$$X + 5 = 8.$$

Solving for X:
$$X = 8 - 5 = 3.$$

Substituting in Eq. 2:

$$3^2 + 10(3) = 39.$$

Zemanek pointed out that al-Khorezmi failed to consider negative square roots. In the example, the square can be completed as the square of a negative number, $(-X - 5)^2$, which yields $X = -13$. Substituting in Eq. 2:

$$(-13)^2 + 10(-13) = 169 - 130 = 39.$$

However, although the solution based on the negative square root is clear in an algebraic notation, such as:

$$[\pm X + 5)]^2 = X^2 + 10X + 25,$$

it is not possible in al-Khorezmi's algorithm, which was spatial.

Problem Solving by Algorithms and Heuristics

Two algebraic tricks. The following algebraic trick can be used to "prove" that any number is equal to twice itself. Let n be the number, and let $n = X = Y$. Then:

$$X = Y.$$

Multiplying both sides by Y:

$$XY = Y^2.$$

Subtracting X^2 from both sides:

$$XY - X^2 = Y^2 - X^2.$$

Factoring:

$$X(Y - X) = (Y + X)(Y - X). \tag{Eq. 6}$$

Dividing both sides by $(Y - X)$:

$$X = Y + X.$$

But $Y = X$; therefore:

$$X = X + X = 2X.$$

Substituting for X:

$$n = 2n.$$

The "proof" depends on an illegitimate arithmetic operation—division by zero. As can be seen by substituting X for Y in each equation, the equality holds until Eq. 6 is divided by zero (i.e., $Y - X$). The trick in the next "proof" is more subtle.

The following algebraic trick can be used to "prove" that any two numbers are equal. Let the numbers be, for example, 3 and 7, and let:

$$X = 3 \tag{Eq. 7}$$

$$Y = 7 \tag{Eq. 8}$$

$$S = 1/2\,(3 + 7) = 5. \tag{Eq. 9}$$

Then:

$$X + Y = 2S. \tag{Eq. 10}$$

Multiplying both sides of Eq. 10 by $(X - Y)$:

$$(X + Y)(X - Y) = 2S(X - Y).$$

Carrying out the multiplication:

$$X^2 - Y^2 = 2SX - 2SY.$$

Adding Y^2 to both sides and subtracting $2SX$ from both sides:

$$X^2 - 2SX = Y^2 - 2SY.$$

Adding S^2 to both sides:

$$X^2 - 2SX + S^2 = Y^2 - 2SY + S^2. \qquad \text{(Eq. 11)}$$

Taking the square root of both sides:

$$X - S = Y - S. \qquad \text{(Eq. 12)}$$

Adding S to both sides:

$$X = Y.$$

Substituting from Eqs. 7 and 8:

$$3 = 7.$$

Let me assure readers not fluent in algebra that every one of the algorithms used is legitimate, and that the "proof" rests on a hidden error in the application of one. The following "proof" may indicate the algorithm in which the error occurs. Given Eqs. 7 through 10 and subtracting Y and S from both sides of Eq. 10:

$$X - S = S - Y.$$

Squaring both sides:

$$X^2 - 2SX + S^2 = S^2 - 2SY + Y^2. \qquad \text{(Eq. 13)}$$

Rearranging terms on the right side:

$$X^2 - 2SX + S^2 = Y^2 - 2SY + S^2 \qquad \text{(Eq. 14)}$$

which is identical to Eq. 11. Taking the square root of both sides of Eq. 14:

$$X - S = Y - S. \qquad \text{(Eq. 15)}$$

Adding S to both sides:

$$X = Y.$$

This version has perhaps made the error clearer: The relevant rule of algebra is that an equality will hold if the same root is taken on both sides of an equation, but in this "proof" the positive root is taken on the left side of Eqs. 11 and 14, that is, $(X - S)$, and the negative root is taken on the right side, $-(S - Y)$. The trick is that this error is very hard to see in the first version of the proof. If the positive root is taken on both sides of Eqs. 11 and 14, then Eqs. 12 and 15 are:

$X - S = S - Y.$

Adding Y and S to both sides:

$X + Y = 2S$

which is the same as Eq. 10 and is true.

These tricks are instructive because they reveal a kind of error that can occur in solving algebra problems—hidden violations of the relevant algorithms (in the examples, dividing by zero and taking different roots on the two sides of an equation). The second violation, incidentally, can occur in problems like the one posed by al-Khorezmi but cannot occur in his spatial solution because it allows only positive roots. In other words, although algorithms are in principle guaranteed to produce a correct solution, in practice they cannot be guaranteed to do so because errors can occur in the use of any algorithm.

The tricks are also instructive for another reason, not yet mentioned: The algorithms in each proof came partly from a *fact* that I remembered and largely from my use of a heuristic rule. I learned the two algebraic "proofs" in the middle 1940s and as best as I can recall I did not think about them after the early 1960s until I began writing this paper. The only fact I remembered for the first trick was that it involved dividing by zero, and for the second trick, that it involved taking different square roots on the two sides of the equation. I worked on the second trick first, and wasted some time trying to work "forward" from Eq. 10 (actually from $X + Y = S$); but then I changed my strategy and worked backward from Eq. 12. I almost immediately solved the problem, that is, found the false proof. (I worked backward from $X - S = Y - S$, which upon arriving at Eqs. 9 and 10 required defining S as one-half of 3 + 7 and of $X + Y$. The proof would be the same if $S = 3 + 7$ in Eq. 9 and $S = X + Y$ in Eq. 10, but it would be cluttered with fractions, such as $X - S/2 = Y - S/2$ in Eq. 12.)

For the other trick, I deliberately worked backward to reconstruct the proof. I identified the needed intermediate step in the second attempt but did not work out the steps to get to that step until the eighth attempt, after which I revised the proof five times to get the version presented herein. The problem was not only to present a "proof" but also to make it look plausible.

The strategy of working backward is a heuristic rule, which can be stated as "Beginning at the end can be more straightforward than beginning at the beginning." This heuristic is often useful in problem solving (Anderson, 1990, pp. 237-239), but the point here is that it can be useful even when the eventual solution involves algorithms. In science, the same point appears in Reichenbach's (1938, pp. 5-7) distinction between the contexts of discovery and justification, and in Kaplan's (1964, pp. 14-15, 17) distinction between the "logic" of discovery and the logic of proof. The discovery of an algebraic proof can result from using the working-backward heuristic, but the algebraic proof itself is presented in terms of algorithms.

Square roots by hand. A person who does not remember the square root of a number such as 144, but who remembers the algorithm for extraction of square roots, could calculate the square root by applying the algorithm.

1. Going from right to left, separate the digits in the number into pairs, including any zeros between the decimal and the first significant digit. For example, the digits in

the number a,b,c,d,e are separated into a, b,c, and d,e. (A concrete example is 573.41, separated into 5, 73, and .41.)

2. Starting with a, that is, the leftmost pair or the leftmost single digit if it is unpaired, find a "multiplier" m such that m^2 that is equal to a or is smaller than a by the least possible amount. ($m = 2$ in the example.)
3. In the locus that will contain the final answer, record the multiplier (m). ($m = 2$.)
4. Double the multiplier ($2m$) and record the result at some convenient locus. (Record a 4.)
5. Subtract the squared number identified in Step 2 (m^2) from the original leftmost pair or digit (a), and append the residual (r) to the left side of the next pair (yielding r,b,c). (173 in the example.)
6. Find a new multiplier m_2 such that m_2 times the number composed of $2m$ and m_2 is as close as possible to r,b,c but not larger than r,b,c. Record this number with the number identified in Step 3. ($m_2 = 3$ in the example, because 3 X 43 = 129, which is less than 173, and 4 X 44 = 176, which is larger than 173. The answer so far is 23.)
7. Repeat Steps 4 through 6 until the digits in the number are exhausted and as many pairs of zeros have been added to the right of the decimal to obtain the desired number of decimal places in the answer, using each new product (e.g., m_3 times $2m,2m_2,m_3$) in Step 6. Record each new multiplier with the numbers identified in Steps 3 and 6. (In the example, r in Step 7 = 173 - 129 = 44; r,f,g = 44.41; and $2m,2m_2$ is 46 [$2m_2 = 2$ x 3 = 6, appended to the old $2m$, 4]. Therefore, $m_3 = .9$ [.9 X 46.9 = 42.21]; and the answer so far is 23.9. The consequent r = 44.41 - 42.21 = 2.20, and r,b,i = 2.2000; $2m,2m_2,2m_3$ is 47.8 and $m_4 = .04$: .04 X 47.84 = 1.9136. Carried one step further, the answer is 23.946.)

When writing this paper, I initially did not remember the algorithm for extraction of square roots, other than that the number had to be divided into pairs of digits and that something had to be doubled. I reconstructed the algorithm by using the working-backward heuristic with a version of the sample problem given above (without the decimal point). However, this time I did not work backward from the final solution (23.946 in the example), but rather I used it to define a series of solutions to sub-tasks. I used a desk calculator to find the square root of the number and used each successive digit in the square root as an end-point for a step in the algorithm. That is, I derived each step by means of the working-backward heuristic: I started with the left-most digit (5) and the answer that the algorithm must yield (2), and I doubled that answer (4). Then I proceeded to the next digit pair (73) and the answer for it (23) and worked out what combination of multiplier and multiplicand would yield this answer. The points of this exercise, in short, are that solving a problem may consist of solving a series of sub-problems, each with its own subgoal, and that the working-backward heuristic may be useful for identifying the sub-goals and hence the sub-problems.

Algorithms in general. The examples considered thus far are algorithms of arithmetic and algebra. These algorithms, and algorithms in any other domain, are rules that will yield the correct solution unless an error is made. The error could be inappropriate application of an algorithm, as in trying to obtain square roots by using the division algorithm, or the error could be a slip in the application of an algorithm, as in taking square roots without regard for sign or writing down an incorrect number. For example, if a person writes down 7 X 4 = 26, then Eq. 1 will yield an incorrect product for 7 X 8.

Newell and Simon (1972) described an algorithm as a problem-solving routine that "has been tailored (1) to guarantee solution of problems of the class in question, (2) to operate smoothly within the limits of the IPS [i.e., the information processing system] with whatever specific EM

ID Problem Solving by Algorithms and Heuristics

[external memory] aids are provided, and (3) to avoid searches as much as possible" (p. 822). The key feature in this description (for the present purpose) is *guarantee*. Anderson (1990, pp. 226-227) used only this feature in distinguishing between algorithms and heuristics, which as noted earlier lack this feature.

The distinction is fairly easy to make in reference to problems in arithmetic and algebra, but it is not so easily made in other domains. An example is the problem of maintaining the correct temperature in a forge by the use of a hand-operated bellows. According to Skinner (1974), the following rule works:

> Up high,
> Down low,
> Up quick,
> Down slow,
> And that's the way to blow. (p. 123)

Skinner called this kind of rule an instruction. It is guaranteed to work unless an error is made, including the errors of forgetting it, forgetting to use it, deliberately not using it, accidentally not using it (e.g., because of fatigue), and depleting the fuel. Given the many kinds of possible errors, the "guarantee" seems about as trustworthy as the guarantee on a cheap watch; but the same kinds of errors can undermine the guarantee on some routines that are indisputably algorithms, such as the paper-and-pencil routine for extracting square roots. Therefore, Skinner's instruction is classifiable as an algorithm.

Reitman (1965) challenged Newell and Simon's characterization that an algorithm guarantees success provided that no errors are made. He said, "there is no such thing as an absolute guarantee in the empirical world" (p. 129). However, Reitman's point is obvious psychologically, and Newell and Simon made the same point in referring to the use of algorithms as a way "to solve a problem in a highly mechanical way and with a low error rate" (p. 822). Al-Khorezmi made the same point in saying that with algorithms "one can solve all problems—without error, if God will" (quoted in Zemanek, p. 63). Incidentally, research suggests that not all the errors that occur even in simple arithmetic problems reflect carelessness; some reflect misunderstanding of the algorithm, such as "borrow from zero" in subtraction (e.g., 103 - 45 = 158) (Mayer, 1983, pp. 369-373). Similarly, Skinner's apprentice blacksmith might move the bellows up too slowly or down too quickly, but is probably more likely to move it up too slowly if that action requires less work than moving it up more quickly.

Reitman also noted that an algorithm deals with a class of problems that are (1) well-specified and (2) well-defined (pp. 148, 154). "Well-specified," as noted earlier, means that the class is narrowly constrained; "well-defined" means that the problem space is explicitly and accurately described.

Heuristics

Newell and Simon (1972) suggested using the phrase "programmed activity" to refer to problem-solving behavior controlled by algorithms, and using "unprogrammed activity" to refer to problem-solving behavior controlled by heuristics (p. 822). They also said that plans are "structurally identical" to programs, hence are similar to the use of algorithms (p. 822). However, a plan is structurally identical to a program only if the plan is precisely specified—unless both the plan and the program contain many hidden mechanisms. An example of hidden mechanisms is Newell and Simon's own theory of human problem solving, which they said contains "a wide range of organizational techniques known to the programming world: explicit flow control, subroutines, recursion [embedded goals], iteration statements, local naming, production systems, interpreters, and so on" (p. 803). Many of these mechanisms are hidden, that is, they are not included in the printout of a computer simulation of problem solving.

Thus, an algorithm may or may not be a program. Furthermore, a heuristic can be characterized as a general plan or routine, and heuristics can be programmed (Newell & Simon, 1972, provided several examples). Thus, programmability does not distinguish between algorithms and heuristics. Algorithms are aimed at precise solution or rigorous proof; heuristics are aimed at the plausible guess, or discovery and invention (Polya, 1948, pp. 102-103).

Heuristics are rules of thumb that do not guarantee a solution (Anderson, 1990, p. 227; Reitman, 1965, p. 129) even if no error is made. They are often applicable across several classes of problems, and they are especially useful for ill-defined problems, although some heuristics can be applied to well-defined problems. For example, chess is an explicitly specified problem—or in cognitive terms, it has a well-specified and well-defined problem space. It has a well-defined terminal or goal state: The king will be captured if it does not move and will be captured if it moves. Many chess players know a general heuristic, "Bishops are stronger than Knights," and use it in deciding between alternative moves in going from the initial state (the starting layout) to the goal state. Players with more expertness know the more precise heuristic, "Bishops are stronger than Knights primarily in the end game" (Newell & Simon, 1972, p. 758); in using this heuristic they will appear to be using the general heuristic selectively. In either case, basing a move on the somewhat greater value of a Bishop than a Knight will often be an error.

Examples of Heuristics

Three examples of problem-solving heuristics are described in the present section.

Product Improvement

Examples of heuristics in real-life problem solving are Alex Osborn's (1963) rules for improving manufactured products, or improving their marketability: Adapt, modify, substitute. "Modify," for example, includes adding, multiplying, subtracting, and dividing. *Adding* could be adding an ingredient, as in adding fluoride to toothpaste; *multiplying* could be the double-your-money-back guarantee; *subtracting* could be decaffeinated coffee or low-fat milk products; and *dividing* could be miniature chocolates or textbook "modules."

"Hill Climbing"

An example of heuristics in laboratory research is the use of a problem-solving rule called "hill climbing." As described by Mayer (1983):

> In hill climbing you continually try to move from your present state to a state that is closer to the goal. Thus, if you are in a certain state, you evaluate the new state you would be in for each possible move, and you select the move that creates the state that moves you closest to the goal. (p. 172)

The hill-climbing heuristic is often undesirable, as shown by the saying "The long way is the short way." An example is the problem shown in Figure 1: The drivers of cars A, B, C, and D want to turn left at an intersection and are waiting for breaks in the oncoming traffic. How can the driver of car D reduce his or her waiting time? One solution that is likely to occur to North American adults is to get in the right-hand lane, drive through the intersection, make a U turn at the next intersection, then turn right at the desired intersection. This solution is the long way in distance but the short way in time. (Some differently socialized drivers use a solution that is short in both distance and time: Get in the right-hand lane and turn left in front of Car A.)

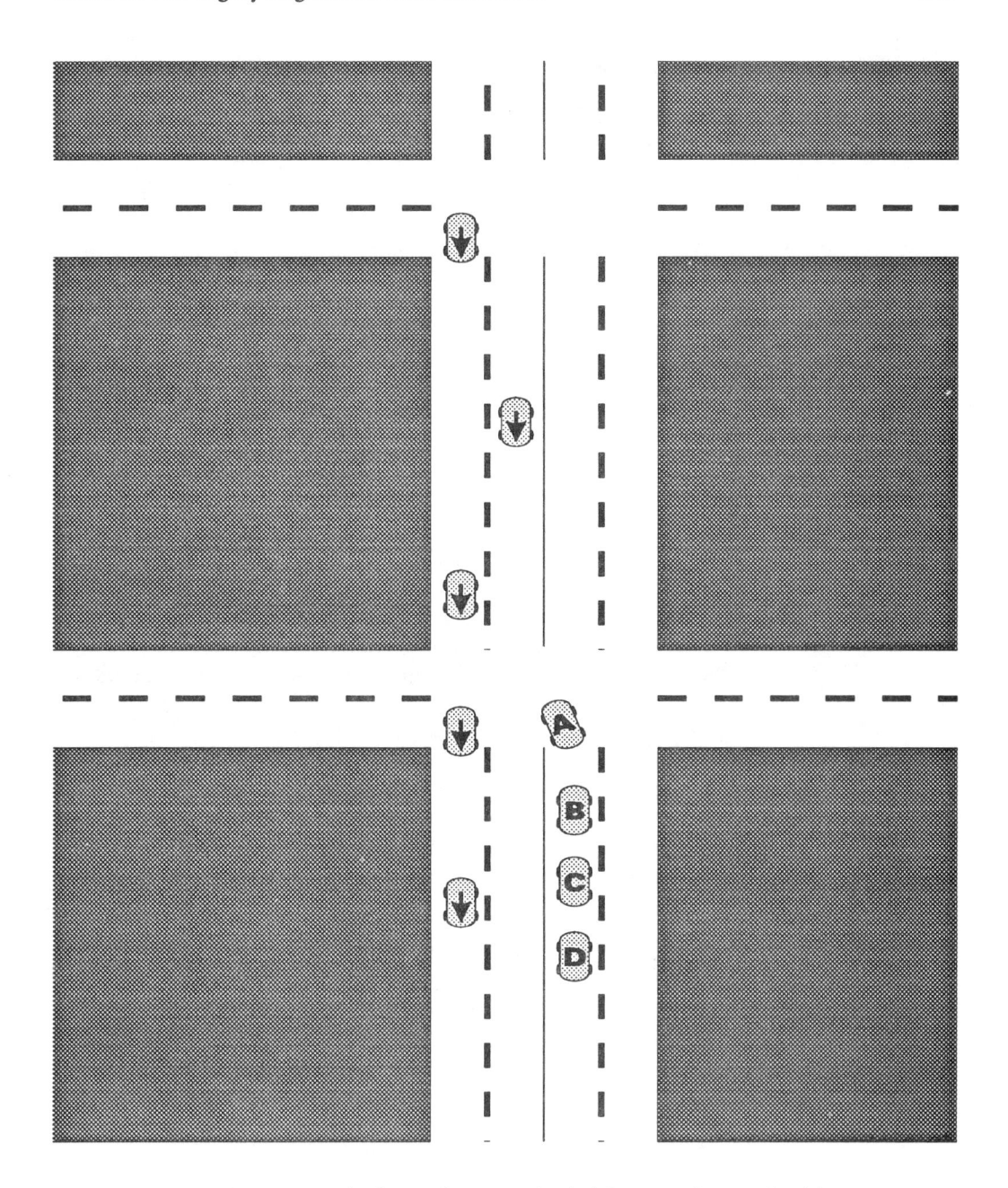

Problem Solving by Algorithms and Heuristics 165

Figure 1. How can the driver of car D make the left turn without undue delay?

Horse Trading Problem

In "hill climbing" and in the driving example, the heuristic is qualitative even though using it involves evaluating quantities—closeness to the goal state and amounts of distance and time. An example of a "quantitative" heuristic is "Symbolize the quantities in arithmetic problems." The usefulness of this heuristic can be seen in a problem described by Maier and Burke (1967, p. 305):

A man bought a horse for $60 and sold it for $70. Then he bought it back again for $80 and sold it for $90. How much money did he make in the horse business?
   a.   lost $10
   b.   broke even
   c.   made $10
   d.   made $20
   e.   made $30.

Let $X =$ buying price, $Y =$ selling price, and $D = Y - X$, with subscripts for the two transactions. The total profit or loss is $D_1 + D_2$. Therefore:

$$X_1 = 60;\ Y_1 = 70;\ D_1 = 10;$$

$$X_2 = 80;\ Y_2 = 90;\ D_2 = 10;$$

and

$$D_1 + D_2 = 20.$$

Thus, the correct answer is "made $20." Maier and Burke found that 48% of the college men in their study and 27% of the college women solved this problem. However, according to Mayer (1983, p. 78), 100% of college students solve a slightly different version with the same multiple-choice answers:

> A man bought a white horse for $60 and sold it for $70. Then he bought a black horse for $80 and sold it for $90. How much did he make in the horse business?

Evidently, emphasizing that the trading involved two different transactions made the problem easy to solve, perhaps by promoting use of the heuristic rule of symbolizing arithmetic quantities.

The Luchins Jars Problem

Another example of the heuristic rule of symbolizing arithmetic quantities can be found in the Luchins jars problem (Luchins, 1942; Luchins & Luchins, 1950). The problem is to take three jars of specified capacity and obtain a specified quantity of liquid. Examples developed by Bugelski and Huff (1962) are shown in Table 1. In the first problem, the solution is to fill Jar B, fill Jar A from Jar B, fill Jar C from Jar B then empty Jar C and fill it again from Jar B. The amount required will remain in Jar B:

$$89 - 43 - 2 - 2 = 42.$$

This is, in fact, the only solution to this particular problem, except for transposing the order of subtraction (e.g., 89 - 2 - 2 - 43). Problems 1, 2, and 3 have the same algorithmic solution:

$$B - A - 2C = D.$$

Most school children and college students given Problems 1, 2, and 3 (or similar problems) solve Problems 4 and 5 the same way:

Table 1
Examples of "Water-Jar" Problems Developed by Bugelski and Huff (1962)

		Jars given		To get
Problem	A	B	C	D
1	43	89	2	42
2	25	59	2	30
3	32	69	3	31
4	17	37	3	14
5	41	86	4	37
6	47	68	4	51

Adapted from Bugelski & Huff, 1962, Table 1, p. 665.

$$37 - 17 - 3 - 3 = 14$$

and

$$86 - 41 - 4 - 4 = 37$$

even though A - C is a simpler solution:

$$17 - 3 = 14$$

and

$$41 - 4 = 37.$$

Furthermore, many school children and college students persist in the algorithmic solution when given Problem 6, even though the algorithm that solves Problems 1 through 5 yields an incorrect answer to Problem 6:

$$68 - 47 - 4 - 4 = 13$$

but

$$47 + 4 = 51.$$

    This example illustrates two noteworthy points. First, the use of a heuristic can include an algorithm or can yield an algorithm. Presumably, "Look for an algorithm" is a heuristic rule that school children and college students use while working on quantitative problems, though they probably would not verbalize the rule that way. A person with a good knowledge of mathematics might verbalize the heuristic as "Express any quantitative problem algebraically." However, the heuristic actually "used" may not be overtly verbalized and may not even be consciously controlled—it may be an unconscious, automatic mental operation. Nevertheless, in any case it is assumed to have a verbal basis, for example in what Vygotsky called "verbal thinking," which is verbal but not verbalized (1934/1987, chap. 4).

Second, the phenomenon obtained in the Luchins jars problem is interpreted to reflect the student's discovery of the correct algorithm in Problem 1, 2, or 3 and confirmation of it in the subsequent problems until Problem 6. The initial problems may be solved by trial and error, and putting the solution in the form of an algorithm takes extra cognitive effort. However, once the correct algorithm is discovered, using it is considerably less effortful than further trial and error. Thus, finding and using algorithms saves cognitive effort in the long run. This point has been made by a number of writers. For example, Matijasevic (1981) said, "Finding an algorithm saves, at least theoretically, the working time of qualified mathematicians since corresponding problem [sic] can now be tackled by less qualified ones or by computers" (p. 441). However, the use of heuristics is also a way to reduce problem-solving effort or, as is also said, to reduce the search needed to find a solution (e.g., Neches, Langley, & Klahr, 1987, p. 24; Newell & Simon, 1972, e.g., p. 138; Tonge, 1961, p. 16).

Example of a Misapplied Heuristic

Several researchers have found that children and adults erroneously use an empirical heuristic rule in a "beads" problem introduced by Murray and Armstrong (1978):

> Suppose the number of red beads in a jar of red beads is the same as the number of blue beads in a jar of blue beads. Suppose that 5 beads are dipped from the red-bead jar and put in the blue-bead jar and that the beads in the blue-bead jar are then thoroughly stirred and mixed. If 5 beads are then dipped from the blue-bead jar and put in the red-bead jar, will the number of red beads in the red-bead jar be the same as the number of blue beads in the blue-bead jar?

Few children and even fewer adults, including college students and older adults, give the correct answer "Yes—same" (Murray & Armstrong, 1978; Odom, Cunningham, & Astor, 1975; Reese, Puckett, & Cohen, in preparation). The reason is that instead of treating the task as a logical problem, with an algorithmic solution, they treat it as an empirical problem involving probability.

When the problem is approached empirically, the answer is "There's no way to know." The probability that any given number of red beads will be returned depends on the number of blue beads, N, with which the five red beads were mixed. The greater N is, the lower is the probability, p, that any given number of red beads will be included among the five beads returned to the red-bead jar. Because N is not specified in the problem, that is, because N is unknown, p cannot be computed.

However, although p in fact cannot be computed, the correct answer is nevertheless "Same" because it depends on logic and not probability. The logic is as follows, and is illustrated in Table 2.

The problem has three states: the initial problem state before any transfer of beads, the second problem state after the first transfer of beads, and the third problem state after the second transfer. The question is about the numbers of beads in the jars in the third problem state.

1. In the initial problem state, each jar contains N beads.

Table 2
Numbers of Blue and Red Beads in the Two Jars in the Beads Problem

	No. in red-bead jar		No. in blue-bead jar	
State	Blue beads	Red beads	Blue beads	Red beads
1. Initial state	0	N	N	0
2. 1st transfer	0	$N-5$	N	5
3. 2nd transfe	n_B	$N-5+n_R$	$N-n_B$	$5-n_R$
Substituting[a]	n_B	$N-5+5-n_B$	$N-n_B$	$5-n_R$
Simplifying	n_B	$N-n_B$	$N-n_B$	$5-n_R$

See text for further explication. [a]Substituting from Eq. 16 in the text.

2. The second problem state is generated by the transfer of 5 red beads from the red-bead jar to the blue-bead jar. In this problem state, the red-bead jar contains $N-5$ red beads and the blue-bead jar contains N blue beads and 5 red beads. However, the number of red beads in the blue-bead jar is irrelevant to the solution, because the problem is to determine whether at the end the number of red beads in the red-bead jar will be the same as the number of blue beads in the blue-bead jar.

3. The third problem state, which is the terminal state, is generated by the transfer of 5 beads from the blue-bead jar to the red-bead jar. These 5 beads include n_R red beads and n_B blue beads, such that:

$$n_R + n_B = 5.$$

Solving for n_R:

$$n_R = 5 - n_B. \qquad \text{(Eq. 16)}$$

In the third problem state, the number of red beads, N_{Red}, in the red-bead jar is equal to the number of red beads left in this jar in the second problem state plus the number transferred back:

$$N_{Red} = N - 5 + n_R.$$

Substituting from Eq. 16:

$$N_{Red} = N - 5 + (5 - n_B).$$

Simplifying:

$$N_{Red} = N - n_B. \qquad \text{(Eq. 17)}$$

After the transfer of the 5 beads from the blue-bead jar to the red-bead jar, the number of blue beads, N_{Blue}, left in the blue-bead jar is the number of blue beads in this jar in the second problem state minus the number taken out:

$$N_{Blue} = N - n_B \qquad \text{(Eq. 18)}$$

which is the same as the number in Eq. 17. Thus, in the terminal problem state the number of red beads in the red-bead jar (Eq. 17) *must* be the same as the number of blue beads in the blue-bead jar (Eq. 18).

For example, if each jar initially contained 100 beads, then in the second problem state the red-bead jar contains 95 red beads. Next, if 2 red beads and 3 blue beads are transferred to the red-bead jar, then in the third problem state the red-bead jar will contain 97 red beads (95 + 2) and the blue-bead jar will contain 97 blue beads (100 - 3).

Heuristics as Rough Rules

One way to reduce search time in problem solving is to settle for a rough solution, by making the goal an *acceptable* solution and not necessarily an *optimal* solution (Tonge, 1961, p. viii). For example, Mayer (1983) suggested that the exact solution to the problem "What is 262 X 127?" involves an algorithm, but that "a heuristic would be an estimate of the correct answer by rounding to manageable numbers" (p. 165).

Paint problem. A concrete example of Mayer's (1983) suggestion can be the answer to the question, "About how much paint will I need to cover an area that measures 262 by 127 inches?" The solution does not necessarily depend on calculating that the precise area is 33,274 square inches; the following rough estimate is probably good enough:

One-eighth of 262 is about 33; therefore, the area is about 33,000 square inches.

The heuristic is to reduce one of the numbers to a simple fraction times a power of 10, then to divide the other number by the denominator of the fraction and multiply the quotient by the power of 10. Here, 127 is close to 125, which is 1000 X 1/8.

In this example, the use of heuristic changes a well-defined problem into an ill-defined one. The problem becomes ill-defined because no way is specified to assess the adequacy of the answer. A better example of heuristic as a rough rule might be to start with an ill-defined problem and to show why a heuristic solution works. The "divisions" task described next is an example.

"Divisions" task. Reese, Puckett, and Cohen (in preparation) developed a problem-solving task based on Plato's method of definition by dichotomous divisions (Plato, *The Sophist*). The research participants were 17 to 99 years old. Each participant was asked to select a "target" card from 32 cards describing events that might occur in one's lifetime (the 32 events used are listed in Table 3). Then the participant was asked to divide the 32 events into two sets of 16 such that the events in each set had some commonality that was different for the two sets. The participant was then asked to divide the set of 16 that contained the target card into two sets of 8, again such that the events in each set had some commonality that was different for the two sets; then he or she was asked to divide the set of 8 containing the target card into two sets of 4, and then the 4 into two sets of 2. For each division, the participant was asked to "think aloud" and to describe the basis for the division, including, finally, telling how the 2 events in the last set differed from each other.

The goal for each division is well defined in the trivial sense that it is satisfied when the events have been divided into two equal sets; but it is ill defined in the important sense that it is satisfied only when the events in each set have an identified commonality that is different for the two sets. The task was intended to be ill defined in the latter sense, and life events were used as the items because they are multidimensional. (Reese and Smyer, 1983, described 35 dimensions that had been identified in life-events research.)

Table 3

The 32 Life Events in Reese, Puckett, and Cohen's "Divisions" Task

---

ACTIVITY DECLINE	IMPROVED MARRIAGE
BECOMING ENGAGED	LEARN WALKING
BEING FIRED	LEARNING HOBBY
BOSS TROUBLES	LEISURE CHANGES
BREAKING ENGAGEMENT	LESSENING STRESS
BUSINESS FAILURE	MARRIAGE RECONCILIATION
BUSINESS READJUSTMENT	RECEIVING AWARD
DEATH AWARENESS	RETIRING
DECREASED STRENGTH	SELF-ACCEPTANCE
DEVELOPING SKILLS	SKILL DECLINE
EMPLOYEE CONFLICT	SPOUSE DEATH
ESTEEM CHANGES	SPOUSE WORKING
GETTING LOST	SPOUSES ARGUING
GOOD HEALTH	STRIKING
HAVE OPERATION	UNFAITHFUL SPOUSE
HEALTH DECLINE	VACATION CANCELLED

The items are listed alphabetically (in two columns to save space); in the research they were presented in random order.

Two different heuristics might work: (a) One heuristic that could be used for any sorting task would be to start by identifying the meanings of the items; for example, the research participant could read them for meaning if they are presented in print. According to evidence from cognitive research, this process should automatically lead to identification of superordinate relations, which could then be retrieved deliberately from memory. The superordinate relations retrieved could be processed in the same way, continuing with the processing of successively higher levels of superordinate relations until a single, all-inclusive superordinate relation, or dimension, is identified. The subjective experience of this mental processing might be reading the items and realizing intuitively that they differ in some specific way. The next step would be to select a dividing point on this dimension, then to sort the items, and finally, if necessary, to reinterpret the meanings of some of the items or to adjust the dividing point on the dimension to achieve sets of the required sizes (in this case, equal sizes). For example, reading the items in Table 3 might lead to the intuitive realization that they differ on the dimension of desirability, and the items might therefore be divided into good events and bad events.

Table 4 shows a possible division. As can be seen, the set of good events is two items short. However, the two events marked with an asterisk can be shifted to the "good" set: ACTIVITY

DECLINE can be interpreted as desirable if the prior amount of activity was too great and ESTEEM CHANGES could mean that esteem improves. These adjustments yield sets of equal size, and therefore permit retaining the division.

Table 4

A Possible Division of the Events in Table 3, Based on the Dimension of Desirability

Good events	Bad events
BECOMING ENGAGED	*ACTIVITY DECLINE
BUSINESS READJUSTMENT	BEING FIRED
DEVELOPING SKILLS	BOSS TROUBLES
GOOD HEALTH	BREAKING ENGAGEMENT
IMPROVED MARRIAGE	BUSINESS FAILURE
LEARN WALKING	DEATH AWARENESS
LEARNING HOBBY	DECREASED STRENGTH
LEISURE CHANGES	EMPLOYEE CONFLICT
LESSENING STRESS	*ESTEEM CHANGES
MARRIAGE RECONCILIATION	GETTING LOST
RECEIVING AWARD	HAVE OPERATION
RETIRING	HEALTH DECLINE
SELF-ACCEPTANCE	SKILL DECLINE
SPOUSE WORKING	SPOUSE DEATH
	SPOUSES ARGUING
	STRIKING
	UNFAITHFUL SPOUSE
	VACATION CANCELLED

See text for explanation of asterisks.

(b) Another heuristic that could be used for any sorting task is to start by reading a few of the items and then to select a likely dimension and a dividing point on this dimension, thereafter proceeding as in the first heuristic. For example, the participant might select the dimension of age-relatedness and start with the idea of events associated with childhood vs. events associated with adulthood. A fairly clear-cut division based on these commonalities is shown in Table 5; but the sets are far from equal in size. If the commonalities are redefined as associated with childhood and young adulthood vs. associated with older adulthood, the events marked with an asterisk could be shifted to the younger set and the sets would be equal.

Table 5

A Possible Division of the Events in Table 3, Based on the Dimension of Age-Relatedness

Childhood-related	Adulthood-related	
DEVELOPING SKILLS	ACTIVITY DECLINE	IMPROVED MARRIAGE
GETTING LOST	BEING FIRED	*BECOMING ENGAGED
GOOD HEALTH	*LESSENING STRESS	BOSS TROUBLES
HAVE OPERATION	SPOUSE DEATH	UNFAITHFUL SPOUSE
LEARN WALKING	RETIRING	EMPLOYEE CONFLICT
LEARNING HOBBY	BUSINESS FAILURE	*VACATION CANCELLED
RECEIVING AWARD	HEALTH DECLINE	DECREASED STRENGTH
SELF-ACCEPTANCE	*DEATH AWARENESS	*SPOUSE WORKING
	*SPOUSES ARGUING	LEISURE CHANGES
	STRIKING	*ESTEEM CHANGES
	SKILL DECLINE	BUSINESS READJUSTMENT
	MARRIAGE RECONCILIATION	
	*BREAKING ENGAGEMENT	

See text for explanation of asterisks.

Heuristics in Teaching

The use of heuristics in teaching is a very complex topic and space herein is limited; therefore, one example must suffice. The example can be found in McIlvane's paper in this volume. He described the real-life problem-solving task of teaching verbal and other behavioral repertoires to nonverbal individuals, and he emphasized the need to tailor the teaching procedure to the individual and the task. For example, he noted that modeling can be effective depending on the individual's prior repertoire and the task. The teacher who recognizes the relevant dependencies and adjusts the procedures appropriately is using, implicitly or explicitly, a heuristic problem-solving rule.

A General Problem-Solving Heuristic

A general problem-solving heuristic is described in this final section. The heuristic can be used for any kind of problem; it can be taught to children and adults; and if used, it can improve problem-solving effectiveness. The heuristic reflects task analysis of problem solving, and in this respect it is amenable to the application of behavior modification principles. However, most of the subroutines are cognitive, and in this respect its use in behavior modification applications or in behavior analytic research requires ingenuity.

Introduction

One kind of heuristic program is intended to be a theory or computer simulation of complex human behavior. Examples are programs that simulate developmental stages in solving the balance-scale problem (Klahr & Siegler, 1978), the Towers of Hanoi problem (Klahr, 1985), and counting (Siegler & Robinson, 1982), among many examples that could be cited.

Heuristic programs have also been developed to provide computer assistance to subject-matter experts, helping them solve problems in their subject-matter. These programs, called "expert systems," are in the realm of artificial intelligence rather than in the realm of theory or computer simulation of human thinking. An example is a computerized heuristic problem developed by Tonge (1961) for assembly line balancing, which is an ill-defined problem that requires assigning assembly-line workers to jobs. The program yields solutions that are "acceptable" rather than "optimal," and Tonge commented that this problem can be solved more cheaply by industrial engineers than by his heuristic program. However, he pointed out that this cost estimate does not take account of an important consideration: Use of the program frees industrial engineers' time for other tasks (p. 63). (Other examples of such programs have been described by Feigenbaum & Lederberg, 1974.)

The Soviet psychologist Tikhomirov (1972/1981) argued that computer simulation of human behavior is useful more as a way to develop expert systems than as a way to understand human behavior. He said, "Making machine methods of problem solving approximate human ones is the strategic goal of artificial intelligence research" (p. 265; all italics in original); and the way to understand human behavior is not "through 'modeling' mental processes, but through the theoretical and experimental analysis of thought processes" (p. 261).

Regardless of how one evaluates Tikhomirov's rejection of computer modeling, one can accept his recommendation of theoretical and experimental analysis. However, I disagree with Tikhomirov's rejection of computer modeling as a way to understand human behavior. When evaluated on its own ground rules, computer modeling is not only useful but also has been successful (for a summary of the ground rules, see Reese, 1989). Nevertheless, this approach is not discussed in the present paper. As Reitman noted in 1965, and as still remains true, the approach has dealt for the most part with how humans solve well-defined problems, but most problems that confront humans are ill-defined (Reitman, 1965, p. 148). A general heuristic that can be used to solve ill-defined problems is described in the next subsection.

Steps in Problem Solving

The steps described in the present subsection constitute a heuristic routine for solving problems. The routine was derived from Dewey's (1933) theory of problem solving and has been used at the Creative Problem-Solving Institutes held periodically by the Creative Education Foundation in Buffalo, New York. (The 36th annual institute was held in June 1990.)

The heuristic includes the seven steps summarized in Table 6. The steps are described more fully below, and are described in the first-person singular in order to make two general points: (a) Rules can influence a person's behavior only if the person uses the rules as self-instructions; and (b) in most conceptual discussions, including behavioral as well as cognitive discussions, rules are expressed in either the imperative voice or the passive voice, and in either voice the agent who must perform the action is obscured. Despite these arguments, however, both versions of the rules can be useful: The rules as expressed in the imperative voice are succinct and should be more useful as guides for analyzing observed problem-solving behavior, and the rules as expressed in the first-person singular should be more useful for training problem-solving behavior.

1. **Identify the problem.** First, I should decide just what the problem is, and put it in the form of a question. Then I should reword the question at least once as a check on whether I have identified the real problem.
2. **Gather information.** Second, I should gather information about the problem and about

Problem Solving by Algorithms and Heuristics

possible solutions. For example: What do I need to know in order to solve the problem? What might have caused the problem? How have I or other people dealt with this problem or problems like it?

3. **Generate possible solutions.** Third, I need to generate a list of possible solutions. I should make a list of all the ideas I can think of that I might use to solve the problem. While I am making the list I should try not to evaluate the ideas; I will decide later which ones are good. At this point, I should just write down whatever comes to mind.

Table 6

Samples of Analyses of Problem Solving into Components

Composite	Bransford & Stein	Frese & Stewart	Skinner & Chapman	Polya	Butterfield et al.
1. Identify the problem	Identify the problem			Understand the problem	
2. Gather information	Define the problem	Select a goal	Set a goal		Set a goal
3. Identify possible solutions	Explore possible strategies	Generate plans	Generate plans and	Devise a plan	Design strategies and
4. Select a plan		Select a plan	select a plan		select a strategy[a]
5. Carry out the plan	Act on the strategies	Execute the plan	Operate the plan	Carry out the plan	Implement the strategy
6. Test the outcome	Look back and evalate	Process feedback and	Evaluate the outcome	Look back	Assess the outcome
7. Change the plan		modify the plan	Adjust the plan		

[a]*Involves the following subcomponents: Estimate outcomes, Compare estimates of goals, and Select strategy with smallest goal/estimate discrepancy.*

4. **Select a plan.** Fourth, I need to evaluate my ideas and select the best one. Which one is best depends on things like how likely I am to solve the problem if I use a given plan, how likely I am to be able to use it, and how much time, effort, and money I am likely to expend if I use it. I need to decide what is best for me to do. Doing nothing might even be my best plan.
5. **Carry out the plan.** Fifth, I must carry out the plan. No matter how good the plan is, I will not solve the problem unless I carry out the plan. In the worlds of business and industry,

this step includes an important substep: Sell the selected plan to the executive officer or board whose approval is needed. This substep also calls for creative problem solving (Osborn, 1963, pp. 204-206).
6. **Test whether the plan is working.** Sixth, I need to check to see whether the plan is working. I need to include tests in the plan to see whether or not I am solving the problem.
7. **Change the plan if necessary.** Seventh, if a test shows that I am not getting anywhere, or not getting anywhere fast enough, or easily enough, or cheaply enough, I should change the plan. To change the plan, I need to start over, beginning at Step 1, 2, 3, or 4.

Two points about the problem-solving steps are that each step constitutes a problem that needs to be solved, and that the solution of each of these problems might be best accomplished through application of the problem-solving steps. Although a philosophical or theoretical analysis might imply infinite regress in this procedure, in practice the problem-solver is likely to use steps only for a few of the step-problems, is likely to use only a few selected steps in solving these step-problems, and is likely to use the selected steps without treating them as problems to be solved.

Another point is that referring to the steps as "steps" is metaphorical in that these components of problem solving are not literally steps of any sort. More to the point, the metaphor implies that like footsteps, the components occur in a sequence; but as Dewey (1933) said, the problem-solver may actually shift around among the components. For example, the test in Step 6 in Table 6 should be developed in Step 3. Also, this test should be considered in Step 4 because a plan that is otherwise excellent but cannot be tested might be undesirable.

A final consideration about this heuristic is its relation to the specificity and definition of the problem space. The goal of Step 1 is to identify the actual initial and terminal problem states, which often are different from the putative initial and terminal problem states. The purpose of Step 2 is to facilitate attaining the goal of Steps 1 and 3. The goal of Step 3 is to generate an effective, efficient plan, that is, an operation for moving from the actual initial problem state to the actual terminal problem state. Step 4 is identifying this plan, and Step 5 is carrying out the plan. Step 6 is a direct monitoring of outcomes in Step 5, hence an indirect check of the adequacy of Step 4 and, more remotely, the adequacy of Steps 1, 2, and 3. Step 7 is taking corrective action, if needed.

Summary: Examples of Heuristic Problem Solving

The issues covered in this paper can be summarized by way of concrete examples of the problem-solving procedures described.

Lecturer Problem

When I gave the oral presentation of this paper in Sao Paulo, at one point I needed a chalkboard eraser quickly, in order not to drag out the time, but the eraser was behind a large projection screen. I used the problem-solving steps without consciously planning to use them. The following reconstruction is based on notes I made about the episode after the presentation.

Step 1 of solving the problem was easy: The initial state of the problem space was the need for and absence of the eraser, the goal state was having the eraser, and the operation was one that would move from the initial state to the goal state with a minimum expenditure of time. Because of the time pressure, I limited Step 2 to immediately available information: (a) I obviously could not reach the eraser without walking behind the projection screen, (b) a speaker's disappearing behind such a screen and causing it to bulge might appear clownish, and (c) if it appeared as clowning, the audience would be distracted from the material being presented. Also because of the time pressure, I combined Steps 3 and 4 by evaluating each possible solution as soon as I thought of it, intending to terminate Step 3 and initiate Step 5 as soon as I generated a minimally acceptable solution. I identified three possible solutions: (a) Walk behind the screen from the other side, which I rejected because the eraser was near the middle; (b) raise the screen, which I rejected because it would take too much time and effort; and (c) walk behind the screen after describing the problem and making it an example of the material being presented. I selected (Step 4) and carried out (Step 5) the last solution. The solution worked (Step 6) with respect to the goal state initially set, in that I obtained the needed eraser almost immediately; but I did not test attainment of the implicit subgoal of avoiding unwanted mirth.

Rug Remnant Problem

A simple problem can be used to illustrate the general problem-solving heuristic:

A rug store is offering a large remnant at $40 per square yard. The price for a new rug cut to the size of a room is $48 per square yard. The remnant is square and has an area of 16 square yards. The Reeses need a rug for a 10 by 12 foot room. They are considering buying the remnant and cutting it to fit the room. What should they do?

The preliminary calculations are easy: The remnant would cost $40 X 16 = $640, and a new rug cut to size would cost the same (10' x 12' = 120 sq. ft., which is 13.33 sq. yd. $48 X 13.33 = $639.84). However, these preliminary calculations do not necessarily solve the problem. If the problem is only to determine the cost of the remnant relative to the cost of a new rug cut to size, then the calculations indicate that the cost is the same. However, another issue might be to add to the cost of the remnant the value of the Reeses' time spent cutting the remnant to size. Or maybe the Reeses prefer to do their own cutting rather than rely on the store's cutters.

Another issue is whether the remnant is too small for the room; and if not, how much will need to be cut off each side. The length of each side of the remnant is 4 yards, or 12 feet, and therefore 2 feet will have to be cut off one side, yielding a 2 x 12 foot scrap. But maybe the Reeses will not consider this segment to be scrap; maybe they could use it as a runner.

Another issue is that the Reeses are considering buying the remnant, and therefore they are presumably satisfied with the color, pattern, texture, and other properties of the remnant. However, an issue might be whether the store has available a new rug that is at least as satisfactory. Also, if the store does not have an acceptable new rug available, two issues are whether the store is willing to order one, and if so, how long the order will take to be delivered, and whether the Reeses are willing to wait that long. Another issue is whether the price includes delivery, and if not, whether the delivery charge is the same for the remnant and a new rug. In short, the answer to the question "What should they do?" depends on what the problem is. "What should they do for what purpose?" Here is where the first step of the general problem-solving heuristic is applied.

References

Anderson, J. R. (1990). *Cognitive psychology and its implications* (3rd ed.). New York: Freeman.

Anzai, Y. (1987). Doing, understanding, and learning in problem solving. In D. Klahr, P. Langley, & R. Neches, (Eds.), *Production system models of learning and development* (pp. 55-97). Cambridge, MA: MIT Press.

Baer, D. M. (1982). Applied behavior analysis. In G. T. Wilson & C. M. Franks (Eds.), *Contemporary behavior therapy* (pp. 277-309). New York: Guilford.

Bugelski, B. R., & Huff, E. M. (1962). A note on increasing the efficiency of Luchins' mental sets. *American Journal of Psychology, 75,* 665-667.

Dewey, J. (1933). *How we think: A restatement of the relation of reflective thinking to the educative process.* Boston: Heath.

Ellis, H. C., & Hunt, R. R. (1989). *Fundamentals of human memory and cognition* (4th ed.). Dubuque, IA: Brown.

Feigenbaum, E., & Lederberg, J. (1974, July). Heuristic programming project. In L. Earnest (Ed.), *Recent research in artificial intelligence, heuristic programming, and network protocols* (pp. 23-46). Stanford Artificial Intelligence Laboratory. Memo AlM-252, Computer Science Department Report No. STAN-CS-74-466. Stanford University, Stanford, CA.

Kaplan, A. (1964). *The conduct of inquiry.* San Francisco: Chandler.

Klahr, D. (1985). Solving problems with ambiguous subgoal ordering: Preschoolers' performance. *Child Development, 56,* 940-952.

Klahr, D., & Siegler, R. S. (1978). The representation of children's knowledge. In H. W. Reese & L. P. Lipsitt (Eds.), *Advances in child development and behavior* (Vol. 12, pp. 61-116). New York: Academic Press.

Knuth, D. E. (1981). Algorithms in modern mathematics and computer science. In A. P. Ershov & D. E. Knuth (Eds.), *Algorithms in modern mathematics and computer science (Lecture Notes in Computer Science, 122,* 82-99). Berlin: Springer-Verlag.

Luchins, A. S. (1942). Mechanization in problem solving: The effect of *Einstellung. Psychological Monographs, 54*(6, Whole No. 248).

Luchins, A. S., & Luchins, E. H. (1950). New experimental attempts at preventing mechanization of problem solving. *Journal of General Psychology, 42,* 279-297.

Maier, N. R. F., & Burke, R. J. (1967). Response availability as a factor in the problem-solving performance of males and females. *Journal of Personality and Social Psychology, 5,* 304-310.

Matijasevic, Y. (1981). What should we do having proved a decision problem to be unsolvable? In A. P. Ershov & D. E. Knuth (Eds.), *Algorithms in modern mathematics and computer science (Lecture Notes in Computer Science, 122,* 441-443). Berlin: Springer-Verlag.

Mayer, R. E. (1983). *Thinking, problem solving, cognition.* New York: Freeman.

Murray, F. B., & Armstrong, S. L. (1978). Adult nonconservation of numerical equivalence. *Merrill-Palmer Quarterly, 24,* 255-263.

Neches, R., Langley, P., & Klahr, D. (1987). Learning, development, and production systems. In D. Klahr, P. Langley, & R. Neches, (Eds.), *Production system models of learning and development* (pp. 1-53). Cambridge, MA: MIT Press.

Newell, A., & Simon, H. A. (1972). *Human problem solving.* Englewood Cliffs, NJ: Prentice-Hall.

Odom, R. D., Cunningham, J. G., & Astor, E. C. (1975). Adults thinking the way we think children think, but children don't always think that way: A study of perceptual salience and problem solving. *Bulletin of the Psychonomic Society, 6,* 545-548.

Osborn, A. F. (1963). *Applied imagination: Principles and procedures of creative problem-solving* (3rd rev. ed.). New York: Scribner's.

Polya, G. (1948). *How to solve it: A new aspect of mathematical method* (5th printing, text "slightly changed" & appendix added). Princeton, NJ: Princeton University Press.

Reese, H. W. (1989). Rules and rule-governance: Cognitive and behavioristic views. In S. C. Hayes (Ed.), *Rule-governed behavior: Cognition, contingencies, and instructional control* (pp. 3-84). New York: Plenum.

Reese, H. W., Puckett, J. M., & Cohen, S. H. (in preparation). *Cognition in adulthood and old age.* Report in preparation.

Reese, H. W., & Smyer, M. A. (1983). The dimensionalization of life events. In E. J. Callahan & K. A. McCluskey (Eds.), *Life-span developmental psychology: Nonnormative life events* (pp. 1-

33). New York: Academic Press.

Reichenbach, H. (1938). *Experience and prediction: An analysis of the foundations and structure of knowledge.* Chicago: University of Chicago Press.

Reitman, W. A. (1965). *Cognition and thought: An information-processing approach.* New York: Wiley.

Ryle, G. (1949). *The concept of mind.* London: Hutchison's University Library. (1950 reprint cited)

Siegler, R. S., & Robinson, M. (1982). The development of numerical understandings. In H. W. Reese (Ed.), *Advances in child development and behavior* (Vol. 16, pp. 241-312). New York: Academic Press.

Skinner, B. F. (1945). The operational analysis of psychological terms. *Psychological Review, 52,* 270-277.

Skinner, B. F. (1974). *About behaviorism.* New York: Knopf.

Steele, R. (Ed.). (1922). *The earliest arithmetics in English.* London: Humphrey Milford, Oxford University Press. (Early English Text Society, Extra Series, No. 118.)

Tikhomirov, O. K. (1981). The psychological consequences of computerization. In J. V. Wertsch (Ed. & trans.), *The concept of activity in Soviet psychology* (pp. 256-278). Armonk, NY: Sharpe. (Original work published in 1972)

Tonge, F. M. (1961). *A heuristic program for assembly line balancing.* Englewood Cliffs, NJ: Prentice-Hall.

Vygotsky, L. S. (1987). *Thinking and speech.* In *The collected works of L. S. Vygotsky* (R. W. Rieber & A. S. Carton, Eds.; N. Minick, trans.; Vol. 1, pp. 37-285). New York: Plenum. (Original work published in 1934; other, less complete translations published in 1962 and 1986 as *Thought and language*)

Zemanek, H. (1981). AL-KHOREZMI: His background, his personality, his work and his influence. In A. P. Ershov & D. E. Knuth (Eds.), *Algorithms in modern mathematics and computer science (Lecture Notes in Computer Science, 122,* 1-81). Berlin: Springer-Verlag.

Chapter 11

Instructing Variability: Some Features of a Problem-Solving Repertoire

Philip N. Chase (1)
Gudfinna S. Bjarnadottir
West Virginia University

A college sophomore enters a small room with bright lights and sits at a table facing a computer screen. On the table in front of her sits two black pads with a small button in the center of each. On the computer screen appears the message: "It is up to you to figure out how to earn points that you may exchange for money. Each point is worth six cents. If you are smart you can earn about $5.00 in the next 15 minutes. Watch the counter on the top of the screen to see how many points you have earned." The individual picks up one of the button pads and presses the button rapidly for 30 seconds. Nothing happens. She then picks up the other button pad and presses it. A beep emanates from the computer. The subject waits a bit and presses again. Nothing happens. She picks up the first button and as soon as she presses it the counter changes from zero to one. She presses the second button quickly for approximately 10 seconds and again the beep occurs. She presses the first button once and the counter changes to a two.

After five minutes of rapidly responding in this manner, she tries pressing the button against the table, but finds that she cannot press it as fast. She tries a number of pressing strategies and each one results in a different rate of responding, but still every 10 seconds the beep sounds and she gains more points. She slows down until she is only pressing once or twice every 10 seconds.

The preceding observation was taken, with some elaboration, from descriptions of typical behavior analytic experiments on rule governance (cf. LeFrancois, Chase and Joyce, 1988). In many rule governance studies, conditions such as these are compared to conditions in which the subject is told how to respond. Comparisons are typically made on the rate of acquiring the response of interest and rate of change in responding when the conditions of reinforcement change. One can also describe this situation as what others more generally recognize as problem-solving. Like Kohler's stick wielding chimp, Weisberg's dot connecting college students and Epstein's banana pecking pigeons, this student was faced with a problem, she had to manipulate the environment until it became discriminative for a particular behavior, and this behavior resulted in the solution.

The conclusion that a typical rule governance experiment is an example of problem solving should not be surprising. After all, Skinner first made the distinction between rule governed and contingency shaped behavior in his essays on problem-solving (Skinner, 1966; 1969). An emphasis on problem solving, however, has been lost in the rush of conclusions that have been drawn from the experiments on rule governance. Most investigators seem more interested in testing whether or not human behavior is rule governed. But another reason for studying rule governed behavior is to determine the variables that produce behavior that adapts to changing environments. This reflects an interest in problem solving.

This chapter will address the relation between problem solving and rule governance with a special emphasis on variability or variation of behavior. We will describe what is meant by problem solving and base that description on the examples that have been given in the problem solving literature. Then, we will argue that the rules or instructions that usually have been manipulated in the rule governance experiments limit behavior to such an extent as to interfere with the variability necessary for problem-solving. The initial steps of the contingency shaping procedures, in contrast, usually produce variable responding for at least a short period of time and if the environment changes during this period of time, the behavior adapts to the environmental changes. Similar effects may be obtained with instructions, but instructions, rules and directions have to be constructed so that they increase variability in behavior. Finally, we will report studies on rules that increased the range of responses subjects made within a problem solving situation and were very efficient in training specific problem solving repertoires.

A Brief Description of Problem Solving

The traditional language used to describe problem solving has always been difficult for behavior analysts. According to these descriptions, problem solving is a distinct class of behavior because it produces outcomes that are identified as being both novel and insightful. Skinner (1969) claimed that if you investigated the history of an individual you would not find novel behavior, the responses have been made before and have been reinforced. Hull (1935) argued that the concept of insight was an explanatory fiction, it reasserted the observation that problems are solved without defining problem solving any further. But these arguments have not convinced other scientists. The problem solving literature continues to point out differences between problem solving and other behaviors. Differences have been described between the simple repetition of behavior and novel instances of behavior, reproductive and productive behavior, and more recently, atomistic responses with discrete defining features and responses that vary considerably from instance to instance (Shimp, 1989). Typically the responses studied by behavior analysts fall into the atomistic category and the responses studied in problem solving do not. It seems important, therefore, to reexamine how problem solving has been described by investigators of problem solving. For example, a translation of terms like novelty and insight as they are used by others might be a first step toward understanding the special characteristics of problem solving.

Novelty. Novelty is simply that which has not been observed and, thus, novel responding ranges from behavior which an individual has never observed to behavior which a society or culture has never observed. This definition of novelty poses some problems for using it to identify problem solving. For example, a first born child may appear to engage in novel behavior to its parents, but the child specialist who has observed many children recognizes its similarity to the behavior of other children. The parents state that the child's behavior is novel; they have observed the child's behavior and know that it has not engaged in the particular response in the past. The child specialist does not see this as novel because the child is engaging in typical behavior. The parents' use of novelty is based on individual history, the child specialist's is based expert normative judgement.

An example of this problem with novelty is revealed in discussions of the various solutions to the famous string problem (Ellen, 1982). In the string problem, two strings are suspended from the ceiling in a room where many other objects are available to the subject. The subjects are asked to tie the ends of the string together, but soon find that if they hold one string the other cannot be reached. Ellen described four possible solutions and specified that only one was considered novel: tying an object to one of the strings, swinging it like a pendulum and walking over to the other string and grabbing the swinging one to tie them together. In this case, Ellen suggested that the experimenter distinguish between his or her experience with the problem as to whether some solutions are novel or not. This analysis suggests that what may be novel to the experimenter is not necessarily novel to the subject. The subjects may have had experience with similar type problems and thus the behavior is not novel. Alternatively the subjects may have never emitted the alternative solutions, for example, tying one of the strings to a chair and walking the other string over to it. The latter would be novel. Granted the experimenter has to judge whether a behavior is novel or not, but novelty has to be judged on the basis of the individual subject's history. Thus, according to a behavior analytic interpretation, novel behavior is behavior that has never been observed to be emitted by the individual under investigation.

Insight. To distinguish problem solving from other kinds of novel behavior, like creativity, investigators have also described problem solving as insightful. The term insightful has been used to describe novel behaviors that appear to have a direction, that seem to be goal oriented, that are not accidental. Scientists have distinguished between solutions to problems that are insightful from those that are due to trial and error. Compare these descriptions taken from Birch (1945) in which chimps solved problems involving reaching food with a stick:

> At 50 seconds, (into the test situation) he returned to the grill, paused and stared intently at the food. Then, he turned away suddenly, rushed into the inner cage, clambered upon the shelf, picked up the stick, leaped back to the floor and carried the stick to the grill and obtained the food... The definite impression produced by his behavior, was that he had suddenly recalled the stick on the shelf, and at once utilized this knowledge in his problem-solving effort. (Birch, 1945, p. 308)

> In the course of his general wandering Art (the subject) entered the inner cage, climbed the shelf and began to play with the long stick. Then upon returning to the outside cage, he carried the stick with him in play and laid it on the floor while he engaged in general activities. Thus, when he returned to the problem, the long stick was immediately available on the floor of the outer cage, and he was able to act routinely, on the basis of his previous stick experiences and obtain the food. (Birch, 1945, p. 311)

Birch (1945) concluded that the first example involved problem solving and the second did not because the first appeared to be insightful. Birch described insightfulness as solutions based upon the perception of relevant functional relations by the individual and the consequent reorganization of these activities in accordance with the requirements of the problem situation (Birch, 1945).

Birch's description of insight, which was influenced by gestaltist descriptions (cf. Kohler, 1925), distinguishes some examples of problem solving from others on the continuum of accidental contact with the solution versus a systematic sequence of behaviors that leads to the solution. Behavior analysts, though, ask: How do we determine the perception of relevant functional relations and reorganization of these activities? How do we know whether this is accidental or not? We observe the individuals behavior to see if they engage in a particular sequence of behavior that leads to the solution and we judge the directness of the sequence by comparing it to less direct sequences of behavior. There is a catch, however. The more we judge a problem solving response to be direct, the more likely we are to find behavior that has occurred previously. Alternatively, the more novel the response that produces the solution, the more likely the solution is due to variability of responding, and the factors that produce the variability may not be understood (i.e. are due to accident).

If we refocus our description of novelty and insight on two different classes of behavior involved in problem solving, then the issue between these two features of problem solving can be resolved. The response that produces the solution has to be a novel response in order for the situation to be called problem solving. The variation in behavior that occurs prior to the solution response, however, can be either a direct sequence of behaviors, uncontrolled variability (i.e. variability for which controlling variables have not been isolated) or somewhere in between these extremes. This distinction suggests three general ways that problems can be solved. They can be solved through a systematic sequence of behaviors that result in a novel response, in which case they have few other novel aspects. Problems can be solved through accidental contact with some critical changes in the environment, in which case novelty is observed in both the solution response and other responses leading up to the solution, and could be called trial and error. Or problems can be solved through a combination of systematic, previously learned behaviors and accidental contact with critical changes in the environment which lead to a novel solution response. If we examine the kinds of problems that are defined by both novelty and insight, we find that they appear to involve some general, but systematic, sequence of behaviors that allows for sufficient range in topography of responding to come into contact with the solution.

A Behavioral Interpretation of Problem Solving

Skinner (1969) posed a question that helps us to see what this kind of problem solving is:

How do they (people) learn to behave appropriately under contingencies of reinforcement for which they have not been prepared, especially contingencies which are so specific and ephemeral that no general preparation is possible? (pp. 141-142)

The answer is that individuals engage in:
1. A class of response relations
2. that occur when an environment establishes a solution as a reinforcer, but
3. the environment is discriminative for a response other than that which produces the solution,
4. the response produces a change in the environment so that it becomes a discriminative stimulus for further responding and
5. Steps 3. and 4. are repeated until the solution is produced.
6. The response that produced the solution is judged by an observer as a novel response and this judgement is justified on empirical or logical grounds for the individuals.
7. The sequence of behavior-environment relations produced by steps 3. and 4. is also judged as a direct systematic sequence of behaviors that is part of the individuals' history and this judgement is justified on empirical or logical grounds for the individuals.

Given this definition, we can examine the example that started this chapter to see how it illustrates problem solving. According to the definition the solution has to be established as a reinforcer. Although not clearly established through deprivation conditions, I assume that a college student's responding will come under the control of monetary consequences, especially if these are described to the subject. Therefore, at the beginning of the example the solution that was established was finding out how to get points that result in money. Later in the experiment a more specific solution, responding every ten seconds, was established as the solution. Only after the subject had responded for a few minutes and had come into contact with the cost (effort) of responding rapidly, did responding "efficiently" become established as a reinforcer.

The environment of the experiment was, at first, discriminative for a response pattern other than one that produced the solution. In this case the response unit of interest was not a single button press, but rather a response pattern. At the beginning of the example the subject tried a few different patterns of responding before reinforcers were obtained. When the second part of the solution was established as a reinforcer she engaged in a number of alternative response patterns before settling on the pattern of pressing the first button once every ten seconds and then pressing the second button. Since the subject did not engage in either reinforced pattern of responding until after trying others, we assume that the environment was discriminative for responses other than the solution in both cases.

The responses prior to the solution response pattern also changed the environment. The computer screen did not change after the subject engaged in button presses and as a result the environment functioned as a discriminative stimulus for other kinds of responding. This relation held until the occurrence of a particular sequence of behaviors that resulted in changes in points on the computer monitor. Thus, feature three and four were repeated.

Feature six of the definition requires a judgement. Has the subject engaged in the behavior pattern that leads to the solution before? As indicated above, the subject did not engage in the pattern of interest until other behaviors had been attempted. Because the monetary contingencies supported discovering the solution as quickly as possible, the evidence seemed reasonable that the final response pattern was novel. To be more sure of its novelty the experimenter could document that the subject had not been in an experiment on human learning before, and she had not taken any courses that taught her about reinforcement schedules and other related experiences. We would never be entirely sure, but the more unique the sequence of behaviors required the more likely that the subject had not emitted the exact response before.

The last feature of our definition is the most difficult one to document, but the kinds of alternative response patterns attempted by the subject indicated that the variation was a member of a general response class learned prior to the experiment. The behaviors appeared to be specifically directed toward different rates of responding with particular alternations of the two buttons. The behaviors were circumscribed sufficiently to suggest that they were not simply trial and error.

Variables That Affect Problem Solving: The Importance of Variability

Having described the subject matter of interest, we can now try to determine what we know about the variables that control this phenomenon. From a behavior analytic perspective or a more general selectionist view (Donahoe, 1991), we might examine three broad classes of variables: variation, selection and maintenance. Variation is produced by changes in the structure of the individual and by changes in the environment. The variation in behavior is restricted or selected by the effect that responding has on the environment. Finally, the behaviors that are selected are maintained by relations among antecedent events and consequences. To understand problem solving, we need to investigate variables from each of these classes.

Like many behavior analysts we have attempted to discover the component behaviors maintained by a number of different problem solving environments. Bjarnadottir and Chase (1988), Danforth, Chase, Dolan and Joyce (1990) and LeFrancois, Chase & Joyce (1988) all started from this perspective. We soon found, however, that one of the factors related to problem solving was variability or behavioral variation. Subsequently we have turned to this factor for further investigation.

From the selectionist model of problem solving we can see the importance of understanding variability of responding. Variability is involved in at least two levels of problem solving. First, some behavioral variability must occur in order for new behavior to be selected by consequences. Second, variation has to be maintained in a systematic fashion if we are to obtain systematic solutions. These aspects of variability are synonymous with the critical features of novelty and insight as described earlier.

The findings of the rule governance literature also reveal the importance of variability for solving problems. One of the major findings of the rule governance literature, that rule governed behavior is insensitive to changes in contingencies, can be described alternatively in terms of variability. The rules that have been investigated restrict variability more than the shaping or differential reinforcement procedures to which they have been compared.

In Joyce, Chase & Danforth (1987) we were interested in fine tuning a relation between instructions and behavior that we had discovered in LeFrancois, Chase & Joyce (1988). LeFrancois et al. had found that instructing subjects to perform differently in the presence of eight different schedules of reinforcement provided the component behaviors necessary to adapt to the presence of a novel schedule (a fixed interval schedule) and under extinction conditions. Joyce et al. attempted to find the minimum instructions that would provide this same repertoire. We

Table 1

Condition	Schedule	Instructions
Variety differentially reinforced	DRL 20 second and FR 40	It is up to you to figure out how to best earn points.
Variety Instructed	DRL 20 second	Wait 20 seconds before pressing the earn button for each point.
	FR 40	Press the earn button 40 times for each point.
DRL Instructed	DRL 20 second	Wait 20 seconds before pressing the earn button for each point.
FR Instructed	FR 40	Press the earn button 40 times for each point.

thought that perhaps instructing subjects to respond to one low rate schedule and one high rate schedule would provide a range that would be sufficient to produce behavior that was sensitive to a fixed interval (FI) schedule. So we constructed four training conditions with differential reinforcement of low rate (DRL) and fixed ratio (FR) schedules as outlined in Table 1:

The differential reinforcement condition did not reinforce successive approximations to the target behavior, but simply exposed the subjects to the contingencies with the minimum instruction, "It is up to you to figure out how to best earn points." These subjects responded to these contingencies until their behavior reached our stability requirement of earning at least five reinforcers in the last two minutes of a session that lasted at least ten minutes. The instructed subjects, on the other hand, were given an explicit instruction and then exposed to the schedule described in those instructions until their behavior reached stability.

The first finding was that it took the subjects much longer to reach stability under the differential reinforcement conditions than any of the instructed conditions. The subjects in the differential reinforcement condition took between 25 and 66 minutes (mean=46 minutes) to reach stability whereas the subjects in the instructed variety condition took between 14 and 29 minutes (mean=19.4 minutes) to reach stability. This was further evidence for the claim that instructions are a more efficient means of training then simple differential reinforcement with sophisticated verbal subjects. These data also indicated very clearly that there was a great deal of variability in differentially reinforced responding before a particular pattern of responding was selected by its consequences.

After each subject reached stability their performance was tested in a session in which approximately half way through the session the schedule of reinforcement changed from a FR 40 to an FI 10 without any stimulus change. We found that regardless of the type of training, only one subject's behavior changed when the schedule changed. This baffled us because the literature suggested that at least the differentially reinforced responding would be sensitive to the change. After reviewing the literature again, however, we found some evidence that a stimulus change might be necessary (Galizio, 1979). So we introduced a stimulus change in multiple baseline fashion across subjects in each group to see what would happen. Just prior to the introduction of the FI schedule, the computer screen gave the following message: "It is up to you to figure out how to best earn points." The data showed that the behavior of most of the subjects in the differential reinforced variety, the instructed variety and the instructed DRL groups changed when the stimulus change accompanied the change from an FR schedule to an FI schedule. The behavior of subjects in the instructed FR group did not change even when the stimulus change occurred. These data indicated that the minimum component skill sufficient to produce sensitivity to an FI schedule was low rate responding. This finding was similar to those of Weiner (1969) which indicated that shaping a low rate schedule was sufficient to produce sensitive FI performance, however, in Joyce, Chase and Danforth (1987) the low rate schedule was instructed.

Though we set out to find the minimum repertoire that we could instruct and still obtain sensitive FI performance, we also made three general observations that are relevant to our discussion of variability:
1. Variability of responding was more an inherent property of the differential reinforced responding then it was of instructed responding at least with the kinds of instructions investigated and with the subjects used (subjects with sophisticated verbal repertoires).
2. Once behavior was stable, insensitive behavior occurred whether the response pattern was specifically instructed or selected by differential reinforcement.
3. A stimulus change was sufficient to introduce variability of behavior as long as the subjects had a history of both high and low rate behavior, and this variation produced behavior that made contact with the new schedule of reinforcement.

These findings intrigued us because they indicated that maybe the differences found between instructed behavior and contingency shaped behavior in other studies were primarily due to a comparison of stable instructed behavior and contingency shaped behavior that was in transition. This appeared to be the case. The studies that clearly showed a difference between instructed and contingency shaped behavior did not report the use of a stability criterion. We wanted to see whether this was a critical variable, so we conducted another series of studies to address this question.

Joyce and Chase (1990) began with an experiment that had the conditions shown in Table 2. After exposure to one of these conditions each subject was tested on an FI 10 second schedule without a stimulus change. We found that only the behavior of subjects with the differential reinforcement short exposure history was sensitive to the FI schedule and that these subjects were the only subjects whose behavior was variable at the moment of the schedule change. Thus, stable

Table 2

Condition	Instructions
1. Differential Reinforcement Short Exposure	1. "It is up to you to figure how to best earn points"
2. Differential Reinforcement Stable (3 sessions, last two minute means vary < 10%)	2. "
3. Instructed Short Exposure	3. "Press the earn button 40 times to receive points"
4. Instructed Stable (3 sessions, last two minute means vary < 10%)	4. "

responding was not sensitive to the change in contingencies regardless of whether it was differentially reinforced or instructed. What we could not determine from this experiment was whether variable instructed responding would be sensitive to the change in schedules. In fact, we manipulated the time that the instructed subjects were exposed to the FR schedule after the instruction. We even reduced it to one minute and we still had performance that looked as stable as the behavior that was required to reach stability. We continued to investigate the variables that might produce some variation in behavior after instructions, but we will present those finding later when the instructional procedures for producing variability are discussed.

We had learned from these experiments and the literature three aspects about variability that are important to the sensitivity of behavior to contingency changes:

1. If a change in contingencies occurred when behavior was in transition, the behavior was more likely to contact that change because it was varying.
2. Once behavior stabilized, whether instructed or differentially reinforced, behavior had to come into contact with an environmental change for the behavior to vary.
3. If there was such contact, behavior was likely to be sensitive to the change in reinforcement if the subjects had a history of varying their responding or a history of the component behaviors that the schedule of reinforcement would select.

These might be the reasons that differential reinforcement procedures have often resulted in sensitive behavior and instructions have not. Often the behavior had been in transition under differential reinforcement conditions and had already stabilized under instructed conditions. When both instructed and differentially reinforced behavior were allowed to stabilize, the differential reinforcement procedures were more likely to have provided the subject with a history of varying their behavior under conditions in which the environment varies, thus when exposed to an environmental change, variation in behavior occurs and contact with the new contingency was more likely to occur. If one provides this same history of variation with instructions, however, instructed behavior is likely to adapt as well.

If these points are examined from the general model of problem solving that we have discussed, one sees some similarities. The first point refers to the initial property of behavior, variation has to occur in order for new behavior to be selected. This variation can occur for a number of reasons, but when an experiment begins, the behavior under differential reinforcement conditions is likely to vary because there have been changes in antecedents, establishing operations and consequences. Behavior under instructed conditions, with subjects who have a history of responding to instructions, is not likely to vary, it is likely to follow the instruction.

The second point refers to other variables that produce variation. In the studies that we have reported, there was an antecedent stimulus change. In other studies there have been changes in the consequences. For example, in Hayes, Brownstein, Zettle, Rosenfarb & Korn (1986), high rate responding underwent extinction when DRL contingencies were in effect, the extinction conditions produced both low and high rate responding, and the low rate behavior puts the behavior into contact with the reinforcers. Other cases exist in the literature. Galizio (1979) and Lamons and Chase (1990) showed that response cost procedures would also produce variation in behavior that eventually made contact with the reinforcers.

The third point is a little more controversial given the data presented so far. Really what we can say is that some kinds of behavior have not changed even when there has been a stimulus change. Whether this was due to the subjects' history of variation in behavior or the component behaviors is still left to investigate. But we do know that the kinds of instructions that have been investigated led to stable behavior very quickly. As far as we can tell, the instructed behavior did not have a history of variation within the experimental context. Single instructions like "respond fast" or "respond forty times to receive points" restricted behavior within a narrow range. This restriction did not allow enough of a range of topographies that would be necessary to contact the reinforcers. So the question addressed next was whether variable behavior could be produced with instructions and whether this behavior would be sensitive to changes in the environment.

Instructions that Produce Variable Behavior

Instructing a Range of Behaviors. The first type of instructional control we investigated involved using instructions to teach subjects a wide range of different patterns of behavior that could be reinforced by schedules of reinforcement (LeFrancois, Chase & Joyce, 1988). In one condition subjects received a specific instruction that accurately described the best way to respond on a particular schedule of reinforcement. They received four minutes of exposure to that schedule of reinforcement. Then, a new instruction was given for another schedule of reinforcement, also followed by four minutes of exposure to that schedule. This training was repeated for eight different schedules of reinforcement. Other subjects were either exposed to one instruction and one corresponding schedule of reinforcement or to no instructions and exposure to one schedule of reinforcement. Finally, all subjects were tested on a novel FI schedule.

The data from this study showed that subjects who had a history of instructions on different schedules of reinforcement varied their behavior during the test schedule and came into contact with the novel FI schedule. Some contingency shaped subjects also varied their responding, and contacted the FI schedule, but the other subjects did not. In this study there was a stimulus change before the test schedule. Before the FI schedule went into effect, the subjects were told "It is up to you to figure out how to best earn points."

As mentioned earlier, Joyce, Chase & Danforth (1987) also indicated that subjects who had been instructed on at least two schedules of reinforcement, one a low rate schedule and one a high rate schedule, engaged in behavior that was sensitive to a novel FI schedule when there was a stimulus change. This study also indicated that instructing a low rate schedule was sufficient to produce the variability necessary to be sensitive to the FI schedule. We speculated, however, that these subjects had essentially the same history as the subjects who had both a high rate and a low rate instruction. All of these subjects started the experiment by responding at a high rate. It took an average of 15 minutes of exposure to the low rate DRL schedule before these subjects responded at a stable low rate of behavior. Thus, these subjects also had a history of low rate and high rate responding.

These data added conclusiveness to our observation that when a stimulus change is programmed, subjects who have had a history of variable responding will be more likely to engage in variable behavior and the behavior is more likely to come into contact with a novel contingency then subjects without this history. This history can be provided by differential reinforcement procedures that produce variable responding or instructional procedures that require variation in responding. But what about situations in which there is not a stimulus change. What history of instructions will produce a systematic variation of behavior even when there is no change in the environment?

Strategic Instructions. To examine this question we have looked at strategic instructions. Strategic instructions are those that restrict responding to a strategy for testing or determining which responses will be reinforced in a given situation. For example, Chase, Joyce & LeFrancois (1987) compared a simple direct instruction about an FR schedule to a strategic instruction. The test involved novel FI, variable interval (VI), and fixed time (FT) schedules that delivered reinforcers at approximately the same rate as the FR schedule, and extinction conditions.

The strategic instruction looked like this:

> Your task is to figure out how to earn the most points with the least effort. Sometimes the points will be delivered on the basis of how many button presses you make, for example, every 20 button presses may earn a point. At other times, points will be delivered on the basis of a passage of time, for example, if you respond once every 20 seconds, you will earn a point. Additional conditions include points being delivered without pressing the button and no points being delivered regardless of button presses. The best way to figure out which system of point delivery is in effect is to vary your speed of responding until you reliably earn points with the least effort.

The FR instruction was like those used in our other studies: "Press the button forty times to receive points."

The data indicated that the strategic instruction was effective in producing behavior that was sensitive to changes in the schedules of reinforcement without any explicit stimulus change. One subject never received a simple FR instruction and his behavior was clearly sensitive to FI 10's, FT 10's, VI 10's and extinction test schedules by the third session. A second subject received the simple FR instruction for three sessions and did not show any difference in performance on the different test schedules. However, on the fourth session this subject received the strategic instruction and immediately showed changes in behavior that were correlated with the changes in the schedules and by the sixth session was engaging in sensitive behavior on each schedule. A third subject received the simple FR instruction for six sessions and showed no change in behavior for each of the test schedules. When given the strategic instruction on the seventh session, this subject's behavior immediately began to vary and show sensitivity to each schedule.

Joyce & Chase (1990) also used the strategic instruction to produce variable instructed behavior. In this study we measured variation in behavior through the use of an interresponse time analysis (IRT). In the first experiment of this study, which we described earlier, only the behavior of subjects who received a short exposure to the differential reinforcement procedure was sensitive to the new contingency and that even as little as one minute of exposure to a contingency after an instruction was sufficient for instructed behavior to stabilize. Therefore, in a second experiment we introduced a strategic instruction to obtain some non-stable instructed behavior.

First the subjects were instructed with the simple FR instruction. Then, a few minutes into the session the schedule of reinforcement changed to an FI schedule without any stimulus change. As in previous experiments the subjects showed no change in behavior. This was measured with cumulative records as before, but also a more fine grained analysis was provided by calculating the IRT's around the point at which the FI schedule went into effect. Then, we provided the subjects with a strategic instruction and after a few minutes of exposure to an FR schedule, the schedule of reinforcement changed to an FI. In these sessions we found that the subjects' behavior varied and the pattern of responding was sensitive to the FI contingency. The IRT analysis revealed that at the moment of the change in the schedule the subjects were engaging in a range of different IRT's indicating considerable variability. We then reversed back to the simple FR instruction and found almost perfect reversals in behavior. The subjects' behavior was now no longer sensitive to the FI schedule. Again, when we returned to the strategic instruction, the subjects' behavior varied and their performance demonstrated sensitivity to the FI schedule.

As with other instructional procedures that we have used, the strategic instruction attempts to establish a range of responses that are made in the context of a specific type of problem. The instructions teach the subject to systematically test what pattern(s) of responses will lead to reinforcement by varying their behavior. This test could be used whenever there is an environmental change or periodically to determine whether the contingencies have changed without an environmental change.

Conclusion

In the beginning of the chapter we suggested that the rule governance procedures involving an emphasis on the patterns of behavior selected by different schedules of reinforcement are a useful way of investigating problem solving. The procedures fit a general definition of problem solving and are not contrary to other examples of problem solving, particularly problem solving involving a general class of behaviors that produce changes in the environment which result in the solution. We might add that one of the benefits of using this procedure as a problem solving task is that each change in the programmed schedule of reinforcement can be considered a new problem and thus repeated exposure to a variety of problems can be observed within an individual subject.

We have also reported on a number of studies that have demonstrated the importance of variation in behavior in solving the kinds of problems that have been investigated in the rule governance literature. Essentially there are two kinds of problems and the factors that produce variability enter into the relation in different ways for each of these problems. The first problem involves an environmental change and a different behavior will produce the reinforcers. For example, sometimes the switch from FR to FI schedules is accompanied by the experimenter saying something like "It is up to you to figure out how to best earn points." The second type of problem involves situations in which changes in stimuli do not occur unless there are changes in behavior. The example we have used is an FR schedule changing to an FI schedule with the same rate of reinforcement and without any interruption of performance or further instructions. The subject can gain the same number of reinforcers for a lot less work if the behavior comes under control of the FI schedule, but in order to do so the behavior must change sufficiently to come into contact with the temporal characteristics of the interval schedule.

In both cases the emission of the correct response is made more likely when an individual has a history of engaging in the component behaviors necessary for coming into contact with the solution to the problem. For example, a history of reinforcement for low rate behavior makes it more likely that low rates will occur in the presence of a stimulus change, and low rates of behavior are more likely to come into contact with the temporal characteristics of a fixed interval schedule of reinforcement. Both cases also require a history of variation in behavior. The first case requires variation in behavior as a function of a stimulus change. Variation in the presence of a stimulus change is sufficiently robust across species and individuals to suggest phylogenetic histories. Whether or not the variation includes behavior that comes into contact with the reinforcer is then dependent on the particular ontogenetic history described above. The second case, however, requires periodic variation of the component behaviors maintained in the absence of stimulus changes. This kind of variation only occurs under certain conditions and suggests that individuals have to be exposed to special histories. One of these special histories concerns the instructions given to the subject.

We have found that if instructions are going to address this problem of variation, they have to tell the subject what behavior to vary, and under what conditions. The instructions have to be specific enough to occasion the responses of interest, but not so specific that they restrict the range of behaviors necessary under all the conditions the subject might encounter. The range of specific instructions and the strategic instructions that we have investigated both appear to provide sufficient variation for the behavior to come into contact with the changes in the environment manipulated in these studies. The strategic instructions used successfully in Chase, Joyce & LeFrancois (1987) and Joyce & Chase (1990) can be called heuristic rules and one of the functions of heuristic rules is to increase the systematic variation in behavior that is likely to put the subject into contact with the changes in the environment that constitute a solution. Giving the subjects a range of specific instructions, as in LeFrancois et al. (1988), may also produce a heuristic rule formed by the subjects. Whether this occurs or not, and whether stating a heuristic rule under such conditions is important for predicting and controlling the behavior of interest, however, remains to be investigated.

Footnotes

1. The authors acknowledge the countless contributions of the members of the Verbal Behavior Laboratory at West Virginia University, especially Sherry Serdikoff for introducing the literature on problem solving.

References

Birch, H. G. (1945). The role of motivational factors in insightful problem-solving. *Journal of Comparative Psychology, 38,* 295-317.

Bjarnadottir, G. S. and Chase, P. N. (1988, October). *Training the components of a novel verbal response.* Presented at the Southeastern Association for Behavior Analysis Conference, Gatlinburg, TN.

Chase, P. N., Joyce, J. H. & LeFrancois, J. R. (1987, May). *Effects of a strategic instruction on fixed-interval performance.* Paper presented at the Association for Behavior Analysis Conference, Nashville, TN.

Donahoe, J. W. (1991). Selectionist approach to verbal behavior: Potential contributions of neuropsychology and computer simulations. In L. J. Hayes and P. N. Chase (Eds.), *Dialogues on Verbal Behavior* (pp. 119-145). Reno, NV: Context Press.

Danforth, J. S., Chase, P. N., Dolan, M. & Joyce, J. H. (1990). The establishment of stimulus control by instructions and by differential reinforcement. *Journal of the Experimental Analysis of Behavior, 54,* 97-112.

Ellen, P. (1982). Direction, past experience, and hints in creative problem solving. Reply to Weisberg and Alba. *Journal of Experimental Psychology: General, 111,* 316-325.

Galizio, M. (1979). Contingency-shaped and rule-governed behavior: Instructional control of human loss avoidance. *Journal of the Experimental Analysis of Behavior, 31,* 53-70.

Hayes, S. C., Brownstein, A. J., Zettle, R. D., Rosenfarb, I., & Korn, Z. (1986). Rule-governed behavior and sensitivity to changing consequences of responding. *Journal of the Experimental Analysis of Behavior, 45,* 237-256.

Hull, C. L. (1935). The mechanism of the assembly of behavior segments in novel combinations suitable for problem solving. *Psychological Review, 42,* 219-245.

Joyce, J. H., Chase, P. N., & Danforth, J. S. (1987). Schedule sensitive performance: Defining training variety. Manuscript submitted for publication.

Joyce, J. H. & Chase, P. N. (1990). The effects of response variability on the sensitivity of rule-governed behavior. *Journal of the Experimental Analysis of Behavior, 54,* 251-262.

Kohler, W. (1925). *The mentality of apes.* E. Winter (translator). New York: Harcourt & Brace.

Lamons, M. & Chase, P. N. (1990). *Rule-governed behavior: The effects of three types of contingency contact on human schedule performance.* Presented at the Southeastern Association for Behavior Analysis Conference, Wilmington, NC.

LeFrancois, J. R., Chase, P. N., & Joyce, J. H. (1988). The effects of a variety of instructions on the sensitivity of rule-governed behavior. *Journal of the Experimental Analysis of Behavior, 49,* 383-393.

Shimp, C. P. (1989). Contemporary behaviorism versus the old behavioral straw man in Gardner's *The mind's new science: A history of the cognitive revolution. Journal of the Experimental Analysis of Behavior, 51,* 163-171.

Skinner, B. F. (1966). An operant analysis of problem solving. In B. Kleinmuntz (Ed.) *Problem solving: Research, method, and teaching* (pp. 225-257). New York: John Wiley & Sons.

Skinner, B. F. (1969). *Contingencies of reinforcement: A theoretical analysis.* New York: Appleton-Century-Crofts.

Weiner, H. (1969). Controlling human fixed-interval performance. *Journal of the Experimental Analysis of Behavior, 12,* 349-373.

Part 4
Other Topics in the Analysis of Verbal Relations

Chapter 12

Language and the Continuity of Species

James G. Holland
University of Pittsburgh & University of South Florida

Natural language is presumably unique to human beings. It is apparently absent in even their closest evolutionary relatives– the great apes. Without language there would be only the simplest of rule-governed behavior (if any). Most thought is predominantly verbal and is typically at a level of complexity beyond the simplest rudimentary verbal behavior and requires instead verbal behavior having the properties of language. "Self" and "mind" are concepts in common language and folk psychologies (and in the current academically fashionable cognitivism), and they are abstract verbalizations established by the verbal community. Such abstractions are unique to the only languaging species; and, originally exist only in the language as an "invention" of the language community. Language is the source of all mankind's capacity for creating mind, culture, technology and the transmission of these across generations. Clearly language and its products have set the human species far part from any other species; yet evolutionary theory demands continuity between languaging humans and other species. Can language really be such a vastly different thing and humans so separate from the nearest evolutionary relatives?

The great apes, most particularly the chimpanzee, are very close to humans in evolutionary time. In looking for continuity, a new biochemical technique, called molecular dating, determines how long ago two species separate. This technique places the separation of chimpanzee and human evolution a mere seven million years ago. This is such a short time for evolutionary change that one might expect only relatively simple biological changes to mediate language. However, a number of substantial biological changes are believed by many to serve in combination as the basis of human language and its absence in other species including the great apes. Biological differences between man and apes related to language production have been suggested and include: (1) larger brain size for humans, (2) brain specialization for production and comprehension including left hemisphere specialization for language (and, for the extreme nativism, innate encoding for language), and (3) vocal mechanism differences. But continuity demands species' differences that are not so great even though the results or product, language, has very sizable consequences.

In keeping with the demands of evolutionary continuity it is here suggested that a simple biological change accounts for species differences in language. The case will be made that the key requirement for a language is a response system with the sufficient speed and flexibility to produce enough different discriminable stimuli in short span of time. Given such a response system, the basic principles of operant conditioning should make possible the shaping of language in the natural environment. Perceptual capacity and an appropriately advanced capacity for complex behavior are no doubt necessary as well; but these may be sufficient in many other species and especially in the great apes. The human vocal response system may be unique in meeting the requirements. The conclusion to be reached in this paper is that the change in the vocal mechanisms is alone sufficient to account for the presence of language in humans (as contrasted with other primates). Only the evolution of the human vocal mechanism was required to enable humans to acquire language in the natural environment. Given the response potential of the humans vocal mechanism, the common principles of operant behavior, as applied by Skinner (1957) in the analysis of verbal behavior, are sufficient to account for the development of language.

Properties of Language

The present concern is *language*, as defined by the psycholinguist, (not the more inclusive and clearly continuous *verbal behavior* which would include simpler communication as well as language). Psycholinguists define language as a set of symbols that can be sequenced according to particular rules so as to convey an indefinite number of meanings from one user to another (Carroll, 1986). While this definition implies theoretical causes lacking identifiable functional variables, a suitable empirical definition is possible. The empirical rendering could be that language is a series of behavioral units in a sequence that can be described by a small set of rules. An individual can emit an unspecifiably larger number of sequences to which different listeners will reliably respond. While the present theoretical framework is that of Skinner's analysis of verbal behavior, the focus is specifically on that subset of verbal behavior involved in this rendering of the psycholinguist's definition of language. While the definition of verbal behavior implies continuity and could include the simpler forms of animal and human communication as precursors to the more sophisticated forms, the linguistic definition excludes these; and the definition seems to have been chosen specifically to set it apart from other behavior.

Verbal behavior is any operant which is reinforced by the mediation of another person. In exploring the evolution of verbal behavior, one could search for evidence of apes having an operant communication system and could speculate on the gradual selection of elaborated communication in the behavior of early man (cf. Skinner, 1987). While this approach is interesting and relevant, the present paper focuses instead on the claimed discontinuity between communication systems and is concerned with that subset of verbal behavior which meets the requirements that psycholinguists have adopted to set language off from simpler communication systems. Moreover, whether or not vocalizations in apes, or other non-human animals, could be precursors to human language, the transition from simple isolated utterances to complex "generative" sequences and rule-described restrictions may require more than a linear progression in a shaping sequence.

Language is said to be generative as evidenced by the ability of a speaker to utter an indefinite number of sequences not previously uttered. Simple communications of animals are not "generative" (Fodor, Bever, & Garrett, 1974). The ape language training research has produced some claims of novel utterances but the results have not yet provided sufficient evidence of "implicit rules" and "indefinite number" of utterances to compel acceptance by the skeptics. Even the training of perfect human language would not be accepted by all as evidence of behavioral continuity (Fodor, et al. 1974). In arguing for the innateness, and the uniquely human specificity of language, they say:

> The fact that we can learn to whistle like a lark does not prejudice the species-specificity of bird song. It is hard to see, then, why a successful attempt to teach a chimpanzee to talk should have any bearing on the innateness of language in people.- What have the chimpanzee studies shown us about language? Literally nothing (p. 451).

Maybe linguistic creationism as a faith is unshakable by facts; but it is true that something more than correspondence of form is needed, and that something else is correspondence of process. Just such a correspondence has been elucidated by Skinner's analysis of verbal behavior (1957). The task at hand is to explore how common functional processes (i.e., functional principles) can account for the apparent discontinuity between human language and other operant behavior of humans and apes, given the existence of a response system capable of language.

The case is to be made that the requirements which a response must meet in order to make a language possible are so restrictive that language could not develop until the human vocal system evolved. Given a response capacity that could meet the stringent requirement for a language, then no new language-specific acquisition principles or separate language modality is required.

Requirements of This Response System

For a language to be possible a response system is required which meets the following requirements:

1. It must be able to produce enough distinctive patterns to yield an uncountable number of different utterances.
2. Listeners must be able to differentially respond to these different patterns.
3. Samples of possible distinctive patterns and listener responses to them must be able to occur within the limits of short term memory (within a time frame of 10-30 seconds that allows a listener to repeat exactly what was said without paraphrasing).
4. The language must be learnable within a few years without deliberate planned or intentional instruction.

The oral-aural response system found in humans meets these requirements and it is for this reason that humans have a natural language. Important physical properties in meeting these requirements are as follows:

1. The response system has a low mass and, therefore, shows little momentum or inertia. In speech moving parts are small, light, and of low inertia; therefore, rapid response onset and quick change is possible. This permits a large number of distinguishable vocal elements in a short time. (Fourteen phonemes a second can be produced, cf., Lenneberg, 1967).
2. Auditory perception of small differences and very short duration events is easy. Moreover, the stimuli produced by the speaker have low persistence. If the stimuli do not fade quickly, discriminations by the listener would be more difficult.
3. There is considerable independence of elemental sounds in this response system so that they can be recombined very freely to produce new stimuli. For example "spot" and "tops" are the same sequence of sounds in the reverse order. It is not, however, the case that individual phonemes are behavioral response units under most conditions; nor is normal speech a chaining of phonemes; rather a single response mechanism produces a fairly small number of identifiable sounds which in various combinations can provide a very large number of functionally defined response units.
4. The response system is not dependent on environmental supports such as is the case with writing or other systems that require the person to be in touch with some object or manipulandum.

Thus the physics of the oral-aural response system provide the possibility of packing large numbers of discrete and distinguishable patterns into a small time span (accommodating the short term memory limits) while using a limited number of movements and sounds–for example, the 40 phonemes of which any English utterance is constituted.

Now there remains the question of whether operant principles will enable the learning of language in the natural environment without deliberate instruction and will meet the characteristics of novel utterances describable by a limited set of rules.

Behavior Analytic Factors

The interaction of verbal behavior by Skinner (1957) is based on principles of operant behavior common to other human operant behavior and other species having operant behavior. It remains to apply his interpretation to the issued of the unique characteristic of the human oral response system and the learnability of language in the natural environment. Given the proper response system, the principles of behavior will account for the presumed distinctive characteristics of language; namely, "generativeness", rapid learning without deliberate instructions, and "implicit rules."

The task would be easier if it could be assumed that adults interacted with the child in ways that reinforced or specifically modeled correct forms. In fact, this author finds no compelling reason to discount this possibility. The reciprocal contingencies between speaker and listeners could well impose a universal basis for the natural social reinforcement of correct language forms as well as early reinforcement of approximations that would later be unacceptable. However, there are additional bases that do not require "intentional" parental corrections or reinforcement. The relative lack of exploration for a natural listener-speaker reinforcement system in language acquisition results from the widely held belief among psycholinguists that mothers do not reinforce or correct syntax and that children do not imitate syntax. Besides a misunderstanding of the nature of reinforcement, a principle source of this belief is a report by (Brown, 1973 and Brown & Hanlon, 1970) claiming little parental correction or reinforcement. However, a recent detailed analysis of the mother-child interactions for one of the three children in the Brown study showed many interactions of possible instructional significance (Moerk, 1983). Extrapolating from his data, Moerk estimated over 3,000,000 interactions of potentially instructional significance per year. This could contribute to much language learning, but because it is unknown whether the instructional nature of these could be culture bound the present argument rests on other aspects which could themselves produce language learning.

Echoic Behavior

Echoic behavior results in the easy formation of new response forms. The close correspondence between the model utterance and the sounds produced by the speaker produces rapid shaping of new forms. This reinforcement for producing a close match could either be reinforced by the listener as described in Skinner's (1957) paradigm for echoic behavior or such imitation could be innately reinforcing or, more likely, both. In either case the correspondence between the stimuli to the speaker (the sounds of the model as heard by the speaker) are especially close for speech and hearing. While similar feedback relationships are found in other response domains, the correspondence is not so close as in speech and hearing. For example, gestures and signing suffer because of the different vantage point with respect to the model's hands and the imitator's hands.

Feedback and Automatic Reinforcement

Rapid shaping can take place without the continued intervention of another person or teacher because of feedback in automatic reinforcement. When someone has learned a certain pattern to be the reinforced one, and later produces that pattern, these response-produced stimuli are like the model pattern. The response-produced stimulus from the individual's own vocalization reinforce that very vocalization. The potential exists for shaping to continue even when the child is alone at play, or in the crib, without the intervention of parents. Thus language learning can proceed without listener correction.

Novel Tact Combinations and the Minimal Tact

The tact is the behavior equivalent of semantics or "meaning." A tact is a verbal response under control of objects or events in the environment acting as discriminative stimuli. It is the behavior of naming or talking about aspects of the environment. The tact is clearly important for the evolution of language since it is one of the main values of language.

Small derived units called minimal tacts play an important role in providing an analysis of what the psycholinguist attributes to "implicit rules." As described by Skinner (1957) at first a functional unit may be a lengthly expression like "I have a doll." After many similar statements "I have a ..." becomes a functional unit which, under conditions of combined multiple control, and with a novel object name, results in a novel statement, "I have a what's it." The process continues until "I" also becomes a minimal tact. Similarly important grammatical units are often minimal tacts. For example, the final "-s" in the "the boy runs" becomes a minimal tact through its repeated presence in a number of other statements. Then later with a different object in action, the action current, and the object singular, the combination of the two controlling stimulus properties produces a novel statement in the form which would be considered grammatical. Minimal tacts carry a great deal of the weight of the implicit language "rules" such as word order and pluralization.

The now classic study by Berko (1958) illustrates the final "-s" as a minimal tact although it was presented as a demonstration of the rule governed generation of a novel statement. She presented young children with a cartoon-nonsense figure and said "this is a Wug." Then the children were presented with two of the figures and the experimenter said, "Now there is another one. There are two _____." The children completed this by saying "Wugs." The utterance as a whole was new, but as a minimal tact it should not be considered generative because the discriminative stimulus for the abstract class "plural" was present as what the newly learned "wug."

The Berko study has been taken as evidence for generation of new rule-governed forms that could not be based on operant conditioning. Ironically a similar example had been used in an operant analysis to elucidate the role of minimal tacts in syntatically important cases. Minimal units such as affixes "are functional units in the behavior of the speaker only insofar as they correspond with particular features of a stimulating situation. The evidence is clearest when a speaker composes new forms of response with respect to new situations. Having developed a functional suffix –**ed** with respect to that subtle property of stimuli which we speak of as action-in-the-past, the suffix may be added for the first time to a word which has hitherto described action only in the present. The process is conspicuous when the speaker completes a form which is not established by the practices of a particular community ... **He singed**" (Skinner, 1957, p. 121).

There is a growing experimental literature pointing toward the controlling environmental variables for novel sequences of verbal responses (Weatherby, 1978, and Goldstein, 1983, 1984). This work has gone under the name of stimulus-matrix learning and has proceeded without reference to Skinner's minimal tact presumably because of the relative obscurity of this feature of his analysis of verbal behavior. In a particularly simple example of stimulus-matrix learning there are four forms and four colors. Each form and each color is assigned a nonsense name. When a colored form is presented to language deficient children, they learn to say the two word "nonsense" phrase for each presented compound stimulus. When a number of combinations of color and form have been taught with each color and each form taught in two or three combinations then when a novel combination is presented the children often correctly say the appropriate color-form phrase on its first presentation. This is a novel utterance of the type often said to be generated; but now the stimulus control is clear. Each of the components has its discriminative stimulus present in a new combination and a novel statement is produced.

Pepperberg (1987) has done similar work with the African Grey parrot. She trained the parrot to name color, shape, and numbers (through five) of various materials. Some combinations were trained and the parrot could on request describe new combinations without specific training. This is of special significance because it is shown in a species that is not known to have a natural language. The parrot emitted novel response sequences appropriate to new stimulus compounds following operant discrimination training with other compounds -- a "generative" sequence in a non-languaging species.

There are several examples in stimulus-matrix learning of novel, "generated" sentences produced after component elements have occurred in other combinations. Goldstein (1983, 1984), in establishing simple agent-action sentences with young children used four hand puppets and four patterns of movement (see Figure 1). Each puppet and movement was given a nonsense name. Twelve of the 16 combinations of agent (the puppets) and action (their movements) were taught. The four in the diagonal were reserved for testing. When presented with these new agent-

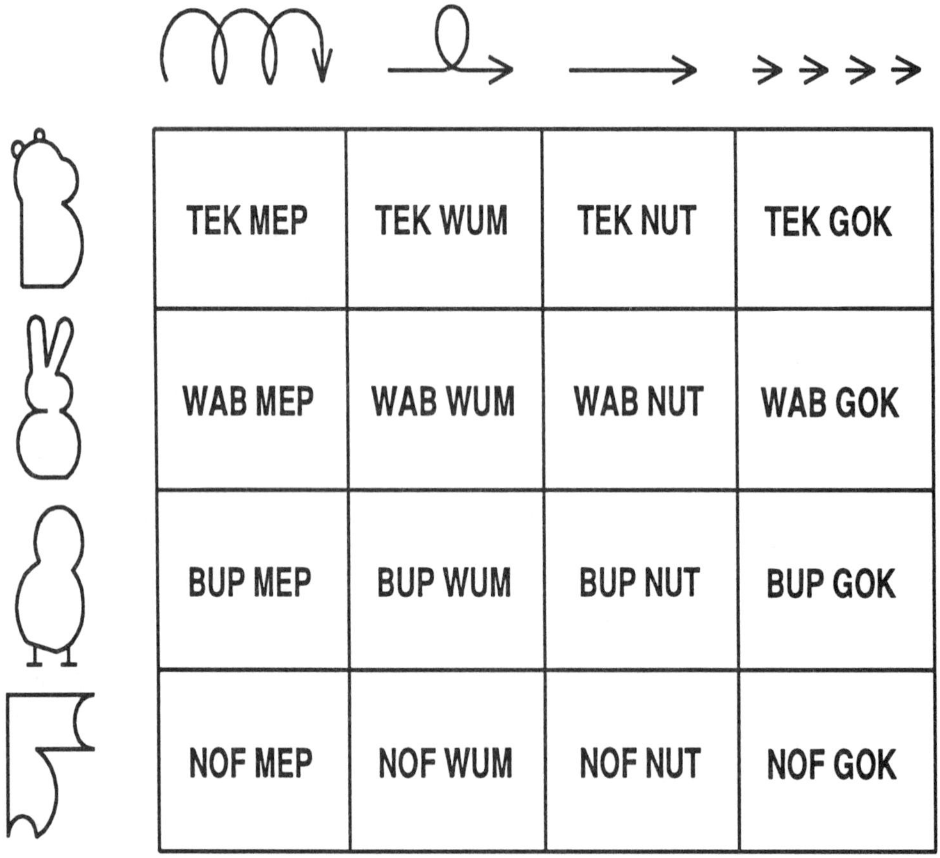

	TEK MEP	TEK WUM	TEK NUT	TEK GOK
	WAB MEP	WAB WUM	WAB NUT	WAB GOK
	BUP MEP	BUP WUM	BUP NUT	BUP GOK
	NOF MEP	NOF WUM	NOF NUT	NOF GOK

Figure 1. The four puppets along the left were named TEK, WAB, BUP, and NOF. The four actions at the top were named MEP, WUM, NUT, and GOK. Children could name the puppet-action combinations represented by the diagonals after being directly trained in the other combinations (Goldstein, 1983, 1984).

action combinations, the children emitted new novel sentences; but the new sentences were not generated in the sense of having no preceding learning history or functional control by external stimuli. They were instead emitted under the control of their separate discriminative stimuli. The constituent parts were learned as fragmentary tacts and later occur in new combinations.

Even simpler are cases in which tacts first occur separately instead of in compounds. Some new "generated" combinations could be of this type. Gardner and Gardner (1975) claim sentence generation for language by the chimpanzee, Washoe, which they taught American Sign. When Washoe's signed "water-bird" on first seeing a swan on a lake, the Gardeners interpreted this as a novel, generated utterance. However, the critics, Terrace, Petitto, Sanders, & Beaver (1979) argue that Washoe is not showing language competence, but was simply responding to two learned stimuli components "water" and "bird". Strangely, Terrace has missed the simplest form of functional control of novel utterances that pre-scientific accounts call "generative". Minimal tacts, either learned separately or as tacts in compounds, are responsible for many of the novel utterances and grammatical forms, but other aspects of language require something more, namely stimulus control from other verbal responses.

Autoclitic Frames and Minimal Intraverbals

The autoclitic frame, in which an element in the utterance itself is the stimulus for another element in the utterance, is another minimal repertoire especially important for such grammatical facts as case agreement and other inflections (see Skinner, 1957). Stimuli from one part of an utterance control minimal units elsewhere in an utterance in producing a number of features describable as grammatical or "rule governed." An example is shown in a stimulus matrix study on inflection for noun-adjective agreement (Holland, 1987). Figure 2 depicts the stimuli. Two forms were given nonsense names ending in "a" and two forms were given nonsense names ending in "o". The ending sound in the name of each form provides the stimulus control for the ending minimal unit for the color name. Again after subjects had learned a few combinations they would respond correctly on the first presentation of a novel combination. In this case the minimal unit was a sound in an earlier part of the subject's utterance.

Summary of Minimal Repertoire

Minimal repertoires are productive and they are essential for the efficient packing of behavior for an indefinite number of behavioral possibilities. Some minimal units are the small single phonemic grammatical elements including inflections and word orders with important grammatical roles such as pluralization and tense signs. Their orderly occurrence is describable by the "rules" of psycholinguistics. These units play a critical role in language because without them only rather simple utterances could be spoken or understood given the limits of short term memory. Thus within a verbal community there are natural contingencies which should reinforce fragmentation and "rules" with productivity or "generativeness." Because the number of different sounds comprising any utterance is limited (40 in English) and memory span is so limited, a speaker can generally be understood and reinforced only through the efficiency gained through the grammatically important minimal tacts.

The minimal tact and minimal interverbal (or autoclitic frame) accounts for the so called "generativeness" of verbal behavior. In a behavioral analysis, however, controlling stimulus elements are identified for the new combinations as tacts, minimal tacts and minimal intraverbals thereby producing novel utterances describable by rules without the positing of internal generation following internal application of rules. The speaker tacts a plural object with the added minimal tact "-s" to the object utterance. There is, in this sense, no generativeness" since the minimal repertoire "-s" and the object name have both been learned in the past. What is novel is the new combination.

Minimal Intraverbal

(or Autoclitic Frame)

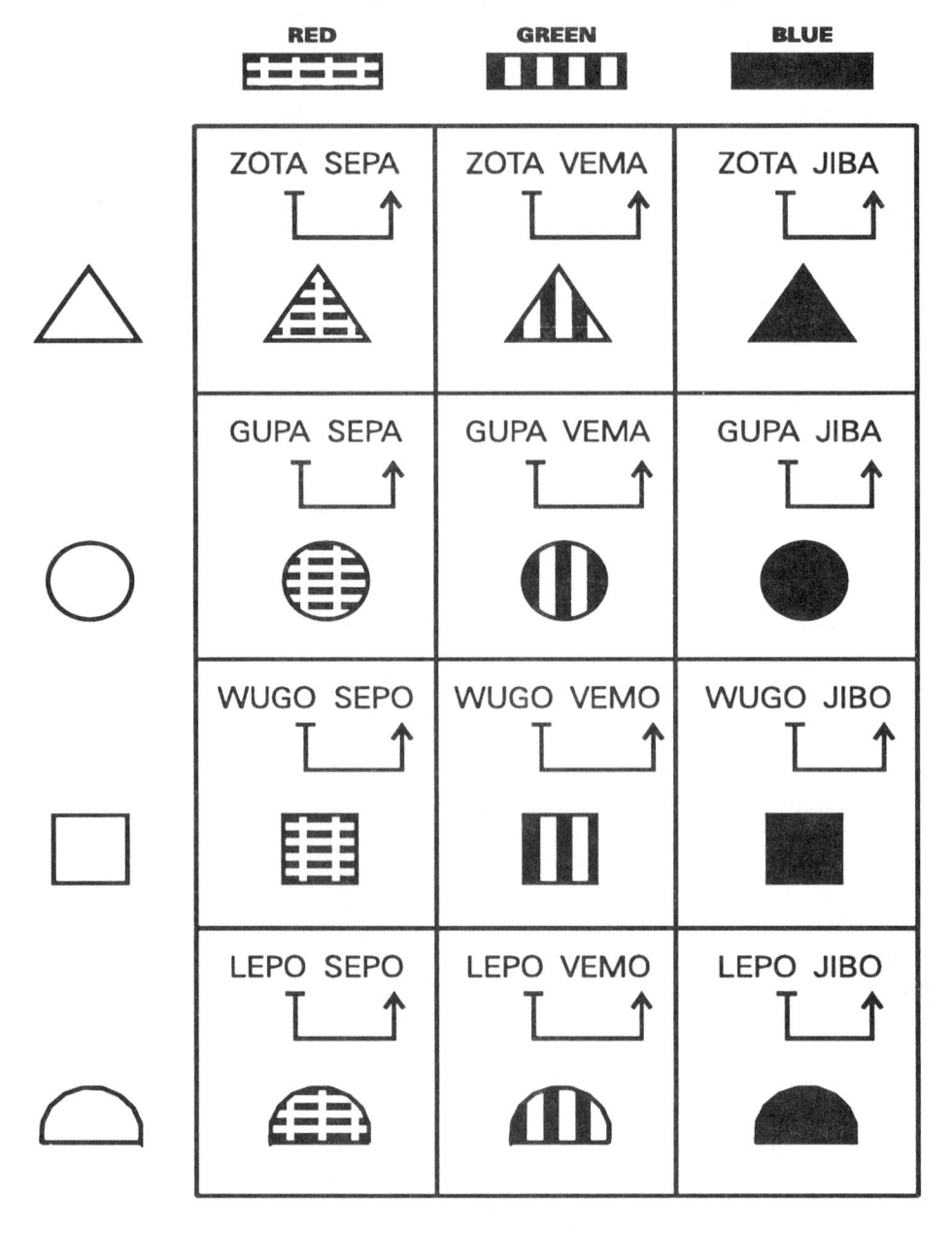

Figure 2. *An example of how word endings in one word can come to control the use of particular endings in other words.*

Possible Biological Bases

From among all the response systems available only the oral-aural system meets the necessary requirements for development of a natural language. Is it also possible that the human vocal system is sufficient in itself to account for the apparent fact that only humans have a natural language? Common biological explanations for the unique language capacity of humans have included changes in the brain size, brain specialization (manifested as left hemisphere dominance), neural changes having to do with "cognition," neural changes having to do with perception of language, and finally changes in the speech apparatus (cf. Harnard, Steklis, & Lancaster, 1976).

Brain changes have been a favorite explanation of why man has language and apes do not (cf. Lenneberg, 1967). The neurological explanations have been favored by the supposition that language is unique in being generative and in following a set of internal rules believed to be special to language. Such a theory requires a sizable array of complex biological changes. The implied discontinuity is inconsistent with evolutionary theory given the recency of the separation of the humans from chimpanzees. Lenneberg (1967), for example, claims that "language is the manifestation of species-specific cognitive propensities" and he devotes much of this classic book on the biological foundations of language presenting evidence for multiple complex neural mechanisms considered unique to man. He acknowledges the problem posed by this assumption of extreme discontinuity in saying, "It is true that this statement introduces some profound problems in the theory of evolution..." (p. 374). But no resolution of the problem is suggested by Lenneberg.

Lenneberg greatly underestimated the potential of principles of operant behavior in accounting for novel utterances and regularities describable by "rules." Recent research has also countered some of the evidence for the claimed species differences in neurological bases. An alternative here proposed is that a relatively small change in the positioning of the larynx and the resulting elongation of the pharynx was sufficient to account for speech and language in humans given the normal working of operant principles. It is true that a sophisticated neural anatomy is necessary for language, but it is quite possible that apes are not so deficient in this regard as to preclude language. They may only lack the one evolutionary change in anatomy that given humans speech.

It is not suggested that just any species with a capacity for operant conditioning would have language if only they had the human vocal mechanism. What is suggested is that other species (at least the great apes but perhaps others as well) are not so limited in any other respect that they could not have developed a natural language if they possessed a response system which enabled the shaping of language.

Vocal Apparatus

Leiberman (1975) provide evidence for the lengthening of the pharynx during evolution as the critical difference between ape and man. However, Lieberman does not view this difference in vocal apparatus as sufficient, and instead posits organizational changes of the brain in accordance with the prevailing psycholiguists theories. Nevertheless, he has contrasted the pharynx of man and ape and the sounds each can produce. In the chimpanzee the larynx or voice box, sits high in the neck with little space before the back of the oral cavity. This area between the larynx and the oral cavity (the pharynx) acts to modify the fundamental sound arising from the vocal cords. The elongated pharynx of man can change shape through muscular action producing several important speech sounds. There is very little space above the vocal chords in the chimpanzee and the ability to modify the sounds emanating from the vocal cords is very limited. Interestingly a homo sapiens infant begins life with the basic primate pattern – a high larynx which takes about a year and a half to descend to the seventh vertebra level necessary for the long pipe and all the language sounds. The lengthening of the pharynx is necessary before the child can utter all the language sounds of their verbal community. Since deaf children have learned a full communication system, sign language, by nine months the delay in beginnings of language development until the second year may be that the infant, like the ape, lacks a sufficiently elongated pharynx.

Lieberman (1975) has demonstrated that the changes in the shape of the pharyngeal cavity result in sound frequency distributions producing three critical vowel sounds, [i], [u], and [a]. The cross sections of the pharyngeal cavity at different distances from the larynx are quite distinctive for the different sounds, and they produce different frequency patterns. The vocal chords vibrate and the resulting sound resonates in the tube which can quickly and easily change shape producing different vowel sounds. So the lengthened pharynx provides a response system which will do all that is needed for a talking ape.

The descent of the larynx in its early evolutionary stages probably had more to do with the development of an upright posture than with the appearance of language (which must have awaited a sizable descent of the larynx before the beginning of a language capacity). In the basic mammalian pattern an animal on all fours is one long horizontal, straight tube. As animals became more upright, the tube began to bend forward with the head arching over into a right angle with the spine. The chimpanzee's head shows some beginning, lesser arch but is not a fully upright animal, and they knuckle walk in a semi-upright fashion without the head arched forward. Man has a head arched far forward and associated flexion in the bone structure (Laitman, 1984). It is this cranial arch which leaves a fossil record permitting inferences regarding the evolution of the response system which makes possible the learning of language.

The australopitecines, a relative of man and ape, lived 4 to 1 1/2 million years ago. They had the basic primate anatomical pattern of a high larynx and thus presumably they had no language. Homo erectus lived one million to 400,000 years ago and had some flexion but not as much as modern man. There may have been some language and evolutionary advantage of improved communication may have been added to those of the upright posture. This increase in flexion, associated with the curving of the head forward, made it easier to hold the head up and look forward while walking upright – an obvious survival asset and therefore an anatomical change that would be favored in evolution. With the flexion came the lengthened pharynx which coincidentally made language possible. The earliest evidence for speech is 40,000 years ago based on finding ritual burials which would seem to require communication among individuals to determine the cultural practices. (cf. Pilbeam, 1972).

Brain Changes

But what about the other popular biological explanations for language as an exclusively human characteristic; namely brain changes in size or organization and changes for cognition and perception? There are differences in the size of the brain along the evolutionary line from early primates to modern man. Some evolutionary theorists and linguists suggest that the brain needed to be much larger before language could emerge. Gorillas have a brain size of about 500 cc; Australopithecus about 500 cc; Neatherthal about 1500 cc; and modern man about 1400 cc. However, the trouble with using brain size to explain the origin of language is that small brained humans and humans who have experienced serious loss of brain mass through injury that occurs in the early years of life (when the brain is highly plastic) also have language. Viewers of the Public Broadcasting System program entitled *The Brain* saw an apparently normal teenage girl with good language even though she had lost a great deal of her brain to hydrocephalitis before a successful shunt operation. A much reduced brain size was sufficient.

The Continuity of Species

Special brain organization is favored as the explanation of human language. Could the evolution of brain specialization account for the origin of language in modern man? Modern man's brain is not only larger, it also has highly organized areas of the left hemisphere which are specialized for speech and language. This hemispheric dominance for handedness and language is widely considered to be the major biological basis for language which is considered unique to humans and is the reason for considering language to be a separate ability discontinuous from other behaviors.

But other species also show evidence of a similar brain specialization including birds and Macaque monkeys. Studies with canary birds songs (Walker, 1980) show that when the innervation is cut from the left side of the brain to the vocal chords, bird song is destroyed, but cutting the innervation from the right side of the brain leaves bird song undisturbed. Thus left hemosphere brain area specialization for communication or voalization is not unique to man.

Recent work with Macaque monkeys (Heffner & Heffner, 1984) also demonstrated hemisphere specialization. They taught a particular vocalization to one visual stimulus and a different vocalization to another visual stimulus. When they ablated only the left temporal lobe, the monkeys lost the discrimination; but when only the right lobe was ablated the performance was unaffected. The left hemisphere specialization for productive language seems to have a close parallel in the Macaque monkey. Again left hemisphere specialization is not unique to humans.

In considering the changes in perception from early apes to modern man, there is not adequate reason to believe that man is specially endowed in contrast with other primates. Rather,

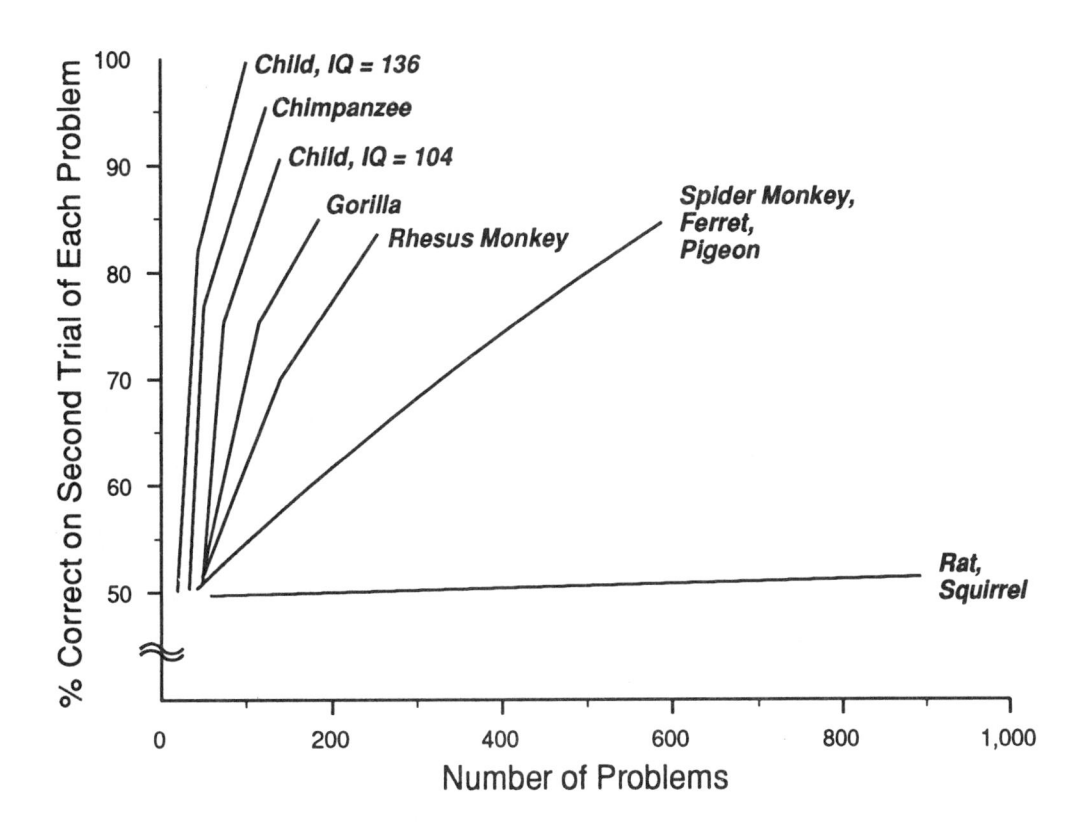

Figure 3. The effect of learning sets in various species.

the evidence (Warren, 1976) suggest that every aspect of perception needed for speech, that does not itself depend on speech, is similar for man, monkeys and chimpanzees.

Similarly, there is little reason to believe that chimpanzees are so deficient in cognitive skill that language would be unlearnable. Although comparative studies across species are difficult and conclusions must be tentative, one of the best means for comparing complex learning or "thinking" has proven to be the learning set procedure developed by Harlow (1949). In this procedure the subject is given a choice between two objects. Choosing one is reinforced, choosing the other is not. The problem is repeated until a correct choice is consistently made; then a new object pair is used. This procedure is continued until the subject performs perfectly on each new pair by its second presentation. (For the first presentation only chance performance is possible.) Figure 3 presents data compiled by Hodos (1975) which compares animals of several species in percent correct on the second trial as a function of the number of different pairs of stimuli previously used. The rat and squirrel do not master this task; the pigeon does respectably well and is similar to the spider monkey; the rhesus monkey does better; the gorilla still better and the chimpanzee is intermediate between two human children. The chimpanzee compares well with humans on this task but might not on some other "cognitive" task. Certainly if the task required language the chimpanzee would be unable to perform it. Nevertheless, there is no compelling reason to assume that the chimpanzee lacks language because of the lack of some prerequisite cognitive skill.

Summary

In Skinner's (1957) analysis of verbal behavior, language is interpreted in terms of processes which are continuous phylogenetically and ontogenetically. A contrary view held by many psycholinguists maintains that language is a special modality which is unique and discontinuous from other behavior because an indefinite number of novel utterances are possible and the utterances are said to follow grammatical rules. The present paper shows how the continuous process of operant shaping and natural selection can produce a natural language; its apparent discontinuity arises from continuity in functional laws. Given a species with reasonably advanced operant conditioning capacity, language might well have been naturally shaped if the species had a response system capable of producing a large number of different responses quickly enough to meet the constraints of short-term memory. Human vocal responses meet this requirement.

The necessary characteristics evolved with the descent of the larynx as a by-product of the upright position of man contrasted with the great apes. The resulting phrangeal chamber permits easy production of some vowel sounds not possible in ape vocalization. The physical properties of the response mechanism (low mass and low inertia, flexibility of sequencing, and non-persistence of vocal stimuli) enable an indefinite number of response forms and permit large units in short time intervals.

The response system of speech has the necessary new potential for the natural environment to shape language. There is rapid shaping of the response forms through feedback in echoic behavior. The automatic reinforcement following discriminated feedback enables shaping without deliberate instruction by adults. Unlimited novel utterances and consistent verbal patterns are produced by new combinations of tacts, minimal tacts and minimal intreverbals (or autoclitics) without hypothesized internal rules and internal generation of language, without the assumption of new modality, and without the resulting assumption of discontinuity with other species or other behaviors.

References

Berko, J. (1958). The child's learning of English morphology. *Word, 14,* 150-177.

Brown, R. (1973). *A first language.* Cambridge, MA: Harvard University Press.

Brown, R., & Halnon, C. (1970). Derivational complexity and order of acquisition in child speech. In J. R. Hayes (Ed.), *Cognition and the development of language.* New York: Wiley.

Carroll, D. W. (1986). *Psychology of language.* Belmont, CA: Brooks/Cole.

Fodor, J. A., Bever, T. G. & Garrett, M. F. (1974). *The psychology of language: An introduction to psycholinguistics and generative grammar.* New York: McGraw-Hill.

Gardner, B. T., & Gardner, R. A. (1975). Evidence for sentence constituents in the early utterances of child and chimpanzee. *Journal of Experimental Psychology: General, 104,* 244-267.

Goldstein, H. (1983). Training generative repertoires within agent-action-object linguistic systems with children. *The Journal of Speech and Hearing Research, 26,* 76-89.

Goldstein, H. (1984). Effects of modeling and correction practice on generative language learning of pre-school children. *Journal of Speech and Hearing Disorders, 49,* 389-398.

Harlow, H. (1949). The formation of learning sets. *Psychological Review, 56,* 51-56.

Harnard, S. R., Steklis, H. D., & Lancaster, J. (1976). (Eds.), *Origins and evolution of language and speech.* New York: New York Academy of Sciences.

Heffner, H. E. & Heffner, R. S. (1984). Temporal lobe lesions and perception of species-specific vocalizations by Macaques. *Science, 226,* 75-76.

Hodos, W. (1970). Evolutionary interpretations of neural and behavioral studies of living vertebrates. F. O. Schmitt (Ed.), *The neural sciences second study program* (pp. 26-39). New York: Rockefellor University Press.

Holland, J. G. (1987). *Minimal interverbals in inflection.* Unpublished raw data.

Laitman, J. T. (1984). The anatomy of human speech. *Natural History, 8,* 20-26.

Lenneberg, E. H. (1967). *Biological foundations of language.* New York: Wiley.

Lieberman, P. (1975). *On the origins of language: An introduction to the evolution of human speech.* New York: Macmillan.

Moerk, E. L. (1983). *Mother of Eve: As a first language teacher.* Idlewood, NJ: Ablex.

Pepperberg, I. M. (1987). Acquisition of the same/different concept by an African grey parrott (*Psittacus erithacus*): Learning with respect to categories of color, shape, and material. *Animal Learning and Behavior, 15,* 423-432.

Pilbean, D. (1972). *The ascent of man: An introduction to human evolution.* New York: Macmillan.

Skinner, B. F. (1987). *Upon further reflection.* Englewood Cliffs, N.J.: Prentice Hall.

Skinner, B. F. (1957). *Verbal behavior.* New York: Appleton-Century-Crofts.

Terrace, H. S., Petitto, L. A., Sanders, R. J. & Bever, T. F. (1979). Can an ape create a sentence? *Science, 206,* 891-902.

Walker, S. (1980). Lateralization of functions in the vertebrate brain: A review. *British Journal of Psychology, 71,* 329-367.

Warren, R. M. (1976). Auditory perception and speech evolution. In S. R. Harnar, H. D. Steklis, & J. Lancaster (Eds.), *Origins and evolution of language and speech* (pp. 708-717). New York: New York Academy of Sciences.

Weatherby, B. (1978). Miniature language and functional analysis of verbal behavior. In R. L. Schiefelbush (Ed.), *The basis of language intervention* (pp. 399-448). Baltimore, MD: Johns Hopkins University Press.

Chapter 13

Some Thoughts on Thinking and Its Motivation

Emilio Ribes Inesta
University of Guadalajara

"Thanks to Ryle and Wittgenstein, we are beginning to understand that the intellectual status of a public performance does not depend upon its being caused, backed or shadowed by a parallel private performance. It would be a sad reversion to a worse-than-Cartesian position if, in a case where a certain kind of performance does have both public and private versions, we were to regard the latter as the only truly thoughtful versions just because they alone were private."

Jonathan Bennett, 1971

"Thinking,' there we have a terrible ramified concept. A concept that comprehends multiple manifestations of life. The *phenomena* of thinking are very different one of each other."

Ludwig Wittgenstein, 1979

Thinking is the most elusive topic in psychology. Partially, its elusiveness comes from the semantic amplitude of the term itself: it includes reasoning, conceptualizing, certain kinds of remembering, imagining, judging, problem solving, and many other ancillary concepts. But there is also a historical background that gives account of this fact: the assumption that the term corresponds to a mental process or entity, hidden from public observation, and consisting in a kind of internal stage where the individual mirrors his or her own experience as a privileged spectator.

Two general problems have emerged from this traditional formulation of thinking. First, the relation between thinking, language, and imagining. Second, the experiential nature of thinking as a covert, silent process or activity, which builds up the representation of the world as meaningful objects and things for the individual. Both features may be criticized on the grounds of a conceptual analysis of the use of thinking as a language game (Wittgenstein, 1953; Ryle, 1949, 1979), or through the historical assessment of the logical and empirical fallacies which have distorted the original meaning of the term in the writings of Aristotle, who is considered the beginner of the discipline which today we refer to as Psychology (Kantor, 1963; Ribes, 1984, 1986).

Although I will eventually resort to both kind of analyses, my intention in this paper is to examine how radical behaviorism–as operant conditioning theory–has addressed this issue, and to propose an alternative approach based on an already developed field theory about behavior (Ribes & Lopez, 1985).

Rule-Governed Behavior: Limitations and confusions.

Skinner proposed rule-governed behavior as the analytic tool to deal with thinking and related problems in *Contingencies of Reinforcement* (1969), although the approach may be traced back to *Verbal Behavior* (1957) and *Science and Human Behavior* (1953). In the earlier, writings rule-governed behavior is implicit in the analysis of the tact and thinking. Some of the shortcomings in these concepts were conserved in the formulation of rule-governed behavior.

I will discuss three problems in relation to the concept of rule-governed behavior:
a) the operational nature of the term;
b) the logical inconsistencies in the definition with respect to operant theory; and
c) the difficulty of distinguishing rule-governed behavior from rule like contingency-shaped behavior.

Rule-governed behavior is distinguished from contingency-shaped behavior in terms of the direct effect on behavior of exposure to contingencies versus the antecedent or indirect control exerted by the verbal specification of contingencies in the form of a rule. Rules are conceived as descriptions of contingencies, and therefore are assumed to be **extracted** from contingency systems as **constructed** discriminative stimuli by the individual or by others. Thus, rule-governed behavior is discriminative stimulus controlled behavior. Nevertheless, the rule as a discriminative stimulus is not the same as the discriminative stimulus forming part of the specified contingency. Because of this, although the topography of the behaviors involved in both cases may be similar, they are conceived to be functionally different. In any case, both types of behavior, to be maintained, must be followed by consequences specified in the contingency. The distinction lies **only** in the locus of control of the behavior.

Rule-governed behavior is related to tacting and thinking because rules as contingency-specifying stimuli normally consist in descriptions and inductions, which extract complex contingencies in the environment. Rule constructing is similar to tacting since contingency specification requires verbal responses, and these responses must "reproduce", in the form of a rule, the properties of the stimulus conditions which define the contingency being extracted. Since most of the time these contingencies are extremely complexthey consist in stimulus properties in relationtacting becomes thinking. Thinking is, to a certain extent, complex tacting (Skinner, 1957).

I will now go through the inadequacies of the concept of rule-governed behavior:

a) The definition of rule-governed behavior rests upon a logic very similar to that being used to formulate the distinction between operant and respondent behaviors.

An operant is identified in terms of an observational relation. If the response follows a discrete stimulus in time, it is called a respondent. If the observer is unable to identify the antecedent stimulus change, the response is called an emitted response, and the introduction of an imposed stimulus consequence allows the observer to identify this emitted response as an operant. Skinner (1935) stressed that an operant may be correlated with a prior stimulus change, but that this stimulus is usually out of the reach of the observer. Hence, the operant-respondent distinction is, in principle, an operational definition based on the observational properties of the relations being thus identified.

The distinction between rule-governed behavior and contingency-shaped behaviors runs along similar lines. If the prior stimulus is the observational referent to establish if a response is elicited or emitted, the consequent stimulus is the observational referent to identity a response as rule-governed or contingency-shaped. If the behavior is directly controlled by consequences it is considered contingency-shaped. If the observer is unable to identify an explicit, immediate consequence, the behavior is defined as rule-governed. The distinction is again established according to the observational properties of the behavioral relation being classified.

Nevertheless, as happens with the operant-respondent distinction when the observer is unable to impose an **arbitrary** consequent stimulus relation to the response, difficulties also emerge with the operationally based definition of rule-governed behavior. First, an operant as an instance of a class, that is, as a response, it may not necessarily be followed by the consequence which defines its membership to such a class. Nevertheless, this definitional property of an operant that imposes restrictions on any observational criterion based upon the identification of a one-to-one correspondence between responses and consequences, does not allow one to distinguish these instances as contingency-shaped or rule-governed behavior. The history of any operant is not observable per se since it refers to a **tendency** of responding and not to single occurrences. Therefore, the occurrence of a response without exposure to a consequence is not a sufficient condition to identify it as rule-governed behavior. Second, it is assumed that the rule as a discriminative stimulus has a **particular** verbal form. Thus, rules are conceived as descriptions, injunctions or some varied forms of softened manding. Nevertheless, the form of the discriminative stimulus does not mean that the response occasioned by it is not under the functional control of present contingencies.

Two conditions do not fit with the assumption that the form of the rule stimulus allows for the identification of rule-governed behavior:

a) when the rule-stimulus controls behavior in similar ways to non-rule stimuli, as does happen with most of instructions; and, b) when the rule itself forms part of a present contingency. These two cases among many others, point out the difficulty of distinguishing rules as **special kinds** of discriminative stimuli. It is not enough that the discriminative stimulus as a rule "includes the discriminative stimulus forming part of the contingency being specified." If this were the case, rule-governed behavior would consist only in a formal exercise of classifying stimulus conditions.

b) There are logical inconsistencies in the definition of rule-governed behavior.

By a logical inconsistency I will not refer to the formal properties of the definition, but to the correspondence between the conditions which are specified by the definition and the empirical circumstances in which the definition is used.

The first inconsistency is related to the very concept of a discriminative stimulus which controls behavior not exposed to direct consequences. I have already commented that the non-occurrence of a consequence does not cancel the generic nature of a response as a member of an operant as a contingency-shaped class. Nevertheless, we face a serious problem when the non-occurrence is systematic and takes place during the **acquisition.** If a discriminative stimulus is defined as a stimulus prior to responding which is the occasion for the response to be reinforced, this means, **by definition,** that the concept of a discriminative stimulus only may be used when there is a contingency including a response being reinforced in its presence, at least during the acquisition state or period. In the analysis of the tact, Skinner (1957) proposed an argument similar to that used for rule-governed behavior. The non-verbal stimulus is assumed to exert control on the tacting response because the later is followed by a generalized reinforcer; since the consequence is not specific to a particular motivational state, the response control is assumed to be transferred to the antecedent stimulus. Nevertheless, the following question remains: how is a strong specific discriminative control developed under generalized reinforcement? (Ribes, 1983). There is no empirical evidence to sustain such statement.

In rule-governed behavior the rule consists of a discriminative stimulus in the presence of which the response is not shaped by the consequence. Even in the case that the consequence is thought of as a delayed consequence, the issue remains the same: the use of the concept of the discriminative stimulus is inconsistent with and violates its fundamental definition. The rule can not be conceived as a discriminative stimulus. If it is so, then it would not be possible to distinguish between rule-governed and contingency-shaped behaviors, or the difference between them would refer to the nature of the stimulus and not to the contingency relation under which a response occurs.

The problem lies in the fact that a concept such as rule-governed behavior is needed to describe complex behavior as that taking place when we usually talk about thinking. But, it is obvious that such a concept can not be built upon the logical structure of the discriminative stimulus relation. The theory must resort to new concepts distinguishing the complexity of the relations to which they have to be applied. This change in the theory must begin with the recognition of the difficulty in defining stimulus functions bound to the concept of reinforcement as a central device in the analysis of contingencies.

A second inconsistency has to do with the role of consequences in the definition of rule-governed behavior as different from contingency-shaped behavior. The basic element in both types of behavior is a contingency system, which is conceived as a system of relations between stimuli, behavior, and consequences. In rule-governed behavior an additional element is included: the stimulus condition specifying contingencies. This makes a double distinction regarding the response: there is a response prescribed by the contingency and a response which follows the rule, responses which may not be necessarily the same. The rule, anyhow, becomes functional to the extent that the response under its control is effective in regard to the contingency being specified. And effectiveness only means that the rule-governed response must be followed by similar consequences to those defining contingency-shaped behavior. If this is the case, and both types of behavior share the same consequences, how is it possible to distinguish among them?

c) Rule-governed behavior as a concept does not allow distinguishing actual rule-governed behavior from rule-like controlled behavior.

The concept of rule-governed behavior entails the construction of discriminative stimuli by the individual, as well as the transmission of constructed stimuli to govern the behavior of other individuals. Both aspects are greatly facilitated by verbal behavior, since this allows for differential responding to stimuli in constructing new discriminative cues and for the social transmission of these discriminative stimuli in the form of instructions, advice, orders, etc. Nevertheless, some problems arise from the definition of rule-governed behavior as constructing and transmitting discriminative stimuli controlled behaviors. One relates to the nature of the process of construction and transmission of discriminative stimuli. Another, to the assessment of the variables controlling the behavior under rule-like stimuli.

When Skinner talks about rule-governed behaviors as a process of constructing discriminative stimuli, he is undoubtedly pointing to the fact that the individual is not responding exclusively to the external stimulus conditions but also to his own behavior or behavior-produced stimuli in relation to them. And, although thinking while behaving[1] necessarily requires that the individual changes external conditions by responding to its own behavior under these conditions, the proposal of a mechanistic-like process supplementing cues to the environment contingencies seems to fall short as a descriptive and explanatory device.

Why so? Because it does not distinguish between responding to **vestigial** cues from **anticipating** forthcoming stimuli. By anticipation I do not mean any kind of fractional response to future stimuli under conditional cues, but responding according to contingencies not present in the situation as physical stimulus elements, and responding to present contingencies **as if** they had changed following the "constructing" response by the individual. The central problem is not the fact of constructing so-called discriminative stimuli, but the nature of the "construction" response.

Verbal responses not only facilitate this process of construction, they are necessary for the construction of new rule stimuli, to take place. The conventional nature of verbal responses[2] allows for their detachment from particular objects, events and situations. They may be emitted in new and different conditions without having to appeal to imagery or memory "processes." To the extent that events are events reacted to verbally, the environmental contingencies are always contingencies mediated by the verbal behavior of the individual (as speaker, listener, reader, writer, marker, signaler, or observer). Rule-governed behavior, if the term has any useful meaning, must be analyzed in terms of the process that takes place when the individual learns and applies verbal responses that modify present contingencies in terms of the conventional function that these responses have.

It is important to point out another weakness in the traditional analysis of rule-governed behavior: the transmission of new discriminative stimuli is not a consequence of changing the private status of constructed stimuli into public, but by their very nature as conventional stimuli and response functions, these new stimuli are always **acquired as consequence of public stimuli-constructing responses**. The difference between "trial and error" behavior and rule-governed behavior lies in the public and conventional provenance of the later. In fact, the only way to demonstrate that a rule-like governed behavior is not a pseudo-type is to show that its acquisition is socially designed to respond to and construct conventional detachable stimuli, and that these relations so established are transmissible through the same behavior governed by externally-induced rules. Obviously, this does not mean that all rule-governed behavior is externally induced. This induction, anyhow, is a necessary condition for its initial acquisition as a non-contingency-shaped behavior.[3]

This argument is connected with the second problem I previously mentioned: the assessment of truly-rule control of a specific behavior. As I have already discussed, the formal features of the constructed discriminative stimuli are not sufficient to warrant that a particular behavior is rule-governed. There are many instances of rule-like stimulus conditions which do not exert truly rule-control on the behavior that follows them. People learn to repeat maxims, to follow and give instructions and commands, to provide examples and models, and so on, and many times the behavior that takes place does not fit to the concept of rule-governed behavior.

Rule-like stimuli normally form part of contingencies that do not require any other participation from the individual besides adjusting to the signalled contingency.

As I have before pointed out, even in Skinner's analysis, rule-governed behavior has to share an effective contingency. In fact, rule-like stimuli come with consequences in most of all the cases of so-called operant behavior. The absence of effective consequences makes an operant analysis of behavior difficult, since rules actually become surrogate stimuli for effective contingencies. How are rules to be detected if they do not substitute for effective contingencies? Although many thinking behaviors are problem solving and, therefore, relate with effective contingencies, many others do not entail **instrumentally** effective behaviors, but only linguistic effective behaviors, and sometimes, there are no specific criteria for effectiveness. Effectiveness in these cases is dependent upon the behavioral relations themselves. This is why the transmission of so-called constructed discriminative stimuli is a test of the true occurrence of rule-governed behavior. Later on I shall examine this topic again from a different perspective.

Thinking as behavior: how is it related to rules and linguistic conventions?

To begin with, I shall discuss very briefly what I consider thinking not to be, in order to propose a tentative definition that may be useful for progress in the analysis of this topic.

Unfortunately, the history of the term "thinking" in psychology is plagued of formal fallacies. These consist in identifying products, procedures and conditions with psychological processes or entities such as mental acts or structures. From this historical use, psychology has been committed to deal with formal fictions such as analysis, synthesis, induction, deduction, transitivity, judgment, reasoning and many other similar concepts.

A careful examination of the ordinary use (or the language games) of these terms shows that they do not "refer" to mental entities, acts of consciousness or extra-episodic hidden activities. They are normally used to talk about features of behavior or to relations in which behavior becomes involved as an essential component. When we talk about thinking we do not talk about a special kind of behavior like talking, for instance. Thinking is not an additional activity, content or entity different from the behavior we are describing through this term. Therefore, thinking is not occurring autonomously from the behavior itself, although it is not identical to one or another component of this behavior. What is thinking about then?

Thinking, as a concept, does not refer to a special kind of behavior, but rather to a special kind of relation in which behavior becomes involved. As such, thinking is not a process. Thinking shares many processes with behavior in general. To identify thinking is not to identify a special course of action in the change of behavior, but rather to identify special kinds of relations in which behavior participates. Wittgenstein (1979) said that "...who **thinks** during his work, frequently incorporates **auxiliary activities**. The words *to think* do not designate in this case those auxiliary activities, as well as thinking is not equivalent to talking... Such auxiliary activities are not thinking, but oneself represents thinking as the stream that must flow beneath the surface of these auxiliary resources if they are not to be just mechanical actions" (p. 23). Because of this, it is meaningless to talk about thinking independently of behavior, but it is equally absurd to identify thinking with a special kind of behavior.[4]

How is thinking to be characterized as a special relation in which behavior is involved? I will define *thinking* as *self-substitutional behavior*.[5]

How is self-substitutional behavior to be understood? First, I will discuss the concept of substitutional behavior.

By substitutional behavior I do not refer to implicit and covert or nonapparent responses, although substitutional behavior, under certain circumstances, may consist of implicit and non-apparent responses. Nevertheless, non-observability or lack of explicit correspondence with stimulus conditions are not the essential features that define substitutional behavior. By substitutional behavior I refer to interactions between the individual and events—normally including the behavior of other individuals—in which functional contingencies do not depend on the presently acting physical circumstances. Because of this, substitutional behavior is tantamount to substitutional contingencies (Ribes, 1986).

Substitutional behavior consists of **conventional** behaviors (responses or response-produced stimuli) which **transform** the situational contingencies under which one or more individuals are responding. This transformation may operate in two ways. One, in which the individual responds to present situational contingencies in terms of contingencies pertaining to a different situation. This substitutional behavior may be characterized as **extra-situational** substitution. Another, in which the individual responds to present situational contingencies in terms of the linguistic properties of the behavior, and thus the contingency becomes dependent on the behavior itself and independent of any specific situation. This substitutional behavior may be characterized as **trans-situational**.

According to these definitions, in order to identify behavior as thinking the behavior must consist of substitutional behavior, extrasituational or transitutional. It is important to stress that substitutional refers to a functional property regarding the transformation of present physical situational contingencies, and the concept has nothing to do with surrogation, replacement or standing for events. However not every substitutional behavior qualifies as thinking. What is the

Thinking and its Motivation

additional restriction? Substitutional behavior must transform the contingencies themselves to which the behaving individual is responding. In other words, the behavior must be self-substitutional.

Let me examine how it is possible to identify these various instances of substitutional behavior and how they differ from non-substitutional behavior.

To substitute for contingencies means the ability to detach particular behaviors from their functional correspondence with present acting physical contingencies in a situation, and accordingly, to be able to attach those behaviors to circumstances not present in the acting situation. This "transference" of functioning contingencies is possible only by means of linguistic responses. Their conventional character allows for detaching them from any situational contingency defined as a perceptual relation, that is, as behaving to the here-and-now apparent physicochemical properties of events and their relations.

Non-substitutional behavior may be covert and implicit to the extent that the responses are under the functional regulation of present physically acting contingencies. The responses may also be linguistic (conventional) without qualifying as substitutional. Substitutional behavior is a matter of functional detachment regarding contingencies, and it is not restricted by the morphological characteristics of the behavior involved in the interaction.

Non-substitutional behavior, therefore, may be identified as behavior that only occurs to specific (variable or invariant) contingencies being present during the interaction. It may consist in apparently "abstract" behavior, but to the extent that it is undetachable to situations in which the functional contingencies to which it is related are working, it does not qualify as substitutional. It is situationally-bound behavior, irrespectively of being linguistic or not, covert or observable, concrete or abstract regarding the stimulus properties regulating the relation.

Substitutional behavior is self-substitutional under two distinctive conditions:

a) When the behavior of the individual affects his/her own behavior to present conditions, according to previous or future confronted situations. It is not implicit behavior to present contingencies, but implicit behavior to non-present contingencies;

b) When the behavior of the individual consists in interacting with linguistic behavior as the contingency events in such a way that linguistic events are independent of any specific situation. Writing up a paper, examining a manuscript, talking to oneself regarding an argument, are instances of this second kind of self-substitutional behavior. To the extent that linguistic relations **as such** are transituational, the linguistic behavior to these relations is the only way to transform them into new relations or contingencies. Linguistic behavior becomes instrumental in creating and transforming linguistic contingencies as functional acting events.

There is a third kind of substitutional behavior that does not qualify as self-substitutional. This occurs when behavior transforming contingencies is directed toward changing the circumstances of a different individual, as does happen in communication episodes or many of the phenomena traditionally studied by social psychologists under the label of prejudice, rumor, social perception, etc.

On different types of thinking

Thinking, as with other kinds of behavioral relations, may be directed or non-directed (Berlyne, 1965). By directed I mean outcome-directed behavior as takes place with any intelligent behavior (Ryle, 1979; Ribes, in press). Intelligent behavior consists in effective behavior. Directed thinking, in this perspective, could be called intelligent thinking and has to do with the general issue of problem-solving. On the other hand, non-directed thinking consists in non-effective self-substitutional behavior.

How are effectiveness and non-effectiveness related with extrasituational and transituational behavior? Only part of extrasituational behaviors are directed, to the extent that allow the individual to respond as being in a different situation without being situationally affected by it. Other extrasituational substitutional behaviors mediate effects on the individual and not by the individual, and therefore, do not qualify as directed thinking. Transituational substitutional behavior, on the other hand, always seems to satisfy the requirement of directedness or effectiveness. Conventional behavior transforming conventional behavioral contingencies is effective and directed due to the very nature of linguistic contingencies, irrespectively of what Wittgenstein (1953) called the language game being played. In our perspective, linguistic contingencies are related to any conventional reactive system which defines arbitrary dependencies among its elements. Therefore, transituational substitutional behavior is not restricted to "natural" languages, but includes also any kind of formal and arbitrary language created by convention, eg., painting, music, mathematics, etc.

Which behaviors take place in extrasituational non-directed contingency substitution? They consist in behaviors which do not adjust to episodes in which the individual "talks" to himself. As Ryle (1979) has pointed out, many of the linguistic behaviors by individuals when alone consist in actions that are not self-directed, but that rather represent adjustments to past or future situations. In this regard, such behaviors affect the present condition of the individual. These non-effective substitutional behaviors might be metaphorically described as "reproductive" and "as...if" actions. I might mention the following behaviors as instances of extrasituational self-substitutions, which do not qualify as directed thinking: to repeat what has been said or done, to "recall" an event or situation, to react as. . ., to rehearse what is going to be said or done, to anticipate circumstances, to recognize an event as being from. . ., to feel as in, with or as doing. The common feature of these behaviors is that, although they substitute for contingencies not present in the situation, they affect the individual as being present in such situation. Needless to say, these behaviors are not strictly verbal, but involve general changes in the activity of the individual. Nevertheless, they may not be characterized as true "soliloquies" (or as Skinner would say: episodes in which the speaker is its own listener).

Extrasituational self-substitution may be conceived as effective or directed when the individual, in a non figurative sense, talks to himself. When talking to himself, the individual does not behave as being in a different situation, but rather substitutes for the acting situation without actually being affected by the substituted contingencies. Some instances of this kind of behavior are: to comment to oneself, to prepare oneself for something, to self instruct, etc. All these behaviors may include some of the episodes which characterize non-effective extrasituational substitution, but to the extent that the latter become component activities of a substituted contingency which does not actually affect the individual, they may become part of effective thinking. True self-talking is the condition which allows for such an adjustment to effective self-substitutional behavior.

As previously mentioned, transituational self-substitution seems to adjust always to the criterion of effectiveness of directed thinking. This is so because "talking about talking"in order to simplify any language game about language is transituational by definition, and unspecific regarding particular events or behaviors. Accordingly, excepting "loose" talk, the relation in which behavior becomes involved in, is always framed by a conventional effect to be searched for or produced. This is the reason why Aristotle in *About the Soul* referred to the intellectual soul as "the place of forms. . . and not of acting forms, but forms in potence". Because of this ". . .the intellect is also able to be self-intelligible" (p. 231 Spanish translation, Third Book, 429b).

To think, in this sense, is to be able to behave in regard to one's own conventional behavior, in order to identify, describe, and apply the relations embedded in the language game as a behavior episode. Ryle's (1979) analysis of thinking as self-teaching is a useful model to follow in order to clarify the process of transituational self-substitutional behavior.

To know something instrumental to solving a problem means that the individual performs effectively in relation to a set of conditions which demand a particular outcome or achievement. Nevertheless, the exercise of such a performance does not warrant that the individual is aware or able to describe the contingencies and behavior relations that took place during such a process. To know something as performance does not entail to know the description of such a performance, and even less, how to formulate a rule, maxim or prescription about that performance. Accordingly, the ability to teach such knowledge is related to the availability of the two latter kinds of knowledge .

Performing effectively is intelligent behavior but does not satisfy the criterion of thinking or "thoughtful" behavior. It becomes thinking when the individual is able to describe the contingencies under which he performed. This description as self-substitutional behavior is an instance of extrasituational substitution. Nevertheless, the behavior is to be conceived as transituational self-substitution when the individual formulates a rule or prescription about the described contingencies, and accordingly, he/she may later apply the rule in a different situation or may transmit it to a different individual as didactic speech (Ryle, 1949). Briefly, transituational thinking as directed behavior consists in searching for and performing linguistic behavior functionally related to a variety of situational contingencies and the corresponding reference to such circumstances, behavior that must not be attached to any of the involved specific performances and situational contingencies.

Which are the behavioral components covered by this process of performance description and rule formulation? Among others, it involves describing, formulating, recognizing, identifying, applying, comparing, distinguishing, relating, fractioning, composing, and course following. These components are not different actions from those occurring as thinking. They actually describe what Ryle (1979) calls adverbial categories, that is, manners of behaving and not types of action.

The actions taking place during performance description and rule formulation may have the most varied morphological features, but they must share their functional integration to linguistic actions relevant to the contingencies embedded in linguistic and non-linguistic effective performances. Formulating a rule is not constructing discriminative stimuli. It is substituting contingencies. As has been previously pointed out (Ribes and Lopez, 1985) to think as transituational substitution is tantamount to **translate** independent conventional contingencies as equivalent.

Some preliminary data about rules and thinking behavior

I shall discuss a series of experiments (Ribes & Martinez, 1990) which deal with the analysis of the influence of rules on behavior, and the distinction between substitutional and non-substitutional behavior.

The three experiments consisted in a matching-to-sample situation in which subjects had to learn a first-order conditional discrimination. The matching task consisted either in a *difference* or a *similarity* relation. In *difference*, the subject had to choose among three comparison stimuli a stimulus different in shape and color from that in the sample. In *similarity*, the choice could be made according to color or shape; the correct stimulus could share one of the two modalities with the sample stimulus and be different in the second one. Comparison stimuli were ordered in three blocks of distinctive difficulty, according to their familiarity or novelty regarding the particular shapes and colors of the sample stimuli being used in each trial.

In the first study, three conditions were evaluated in all the subjects, although the conditions were presented according to different sequences. The experimental manipulation consisted in the instructions given to the subjects regarding the rules to be observed in order to solve the matching task. Three types of instructions were given: a) instructions which correctly informed the subjects about the task, and the correct matching choice among the comparison stimuli; b) instructions which informed incorrectly about the task: subjects were instructed to match according to similarity; and, c) instructions formulated by the subjects themselves during base-line sessions, when they were asked to write down what they thought the rule was in order to respond correctly in the matching situation. This instruction resulted in a different rule from every subject. Subjects were informed at the end of every session regarding the number of correct responses during that session, and they were asked also to write down what they thought was the rule to be followed in order to respond correctly to the matching task.

The type of instruction seemed to be an effective variable controlling performance on the matching task, although some sequential effects were observed. The highest percentage of correct responses was found in the condition where the correct instruction was presented. Responding under self-generated and incorrect instructions generally resulted in poor performance although in some subjects a significant percentage of correct responses was observed in both conditions. Two sequential effects are worthwhile mentioning. First, that the highest correct responding under false instructions was observed **after** the condition of true instructions. Second, that more incorrect responding under correct rules took place when the false instruction condition preceded the former.

These results suggest some tentative conclusions. Experimental subjects tended to adjust to the task instructions. This may be observed in the initial performance under each condition, the sequential effects of the various conditions, and the irregular performance in the test sessions (transference sessions). Nevertheless, in spite of the fact that information about performance in the task was given at the end of every session, this feedback seemed to exert some influence, since during the true-instruction condition the performance was maintained, from the very beginning, at a high level of precision; and in the conditions with false and self-generated instructions, correct performance was observed at unexpected levels of success in some cases. This means that instructions were effective to the extent that they were correlated with performance, even when feedback was not immediate or regularly following every trial. The performance of experimental subjects was higher with low difficulty stimulus arrangements and very poor with high difficulty ones. This suggests that in spite of having responded correctly to the true-instruction condition, the subjects did not really formulate a "rule" or apply it. Moreover it is possible that they could not describe their performance. They just performed the instruction. Otherwise, they would also have been successful with non-perceptually obvious arrangements in the other two conditions, as well as in their response to the transference tests. The descriptions they gave, about the rules being "followed" during the task were, in general too non-specific to consider them descriptions of their performance.

In a second study, the performance of experimental subjects under changing stimulus relations was evaluated in a matching task. Three conditions were presented in different orders: a) a matching task based on the difference between stimuli; b) a matching task based on the similarity between stimuli; and, c) a matching task alternating similarity and difference relations among stimuli between sessions. The instruction given was that subjects should choose a comparison stimulus having a relation with the sample, and the relation might change in different sessions. As in the first study, information about their performance was given at the end of the session, at which time they were asked to write down the "rule" they thought might describe the correct relation between stimuli. Subjects performed under the alternation condition when this was the initial one in the experiment. Otherwise, they responded in terms of a similarity or of a mixed similarity-identity relation, which, were the dominant self-descriptions of the rules being